To: Betty
You no doubt don't need this but may find it fear.
Thanks
John

$5
A455

Finding the Real You

Finding the Real You

Meeting the Most Important Person in Your Life

Neil McK. Agnew, Ph.D. and John L. Brown, Ph.D.

With the reluctant assistance of
Professor Elbert Shiplitz, Ph.D.

Copyright ©2002 by Neil McK. Agnew, Ph.D. and John L. Brown, Ph.D.

Library of Congress Number: 2002090831
ISBN: Hardcover   1-4010-4979-6
          Softcover   1-4010-4978-8

All rights reserved. No part of this book may be reproduced or transmitted in any form or by any means, electronic or mechanical, including photocopying, recording, or by any information storage and retrieval system, without permission in writing from the copyright owner.

This book was printed in the United States of America.

To order additional copies of this book, contact:
Xlibris Corporation
1-888-795-4274
www.Xlibris.com
Orders@Xlibris.com

Contents

Preface 9

Chapter 1: 11
   THE SEARCH BEGINS

Chapter 2: 22
   A FAMILY OF MINDS

Chapter 3: 40
   SUSPENDED IN A NETWORK OF
   ALLIANCES

Chapter 4: 54
   LINKING AND DEFENDING ISLANDS

Chapter 5: 73
   A PLACE TO STOOD

Chapter 6: 85
   Hey Hey IT'S THE RHYTHM
   NOT THE WORDS

Chapter 7: 106
   THE SHIPLITZ FORMULA

Chapter 8: 128
   YOUR RHYTHMS DANCING WITH THEIR
   RHYTHMS

Chapter 9: 157
   YOUR DANCE CARD

Chapter 10: 179
   DANCING WITH THE FUTURE

Chapter 11: 214
   RIGGY JIGGING WITH THE UNIVERSE

The authors would like to acknowledge the following individuals for their invaluable help and support in seeing our book through to completion. Neil Agnew would like to thank his wife Mary for the same unfailing support through the difficult stages of writing as she has provided throughout their entire married life. John Brown would like to thank his mother Doris Jones who has always been there with a helping hand, no matter what. Finally, both authors wish to acknowledge the help of their graphic assistants. Ryan Howarth for designing and developing the cover and Nick Rudnicki for putting the graphics into an acceptable format for publishing.

PREFACE

Let's face it. Most self-help books promise a lot more than they deliver. Given their popularity they must be filling a humungous need. Like miracle diets—that also don't work—such books capitalize on the fact that hope springs eternal.

Since most miracle diets and self-help manuals deliver much less than they promise, we decided to write one that delivers much more than it promises. At no extra charge. The title promises that we'll help find the REAL YOU. Instead, we help you find a whole gang of Real Yous. We promise you the wisdom of two ordinary Joes and yet we locate a crazy genius, steal his brilliant stuff and sneak it to you. Again at no extra charge. What a deal!

Naturally you expect a normal book where one chapter links in a clear and logical fashion to the next with a neat, all encompassing conclusion tying together all the loose strands. The way life is supposed to, but doesn't. Instead, we secretly introduce you to a leading edge model of the universe—The Shiplitz Formula. This theory deals not with the superficial stuff of life where A leads to B leads to C, beans lead to gas, but with the richer, deeper stuff—like the emergence of self—where A,B,C and the rest of your personal alphabet, keep getting out of order, running around in circles, bumping into each other. Does that sound like your life too, or is it only our's?

Have you ever seen those pictures taken with a miniature camera of sperm trying to find the egg? Some of them swim in circles, some have two tails, some have hardly any head, they're swimming off in all directions, bumping and crowding. You look and ask yourself: "Can this be the beginning of life, of me—Jeez!" Yet it only takes one of these mindless idiots to get to mother egg. This is the essence of what we think in a nut shell—unpredictability in the short run, but in the long run miraculous patterns emerge, life appears and unfolds—never in a straight line, never with A, B and C in order, but nevertheless as it should.

We want to help you identify a pattern for yourself and what is important for you in that pattern. If you find you like your pattern, we have suggestions on how you can defend and maintain it. However, as often happens to us we find the pattern no longer works. We would like to rearrange our life's furniture. We may even want to break out, get new furniture, or even move house. If so we have ideas to help you in the relocation. Our intent is not to tell you where to relocate but to help you in the search for the new location.

We hope you have some fun in the process and along the way get to know a few of the Real Yous. Some who are familiar friends, others you may never have really got to know before. We had fun writing the book and guess what, it helped us to meet a few of our own Real Yous and we are even still the best of friends.

If you do keep going and you do finish our little book don't forget to send for your Baccalaureate of Rhythm, gold embossed certificate—suitable for framing. And visit our web site for regular 'wise bites' at www.RealYou.ca.

CHAPTER 1:

THE SEARCH BEGINS

You may not know it but you're an unsung hero.

Whether you're the work of God or Evolution, you're a work of art.

Whether you're male or female, short or tall, you're a wonder.

All the King's horses, all the King's men, all the Nobel Prize winners and computer whizzes couldn't put you together again—you're unique in all the world.

Bill Gates would give mega bucks for a computer that could move and learn like a kitten. You're a million times smarter than a kitten so think how much he'd pay for a reproduction of you? You ARE a wondrous work of art!

How come you're so special? Well apparently it has to do with at least three things: Your brain, your heart, and your soul—or spirit, or character, if you prefer. But because we usually rely, not always wisely, on our brain to keep us informed about the goings on of the other two we'll start with it.

YOUR BRAIN

Talk about wonders. All we have to do is encounter someone with a damaged brain or Altzheimers to know how lucky we are. But given

Neil McK. Agnew, Ph.D. and John L. Brown, Ph.D.

a normal brain you probably feel that there's nothing so special about your brain. And in a way you're right. Think about it, you have the same sized brain as Og and Oola, your cave-dwelling ancestors. And yet you'll admit that modern caves and their surroundings have grown astonishingly in size and complexity. In our caves Og and Oola would be totally lost. How come with the same sized brain as theirs you're not—well not all the time anyway? If it's not your brain that's changed, what is it? Your mind?

Your Magical Mind

The human race travels through centuries, and individuals through a lifetime, following mind maps—chasing their hopes. So even if brain size doesn't change, the territory and the maps sure do. In a small cave or territory you can get by with a simple map, a simple mind. As the size and complexity of our world increases so too does the division of labor, both inside and outside our heads.

So brain/mind experts are telling us that you don't have A mind. You have MANY minds—some specializing here, some there. But what they're not telling us yet, is what holds them together, other than your skull.

A JOURNEY INTO NEW TERRITORY

We're about to start a journey exploring this intriguing notion of your many minds and the puzzle of what holds them together. On the trip be prepared for some different notions. The first time one of us went to visit a friend in England we complained about almost everything: driving on the wrong side of the road; warm beer; funny telephones; lousy coffee. He put up with our moaning and groaning for a day and then said quietly: "If you wanted everything to be the same you should have stayed home."

Think of this little book as a holiday from your usual way of thinking. And like any good holiday it should involve a change. It should involve seeing new things, meeting some new people. It should also involve having some fun, stepping out of yourself and even acting a bit silly. And finally, from any worthwhile holiday you should return with vim, vigor and vitality. Well at least with one of them—with enough added juice to take a renewed shot at The Life Game.

As we travel, you'll start meeting some of the central figures on this mental holiday, some similar to yourself, some very different, as well as the first of a series of famous characters (warts and all). You're welcome to come along as an invisible observer, but feel free at any time to emerge and join the fun. Also, you'll be given ample opportunities to go exploring on your own—be sure to bring some comfortable brain wear—nothing too tight . . . on a journey like this a person's mind expands.

THE SEARCH BEGINS

Most of us don't appreciate that we're one in a billion. Instead, when we look for our Real Self we either discover someone we don't like very well, or a mob—like a classroom of kids, all waving their hands and snapping their fingers, wanting to be chosen. I suppose you could always go to a shrink to help in your search but that doesn't always work as the following case indicates.

A friend makes a New Years resolution: "I'll be true to myself . . . when I find me!" They seek help.

Client: "Doctor. I'm not feeling myself."
Doctor: "You want me to help you find the real you?"
Client: "Of course . . . but how much will it cost?"
Doctor: "Only a thousand dollars."
Client: "A THOUSAND dollars! If this is not the real me why should I pay you all that money? Let's wait till we find the real me and let them pay you a thousand dollars. Furthermore, how can we be sure we've found the REAL me?"
Doctor: "Trust me, I'm an expert, I'll know if it's the real you."

Neil McK. Agnew, Ph.D. and John L. Brown, Ph.D.

Client: "But experts make mistakes. How can I be certain we haven't found another pretend me?"

[Psychologist starts to say something but client interrupts]

Client: "You know Doctor, if the person we find pays you a thousand dollars . . . I'll know it's not the real me."

WHERE ARE YOU HIDING?

In its various versions this old "shrink" joke pinpoints the challenge facing us all and is the central theme of this book. Who am I, REALLY? And, who are you, REALLY? Who did I REALLY marry? Who is this kid I've sired, REALLY? What makes my boss tick, REALLY?

Like scientists, we're trying to peel back all the layers and discover "the truth" —like who is the core person inside. But in our search we lack the scientists time and money. We have to do it on the run. No white coats, no fancy instruments, no sabbaticals.

Nevertheless, we're not too bad at pegging certain people. Particularly if they're not too close to us. Even if you're not a psychologist you get a pretty good idea of what makes some co-workers or neighbors tick. That's because you don't have the overwhelming amount of conflicting information and emotional baggage that camouflages your "near and dear" ones. It often takes years for you to discover the "real thems".

So it isn't that you can't, you just can't do it so well up close, in the noise of life's traffic. That's maybe why the wise advice you give so often falls on deaf ears. Maybe you're not talking to the REAL THEM. When was the last time someone said to you: "Wow that's really brilliant advice, I wish I'd thought of that?" On the other hand, when was the last time to your words of wisdom, the recipient sprayed you with a bunch of "yes buts . . ."?

Speaking of delivering chunks of wisdom to 'up close' people, who is really, really up close? YOU! You are the closest of all! And how often, pray tell, do you take your own astute advice? So much for New

Finding the Real You

Year's Resolutions! Ah, but ignorance can be bliss, self-knowledge can be so depressing. To ignore conscience can be so sweet.

In the rest of this book we'll help you look for and even find the Real You—and for a lot less than a thousand dollars.

In the search we'll capitalize on some of the effective psychological telescopes and microscopes already in your repertoire, as well as introducing you to some simple but powerful mental radar for reading the future, and even sonar for locating strong stuff below the surface.

THREE KINDS OF PEOPLE

There are three kinds of people:
>   People who believe in zero;
>   People who believe in one;
>   People who believe in many.

The ZERO people or skeptics don't believe in anything, or so they say.

The ONE mind people believe that everything can be explained with a single idea—like the scientific method, or God, or money, or vegetarianism.

The MANY minds people believe there is not just one answer and so in their head space they harbor many different minds to help them navigate the boring, the wondrous and the weird worlds they encounter along their wondering way.

ZERO mind people, you will be very happy with this book. It includes a bunch of stuff you can disagree with . . . and about which you can even teach us a thing or two with a few of your well placed: "**Yes buts** . . ."

ONE mind people, you will find this book a challenge. We'll keep trying to sneak into your heads several different kinds of minds, into a space where you KNOW only one mind belongs. Of course, being of ONE mind, you will keep a weather eye out for "master mind"—the big boss who keeps your mini-minds in order.

Neil McK. Agnew, Ph.D. and John L. Brown, Ph.D.

We know it's heresy but you may even find that the "master mind" is usually the situation you're in: like the bathroom; the church; in front of the TV; in bed; in the car; at the office. Have you ever thought that maybe it's not you but the situation in which you find yourself that really determines which YOU has center stage? Even the strongest habits go into hiding in certain situations. Like? Well how often do you smoke in church or fart at a funeral. But you say: "**Yes but** . . . for really important stuff the BIG ME is really running the show!"

Now, those of you who already entertain the notion of many minds will find yourself in some familiar territory. You've already decided or suspected that you need a team of different minds: one to deal with children and dogs; another for cats; another for hard edged things like needles, barnacles, used car salesman and the internal revenue department; but a different mind to deal with kittens, loved ones, and hot fudge sundaes; and still another to deal with spirits, Gods, and loon calls at sunup on a misty morning.

> In looking for the Real You:
> The ZERO mind people will be even clearer who
>   they aren't.
> The ONE mind people will find a Master Mind that
>   manages the mini-yourself.

The MANY minds people will add a few more helpful, weird, even hilarious characters to the menagerie already rattling around inside their head, heart and soul. Because? Well because they KNOW something. They know that your mind has one rule: "I am a group". Hey, maybe that makes them ONE mind people? Or maybe the mind is a democratic—rotating leadership?

DEMOCRATIC?

In a pigs eye! You know better than that. You know that some of your minds boss or bully others. Like? Like when one mind says:

Finding the Real You

"Don't do it!" And another says: "I gotta, I just gotta. Gotta have it (the latest golf club, hot fudge sundae, pair of shoes, my own way). Gotta do it (watch TV NOW, have sex NOW, avoid doing the report NOW).

Not only does one mind bully another, but some bullies, boss other bullies—it's like the army or a corporation—a whole shifting hierarchy of bullies, each protecting and expanding their turf. So who is the Real You? The "current" C.E.B (Chief Executive Bully?) Or, The "current" executive committee of senior bullies? And who will be running the show next week, next year?

INSIDE BULLIES, OUTSIDE BULLIES

Where do your biggest bullies live? Inside? Inside your genes, your jeans, your head, or your heart? Like? Well like a big optimistic bully that cons your other minds into seeing the world through rose colored glasses. Or conversely, a pessimistic C.E.B. that cons your other YOUS into seeing the world through poop colored specs.

Or maybe your biggest bullies live outside your noggin. Like? Well like in your mate's head. She/He lets you make little decisions (which fork) but their THEMS make the BIG ones (what you eat).

Or maybe, as egghead economists and sociologists claim, the biggest bullies of all aren't localized inside our head but permeate THE CULTURE. Big government, big corporations, big educational systems pull your strings. So, according to this ivory-tower perspective, don't look for your Real Yous inside but look outside. What a repulsive idea!

But any bully's manner—overbearing and mean—can eventually generate revolts. "Mini-minds rise up, the only thing you have to lose are your chains . . . or your mind."

As we start the search what's your hunch? Where will you find your biggest bullies? Inside your genes? Inside your head? Inside your heart? Inside somebody else's head? Inside your culture? We'll see.

We start right off by making deposits into your bank account—your brain power bank account. Distilled from the smartest gurus we know, these deposits, 'wise bites' and 'wise bits', can serve as your personal investment portfolio. You can pick and choose which deposits pay off, which ones compound your wisdom and help get a better fix on the real YOU or YOUS.

MIND DEPOSIT #1

Adopt the "many minds" perspective. Humor us, at least in the beginning. Consistency or logic tight categories are fine when dealing with stable bits and pieces of the physical world. But when dealing with live critters, with silly circumstances and poopy people, it's not neat and tidy, it's like fighting bees. Therefore, one neat and tidy mind has trouble. The more good minds you have the better the chances are that one of them will manage and even enjoy the changing scene. Many minds mean a wise division of labor.

Otherwise, with only one mind to do all the work, you're like the nervous rider galloping off in all directions at once. With only one mind you have to keep twisting it torturously out of shape to fit the zigzagging flow of experience, and periodically exclaim: "I give up—I'm outta here, I'm heading down to the end of the garden to eat worms, or to the nearest bar, or to yet another TV guru".

Well yes . . . Hey, Bertha not a bad analogy, a "family of minds" with all the strengths and challenges of a family. Actually another genius came up with the notion of 'A Society of Minds' as we'll see in the next chapter."

Finding the Real You

For those of you who enjoy a turn in the captain's chair we provide an opportunity for exploring and mapping your own mind(s) at the end of each chapter.

Map #1: Lifestyle Analysis: The following activity matrix enables you to start the search for the Real You with a personal audit of the "payoffs" produced by your major activities and the MINDS that drive them. Some of your YOUS live for today, go for short-term gains (like pigging out and boozing up) and to hell with the long-term consequences. Other YOUS tolerate short-term pain for long term gain (ahem . . . like buying this book and completing this mind-mapping program!). (See Figure 1.2).

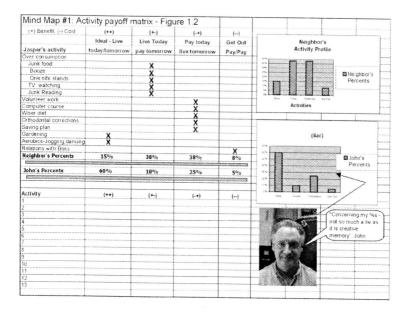

In the left-hand rows you have space to write in your major activities. You will then notice four columns for categorizing each activity. For example at the top of each column a positive sign (+) indicates a benefit, and a negative sign (-) a cost. The column header (+-) means a short-term benefit and a long term cost, conversely (-+) means a short term cost and a long-term payoff.

The first column is for activities that provide both short and long-term benefits (the ideal payoff—like making luscious love and producing ideal children that cheerfully do your bidding and support you in your dotage). Right!

The second column includes activities that are great when you do them but later you pay the price (Live today—pay tomorrow . . . like the eat now—diet later roller coaster).

The third column is for activities that produce some mental or financial pain in the short run but big payoffs in the long term (Pay today—live tomorrow . . . like struggling through a course in creative writing and then publishing the great American novel).

The fourth and last column is nightmare alley (Short term and Long term pain . . . like a dead end relationship or job). Get out!

In Figure 1.2 we provide two examples plus graphs: one for Jasper, a neighbor who lives across the street. We also include a second example created by one of the authors—John—just showing his percentages in each column—needless to say he was in a truth-stretching frame of mind when he did it.

Notice, the number of X's in each column tells you what kinds of payoffs the person is getting from their repertoire of activities or Selves. In the first example, Jasper, our neighbor, has 15% of his activities falling in the Ideal or (++) column; 38% in the Live Today or (+-) column; 38% in the Pay Today/Live tomorrow or (-+) column; and 8% in nightmare alley or the (— —) column.

In John's example he claims 60% of his activities fall into the Ideal column, only 10% in the Live Today column; 38% into the wise Pay Today/Live tomorrow column, and only 5% in nightmare alley. Yeah, in his dreams.

Now you get a chance to make a start at a lifestyle analysis by filling in the bottom matrix. Go to Figure 1.2 and start by writing in your major activities on the left, then place an X in one of the four payoff columns. Try to be more honest than John—in fact do it in pencil—

Finding the Real You

you'll probably want to change it several times as you go along, as your self-knowledge grows . . . and grows. . . . Wow!

Don't be discouraged if you don't like the number of X's falling in columns two and four . . . remember they're only done in pencil. All it takes is an eraser to shift the balance. Or better still make some real changes by getting the cooperation of inside or outside bullies to help you rearrange the percentages.

Also, if you take a crack at all the Mind Maps at the end of each chapter you can even earn a Mind Mapping Certificate. Wow!

CHAPTER 2:

A FAMILY OF MINDS

"Big sisters are the crab grass in the lawn of life."
—Charles Schulz

Max: "All birds fly"
Kate: "What about Ostriches—they don't fly?"
Max: "Ostriches are birds who don't fly."
Kate: "What about Penguins, they don't fly."
Max: "Penguins are birds that swim instead of fly."
Kate: "So all birds don't fly?"
Max: "Go stuff it in your ear!"

Here we have my eight year old son Max being operated upon by his eleven year old sister Kate. Ah, the family. Will we ever forget the interpersonal surgery we performed on each other? The exhilarating times around the table discussing the nutritional benefits of broccoli and brussels sprouts. The fascinating discussions of balancing freedom and responsibility. The joy of family holidays?

Just when you discover a little island of truth like: "all birds fly" or "all Russians are red" or "all men are horny", right away an older sibling or a smart Alex invades and demolishes your nice little con-

Finding the Real You

struction. And even within the privacy of our own heads it's difficult to protect one truth from firing at another—interneural warfare. Maybe the metaphor of a family of minds isn't such a hot idea. Well, let's give it a try and see.

DR. SHIPLITZ ARRIVES

Speaking of families, a new one moved in next door. The husband is kinda weird, Professor Elbert Shiplitz who walks around in snowshoes all the time so he won't fall down the spaces between the atoms (See Figure 2.1).

Fig 2.1 Professor Elbert Shiplitz

Yes, you probably guessed it, he's one of those theoretical physicists who's so brilliant that the students and most faculty can't understand him. He's so strange that the University pays him to stay at home and write books. Unfortunately, Professor Shiplitz, suffers from periodic writer's block. His wife told my wife the reason he's 'different' is because he can't forget he's an orphan. As a newborn baby he was left on the New York sub-way in a violin case. Funny, he reminds us of someone but can't put a finger on who? If Shiplitz is so smart maybe we can get some ideas from him for this book—we haven't got writer's block... just thinker's freeze.

And we have other problems too. I feel sorry for John, my handsome co-author. He and his young girl friend are off surfing in Hawaii. Sadly, he lacks the security of us married types, so he lives day-to-day, pogo sticking about seeking, and usually finding short term pleasure wherever he lands. Unfortunately, this live-for-the-moment attitude prevents him from locating and luxuriating in the endless cornucopia of intellectual and emotional coupons flowing from marital bliss. Poor John.

Anyway, I'm at the office alone with my minds tossing up nothing but word salads so I head home early and what do I find? I find my new neighbor, Herr Dr. Professor Shiplitz, reclining in my lazy-boy—snowshoes and all—drinking my gin, and watching my wife Bruney up the ladder painting the family room ceiling. Surprisingly, he's almost sociable and intelligible. No doubt my gin has temporarily shut down half his neurons so, for a few minutes, his brain size is the same as mine and he can think simple like the rest of us living down here in the intellectual basement of life.

Apparently my wife Bruney told him about the book John and I are writing about how to find the Real You. Before Shiplitz clatters off home he says: "Read Marvin Minsky, he's almost as smart as I am." So we check out Minsky on the Internet.

SOCIETY OF MINDS

Marvin Minsky, a brilliant and puckish Professor at MIT, invented an electron microscope, helped father Artificial Intelligence, and thinks your head is full of a society, a society of mental islands. Each island is a collection of consistencies that your fallible common sense

Finding the Real You

has constructed from all the messages you encounter . . . like all birds fly, all single men are unhappy, etc.

But the flood of experience is too complex and conflicting to let you fit it all neatly together on one big island or one mind. Nevertheless, "the ONE mind people" are still looking for "one theory of everything." We'll leave them to it and go with Minsky who's not trying to make sense of the whole world with one big consistency, but instead relies on a personal collection of smaller ones.

What might some of these islands of consistency look like? Here are some examples so you can start mapping a few of yours. Do so by merely completing the following:

Women are: _____
Men are: _____
Democrats are: _____
Republicans are: _____
People on welfare are: _____
Blondes are: _____
Politicians are: _____
Lawyers are: _____
Telemarketers are: _____
Customers are: _____

How did it go? Did you notice how most of our common sense islands have noun names? Nouns freeze things, keep them stable, keep them from leaking all over the place. We'll come back to this important observation later in the book.

To get a peek at a few of someone else's islands, or minds, simply ask a **male** friend to talk about women: "Women are emotional illogical, and suckers for compliments." What about men?" Men are objective and analytical, and suckers for tears".

Now listen to a **female** friend: "Men's minds are right behind their zippers; without the protection and promotion of the old boys' network they'd all be dishwashers. In exchange for letting males pee standing up the Goddess gave women multiple orgasms; the hands that change the diapers will rule the world."

But you say: "Hey these are stereotypes, and stereotypes are bad, right?" Of course . . . but we have a wee problem here. I warned you Minsky was smart but puckish. What's the alternative to his society of islands of stereotypes? A different island for every woman you know, for every man, every politician, and every bird? Well no but . . . But What?

Observe successful leaders: politicians, entrepreneurs, and even scholars. They rely on powerful simplifications like 'evil empire', 'equality', 'market economy', 'compassionate conservatism', etc. and by various means these people lure us on to their islands. They do it with promises, persistence, guile, or even logic, and often like good little sheep we jump between the brackets of their prize stereotypes or islands.

Furthermore, successful shepherds, con-artists, or gurus possess the energy, skill and brass to deflect assaults on the boundaries of their island stereotypes. At least for awhile, until a new charismatic pied piper dances in and lures us camp followers away. Well not us, but all those other sheep who slavishly follow the fads and fashions.

BEARS OF SMALL BRAIN

Winnie the Pooh acknowledged he was a bear of small brain. Apparently he's not alone. As noted earlier we have the same sized brains as our distant ancestors—the early cave dwellers, Og and Oola. Our brain is only big enough to get to really know four or five of the other grimy humanoids occupying our cave or office. Then with our few surplus neurons we rely on very simple codes to label the other members of the tribe: "loud snore", "one eye", and "big bum".

To save precious brain space Og and Oola also relied on stereotypes for everyone outside the cave, the out-groupers: the egg suckers, the blue faces, and the fuzzy wuzzies. We do the same but use different labels. Egg suckers become: Democrats; Republicans; blacks; street-people, etc. Sounds like Minsky's Islands of Consistency.

Finding the Real You

In fact some experts claim, that like our cave squatting ancestors, we can only handle—cognitively and emotionally—about 7, plus or minus 2, close relationships. How does that compare with your experience?

Only in familiar, small face to face groups, can we afford to recognize and remember a lot of individual characteristics about each other: that is, establish multiple personal codes for a few special members of our tribe. As we grow up we keep encountering more and more individuals and groups so our poor brain has to drastically ration its mental space. The larger the number of people we try to think about the more we rely on stereotypes. Once you go beyond your close face-to-face contacts you too must rely on fewer codes, on fewer distinctions until you rely mainly on ciphers, on colors, on classes, on labels. Anyone who tries to tell you differently is an egg-sucker.

Our small brains evolved only far enough to handle small worlds—our cave and it's immediate surround. Nevertheless, ready or not, gradually our world got bigger, but not our brain. So, since we haven't yet had time to grow bigger brains to handle much bigger caves and worlds, human heads have to radically simplify and protect our constructed **Islands of Consistency**.

Recognizing our small brain/big world dilemma, Minsky also claims that your various minds or islands possess protective breakwaters and nasty immigration officers to keep out undesirables, to reject ideas and people who don't fit into our categories, to turn away inconsistencies or exceptions. That's why it's so hard to change most people minds. We protect our limited brain space by defending our manufactured truths, our mind maps. We can't mentally afford to clutter up our islands with too many exceptions, protesters, trespassers, cranks and skeletons.

Remember how we opened this chapter with Max and his innocent island of consistency: "All birds fly" only to have Kate, his big sister, lead in assault troops loaded with non-flying ostriches and penguins. He, of course, drove off the invaders by firing his bazooka: "Stick it in your ear." Well, some defensive maneuvers are less sophisticated than others. But notice most of the time that's the economical way to think of birds—as flyers.

Only when we encounter a smart-ass, or an expert, do we go to the trouble of fleeing to the other end of our island, unlock our shed of exceptions, and see what's there. If it were otherwise our minds would be a clutter of inconsistencies. Sure we grant one or two of our minds extra space for pet projects in which we display details and even pet exceptions. But only one or two, or else we produce brain smoke and meltdown.

BOUNDED RATIONALITY

Yesterday, I spied Shiplitz over the fence beating his lawnmower with one of his snowshoes. Like a good neighbor I went over and started his machine and also thanked him for the tip on Minsky. For my reward he gave me the name of another smart dude I should check out . . . a Nobel Laureate no less!

Herb Simon got his prize for studying how we make decisions. Simon concluded that we are bears of small brain—that we don't have a lot of 'on-the-spot' rational capacity. First, we have very limited short-term memory. For example try keeping a new phone number in your head while walking across a noisy room. Or try to recall what the computer salesperson told you about the bits, bites, roms, rams, and Hertz—whatever car rentals have to do with computers.

Not only do we lack a large short-term memory store, but Simon's second discovery established that we have limited rational or analytic capacity. Except for one, or maybe two pet projects, we lack the brain power to understand important details and evaluate more than one or two points of view about: the Democratic or Republican platform; different mutual funds; diets; computers; or laundry detergents.

On this point Shiplitz told a reporter: "The role of reason in human affairs is grossly over rated. At best 1% of our thinking and acting is controlled by reason. The rest of the time we run on automatic—

automatic thinking, feeling, acting. So most of the time we behave like robots—one damn ritual dance after another."

He said a lot of other stuff too. Like in order to cut down our thinking load, to stop our neurons from smoking, we rely on mind-saving tricks. Like? Well like relying on simple categories (all birds fly); like thinking in stereotypes (Democrats are soft headed, Republicans are hard hearted, Apple Computers are cool, made in the U.S.A is best). Because we can't handle too many complexities we go for simple stories about how the world works: women's minds play naive "goddess" or "homemaker" tapes, and guys minds play immature "playboy" and "mummy tapes".

He says we play our mind tapes not because the simple stories do justice to experience, but because they are mentally affordable, because they're easy to store and retrieve, because we only have brain space for rich information about a very few high priority islands. So, usually most of the other stuff in our heads we keep on Mickey Mouse simple islands like "all birds fly", "all Republicans are hard hearted" "All Democrats are soft headed," "Guys are only interested in one thing . . . plus sports."

Wise bite: Of the small amount of rational capacity we do possess, our superficial selves have captured most of it. This shallow mob uses it for drawing overly simple maps (caricatures and stereotypes) of your on-going experience. That leaves your small surplus brainpower for your Real Yous to do important stuff. Like? Like exploring and mapping in greater detail a treasured person (child or lover), or topic (winemaking or physics), or activity (publishing a novel on the net or playing jazz on the tenor sax).

MINDS AS CONCENTRIC CIRCLES OF ISLANDS

If, for a minute, you give these power thinkers—Shiplitz, Minsky and Simon—the benefit of the doubt a weird image starts to emerge of what the Real You must be like. You get the picture of a relatively small brain desperately trying to continuously update maps of a very big moving world. The only way to map a big complex world onto a small brain is to ignore most of the complexity, except for a few treasured places.

So, as a first approximation of The Real You we start with an image of a network of mental islands spreading out in concentric circles. In the center we find your high priority, information rich and treasured islands: ones containing your favorite self-images; your child; your dog; your best friend, your lover and/or your mate; your treasured baseball team or author. Figure 2.2 gives an example of one mapping.

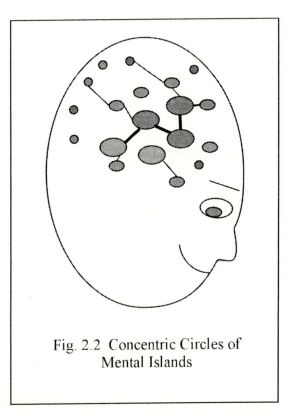

Fig. 2.2 Concentric Circles of Mental Islands

Finding the Real You

Spreading out from this central core of priority islands we find the next ring which contains less familiar other people, events, or objects. The maps of these peripheral islands contain less detail for they describe less loved or less hated family members, co-workers, neighbors and their dogs, restaurants, ski resorts, clothing stores, etc.

Then, moving still further out through the concentric rings we encounter even more crudely mapped islands including stereotypes of low priority contacts: lawyers; politicians; bankers; salesmen; communists; ancestors; ghosts; lawn mowers . . . all the way out to Jupiter and Martians—unless you're a Sc-Fi addict and then Spock and kin live on one of your center islands.

Be aware of bridges between some islands—the mental traffic flows readily from one to another. While others are more isolated, less populated, less familiar.

Notice too that as far as most of your casual acquaintances are concerned they have you living on one of their outer islands. As far as large institutions are concerned—like governments, banks, and insurance companies—you're way out. Your basic code is a number, a cipher.

But also notice with the aid of public relations experts and computers, institutions try to con you into thinking that you're special, that you're 'central'. Of course they don't want to actually see you, they don't want you messing up their doorstep.

The only bridge they want between you and them is electronic with them controlling the switch. That's why they want you to line up at ATM's, that's why they program computers to automatically type your name into their correspondence. Some even use gold ink "because you're so precious to us!" GAWD! That's why they love recorded messages—to keep you at institutional arm's length, but remember: "Your call is important to us. . . . I'm away from my desk for the moment . . ." Yeah right, discussing re-runs of Seinfeld with all the others who are also away from their desk for the moment, or hour, or day.

Neil McK. Agnew, Ph.D. and John L. Brown, Ph.D.

REAL YOU NOT WILLFULLY IGNORANT

But before we OD on self-righteousness, remember institutions are only doing what we also do with large groups. According to Shiplitz and Co. we have no choice but to map most of the big world by going "code simple". Neither we, nor they, have any alternative in managing the potentially overwhelming flow of experience but to avoid or block out most of it, categorize and stereotype the rest, except for four or five very special people, objects, or events. So the Real Yous are, and must be, "ignorant" about most things. Not willfully ignorant, but being bears of small brain necessarily so.

LOW COST ELABORATIONS

Sure, we can commit a fraction of a percent of our precious mental computing power to handling a few exceptions to one of our stereotypes by adding a code or two to some of our second or third ring islands ("not all bankers are heartless . . . just 99%"). We can even buy a video from one of the big-smile-white-teeth TV hucksters telling us how to remember names and identify people's central islands so we can temporarily trick them into thinking they're special: ("Hello BILL how's that great little wife of yours? . . . Ah . . . you're divorced . . . nine months ago . . . sorry I hadn't heard.")

As we said, computers let institutions add multiple codes to your name and not only automatically send you "overdue" notices but "sincere" birthday cards as well—isn't that sweet? But notice it isn't their brain you're occupying, it's one of their computers. The computer is like a prosthetic extension of the institutional brain—with all the intimacy of being stroked by an artificial limb. Ever wonder why it is so hard to tickle yourself?

Finding the Real You

ISLAND RENOVATIONS

Of course, even though you have to radically ration your mind space, unless you're in crises you have enough for some island innovations. Not only can one of your Yous manage some superficial coding of a few new individuals (remember their first name using some memory trick) but occasionally at great cost you can actually clear out one central island with it's connecting bridges and replace him/her/it with another from the second ring. But breaking an alliance based on a web of well-established mutual expectations creates BIG Stress.

Such demolition and reconstruction requires the costly services of mental wrecking crews and building contractors. During such cognitive-emotional renovations most of your Yous, and some Yous of your friends and family, have to drop whatever they're doing and help you collect and empty garbage and carry bricks.

Moving a new individual into the central core takes time, while moving into the real center of a new group takes forever. We typically avoid it unless we're desperately lonely, or we move to a new job, or town, or country. Such engagements are Godzilla sized mind stretchers because they involve clearing out so many of your central and second ring islands and repopulating them from the ground up.

Have you ever wondered why it's so difficult for adults to REALLY learn a new language? It involves literally rewriting millions of codes on the central islands. So typically we give up, or merely learn the foreign phrases for a few necessary activities: "Ou est le biere?" and "Ou est le toilet?" And of course you put 'le' in front of everything! Saves memory space.

STEREOTYPES ARE BAD BUT . . .

What do we do about the fact that most of our head is filled with islands littered with Mickey-Mouse-simple and mean-minded stereotypes? Well, we could go for positive oversimplifications, instead of

Neil McK. Agnew, Ph.D. and John L. Brown, Ph.D.

negative ones: all pinks are kind; all males are sensitive; all politicians are good Samaritans. But that's kind of like putting out a welcome mat to everyone: open house for come-one-come-all mind guests. But hey, can you really put out such a humungous invitation—everybody welcome—into such a small mental house?

Notice, negative stereotypes solve the mental space problem, they signal a full house! No Vacancies! No Entrance without a pass!

Also, have you noticed most of us have a perverse curiosity concerning bad news about others? Like? Like Dorothy Parker who said: "If you can't think of anything nice to say about anyone come and sit by me." It's almost as if we reserve one island for receiving and storing bad news about almost everyone, particularly about outer island folk.

To be fair, while we rely mainly on stereotypes—mentally manufactured islands of consistency—as noted we also provide a tiny space on each island for exceptions, for special cases: for the generous Scot, the sober Irishman, and the smart blond—space for the odd exceptions that prove the rule. But don't entertain too many exceptions or they cause mental traffic jams, and if there are enough of them they may even revolt and try to take over the island, block bridges, cause inter-island wars.

Watcha think? Can you buy the notion that the Real You consists of concentric circles of islands, a few relatively sophisticated, well connected and well defended ones at the center. All surrounded by spreading rings of others that are populated by increasingly superficial stereotypes?

Of course, some of your "Yous" are located on the islands of other people, pets, and institutions. On a few special islands your Yous occupy a central place—for your Mum, your dog, your mate. On others only one or two of your Yous actually appear, known for example to your hairdresser or barber. But on most you're merely a simple code—a cipher like a credit card number. And, of course on most islands in the big world you don't exist at all . . . try losing your wallet in China.

So in looking for the Real Yous, in searching for the warmly regarded and richly detailed Yous we know where to search don't we?

Finding the Real You

We focus on the center islands—yours and those of your trusted buds... Unfortunately so does the phony gladhander, newly graduated from the latest spin on "How To Win Friends and Influence People".

MIND DEPOSIT #2

Think of your different minds as a family or society of islands. Each island is a collection of common sense consistencies. The center contains a precious few, mentally expensive islands reserved for high priority stuff (your self-images, your children, dogs, lovers, sports teams) each endowed with multiple distinctions or codes. But most of the islands are populated with simple categories, stereotypes or consistencies—plus a few inconsistencies (exceptions) that sneaked ashore and are usually locked away in a tool shed—out of sight, out of mind.

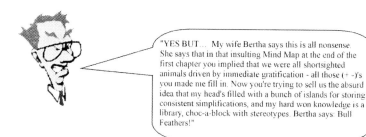

"YES BUT... My wife Bertha says this is all nonsense. She says that in that insulting Mind Map at the end of the first chapter you implied that we were all shortsighted animals driven by immediate gratification - all those (+ -)'s you made me fill in. Now you're trying to sell us the absurd idea that my head's filled with a bunch of islands for storing consistent simplifications, and my hard won knowledge is a library, choc-a-block with stereotypes. Bertha says: Bull Feathers!"

"Furthermore, Bertha says you better ask your crazy neighbor with the snow shoes one question: If the Real Me is a family of minds then what holds them all together? What makes me so absolutely certain there's one me? Because there is! Here I am. Look at me. Touch me... there is only one me... isn't there Bertha?"

Well yes... Bertha has a point about what holds your minds together. I asked John and he says to tell you that just like a house holds a family together, your skull holds your mind together. I asked

Shippy too and he said: "A society of minds, like any society is held together both by physical location—inside your head [hey John got half of it right], and by a network of short and long term alliances between your various minds, and also alliances with those of others in your cave and culture".

So we should start looking for the Real Yous among the long-term alliances between islands, inside your head and outside. We will eventually end up with a moving "map of YOUS" drawn on the big seething sea of life. Wow! Think of the metaphors that opens up to us; stormy seas, tranquil seas, heaving seas. The list could go on . . . but enough already!

Wait until the next chapter where we corner Shiplitz and get some really neat stuff. But without waiting let's start right now by mapping some of your own alliances. It's suspended in that network you'll find some of the most important Yous.

MIND MAP #2

One of the things that holds your mental islands together, in addition to your skull and some of it's inside alliances is your network of friends and loved ones. So if we're going to get to meet the Real You we have to meet your mates and buds.

You, and we have to get a feel for the rigid or flexible web of mutual expectations in which you're suspended. To get a crude initial estimate of that network we ask you to indicate from among your acquaintances the ones you choose for close face-to face relations and the ones who choose you, the seven plus or minus two close relationships we bears with small brains can manage. In Mind Map 2.1 we provide an example filled out by Jasper, the same neighbor who did the Mind Map in Chapter 1.

Finding the Real You

Ch. 2 Mind Map #2.1 Jasper's Example

Relationship Map	Two-Way Choices			One-Way (+)		One-Way (-)		
Tribe members:	Mum	Boots	Bill	Simon	Esther	Dad	Gerty	Paul
He Chooses them	X	X	X			X	X	X
They choose him	X	X	X	X	X			
Match/Mismatch	Bingo	Bingo	Bingo	No Way	No Way	Sob	Sob	Sob

Ch. 2 Mind Map #2.2: Yours

Relationship Map								
Tribe members:	1	2	3	4	5	6	7	8
You Choose Them								
They Choose You								
Match/Mismatch								

Mind Map #2.1 shows that Jasper has three, two-way or mutual relationships (Bingos): his Mum, his dog, and his friend Bill. He also has two one-way positive choices—Esther and Simon—both want to be his friend but currently he has no island space for them (No Way). Nevertheless, he thinks he has space for Dad, Gerty and Paul, none of whom have space for him (Sob). Here's a crude test of whether you have real space for someone: "would you leave your nice warm bed, at three in the morning, on a cold wet night in answer to their phone call saying they're feeling down in the dumps and need someone to talk to? Or would you underwrite their mortgage? Or donate them one of your kidneys?"

Anyway, our neighbor has a core network of two people and a dog, and the open opportunity for adding two more—Simon and Esther. Five out of the "standard" seven (plus or minus two) isn't bad. He might even add Gerty who has just broken up with her sometime lover—any port in a storm.

Mind Map #2.2 Now it's your turn. Map your current relationship network in the spaces provided in Mind Map #2.2. There are at least two excellent reasons for doing so: 1) Other people help us define who we really are; and 2) If you're trying to make important changes the significant others in your life can really help or really, really hinder.

Neil McK. Agnew, Ph.D. and John L. Brown, Ph.D.

Once you complete the above matrix you have a crude map of some of your central and peripheral islands, and of some of your established and potential alliances. The two-way choices constitute a powerful web of mutual expectations in which some Real Yous are suspended.

If you don't think so just try going against one of yours or one of their expectations and see what happens. Try changing your eating, drinking, or love making habits and sooner than later you'll feel the force of the web. Those networks help locate you, help define who you are, help keep your islands in place, help keep you who and where you are! If you're going to make a move you need resources, you need mental and emotional moving expenses—a lotta people can't afford to move. But with our help you can! So hang in there with us.

Mind map # 2.3 Now review the life-style activities you mapped out in Mind Map # 1 at the end of Chapter One. Focus on those activities that provide short-term gain and long term pain (+-). Next select ONE of those activities, not only one that you want to change, but in doing so would be supported by someone in your core network. For example, such targets for change are often over-consumption activities—TV; booze; food; sports; sex. Did you find any activity that your mutual choice network would help rather than hinder you in the process? If so you're halfway there.

Here's an example in Mind Map 2.3 for our neighbor Jasper who wants to make some life style changes. He's found that he'll get most of his support from Mum and his buddy Bill and possibly Simon if he wants to spend more time with him and switch him from a No Way to a Bingo relationship. And while he would like to have Gerty in a Bingo relationship he realizes she is only interested in him for one reason—a one night stand.

Finding the Real You

Ch. 2 Mind Map #2.3: Jasper's Change

Relationship Map								
Tribe members:	Mum	Boots	Bill	Simon	Esther	Dad	Gerty	Paul
Junk food	+	-	-	-	-	0	-	0
Booze	+	0	-	-	-	-	-	0
One-niters	+	+	+	+	+	0	+	0
TV watching	-	-	+	+	-	+	-	0
Junk reading	+	+	+	+	-	-	-	+

Of course Jasper could pick one of his (+-) behaviors that doesn't require much active support of any of his core network—like his junk reading, and his one-night stands. For example he can work on reducing his junk reading by raising the quality from blood and guts action thrillers to biographies of famous sport figures. Any ideas about reducing the one-night stands? No?

Now, after this example, your problems seem to shrink by comparison. Right? So which one did you choose? Do you have at least one supporter or are you on your own? Take heart, help is on the way!

CHAPTER 3:

SUSPENDED IN A NETWORK OF ALLIANCES

> **"With friends and family like these who needs enemies."**
> —Anonymous

John's back from Hawaii shoving his preposterous tan and self-satisfied grin in everyone's face. One of my self-images shrinks. I close my eyes and think about the ape-like Herman in the next office with his potbelly and curly black hair everywhere but his head. I almost succeed in stretching me back into shape.

Humming the tune 'Hawaiian Holiday', John reads my draft of Chapter 2. "Too many big names, too much theory, too many words. Keep it simple. I've got jet lag. Going home to crash. See ya."

My Author Image—hopeful, yet fragile—collapsed into a fetal position. But salvation is at hand. My self-righteous Me rides to the rescue: "That SOB's got his nerve. After two weeks of lounging, surfing, wining, dining and . . . and . . . who knows what . . . he glides in here and casually pees on my little parade. Well . . . well . . . I'll show him." So savoring a deliciously sanctimonious pout I go home early too, but make a mental note to find a more articulate, aggressive and regal Me. A real dragon slayer.

Get home to find Bruney once again up the ladder finishing the ceiling and Shiplitz yet again reclining in my Lazy Boy, guzzling my gin. Even that autistic egg-head recognizes Darth Vader has arrived and desperately struggling to rise gets one snowshoe caught in the chair's mechanism. Darth exits stage right and whimpy ME extricates Shiplitz who shuffles off home mumbling: "Why? Why? Why?"

Unconcerned, Bruney keeps painting away—whistling 'I've got a wonderful feeling.'

"Well I'm glad someone has. Have you been drinking?"

"Oh" she says, "Just a teensy weensy sip to keep the Professor company. He just hates drinking alone. He's really a sweet little man. I had him hold the ladder for me and you'll never guess what he did—he ran his hand up my leg . . . all the way!"

"I'll kill em . . . I'll kill em" I scream heading after Shiplitz.

"Now don't be silly, he's just a harmless little fella—I'm sure his warm, trembling hand just slipped. Anyway, who's going to hold the ladder for me when I paint the dining room?"

Just as the waves dissolve against the rocks, so my heroic self-image shatters against a hardened heart. I wonder how many more ME's can get clobbered in one day? With friends and family like these who needs enemies. If the real ME's are supposed to be safely suspended in a network of alliances I'd better buy them all parachutes, speaking of which I poured myself a large gin. Bruney joined me. Later we re-established a neglected alliance between two of our barely civilized selves.

YOU AS AN EVOLVING NETWORK OF MENTAL ISLANDS

In the last chapter we indicated how the Real Yous are located on a Society of Islands arranged in concentric circles. What holds a society together? Habits and alliances?

Neil McK. Agnew, Ph.D. and John L. Brown, Ph.D.

For example some of us have the habit of sniffing around our network with a nose for details. Others, just as predictably rubberneck about with an eye for the big picture. Not only individuals but cultures have mental habits—the Northern hunger for 'truth' and the Southern eye for 'beauty'. The stability of personal and cultural habits provide constraints, provide guidelines, provide social structure.

More obviously though, trusted alliances—short term and long term—serve as social glue. An alliance with Darwin lead us out of the 19th century, one with Freud lead us into the 20th, Shiplitz is leading us into the 21st.

MENTAL ISLANDS INSIDE YOUR HEAD

Some alliances exist between the array of mental islands inside your head, while others connect your islands with those inside the noggins of others.

First we focus on your internal islands. For example in the center we find the alliances and territorial struggles between your various selves—ranging from the ideal to the ones with warts, whines and gas. Which of your Selves hog center stage: 'Nobody wants me' or 'Too many people need me'; 'Look at what I've accomplished' or 'How come people don't wave and cheer when I go by?' 'Why wasn't I born beautiful?' or 'Those pigs just want my body'?

Remember the matrix of interpersonal relationships you mapped at the end of Chapter 2? What if you did the same thing again, only this time mapped the happy and not so happy networking between your many selves: between your ideal physical image and the lumpy one reflected by your mirror; between the one with saggy bits and the svelte, flawless designer skins inhabited by movie stars; between your ideal intellectual self and the tongue-tied one who repeatedly mangles your brilliant thoughts; between the spendthrift and the budgeter; between the self that craves to be invited and the one who 'vants to be alone'; between the 'successful' self image and the one

Finding the Real You

who fails to get the promotion, can't manage the children, loves the wrong person, has yet to break 100 in golf—and like Charlie Brown, never does get to kick the ball.

We need practice mapping someone's islands. I suggest we do John's. He suggests we do mine . . . We both decide to go to the next office and map Herman's.

HERMAN'S ISLANDS

What would the mental islands inside Herman's head look like? After several expensive interviews with him in his favorite bar we drew the following Mind Maps. The first is in Figure 3.1

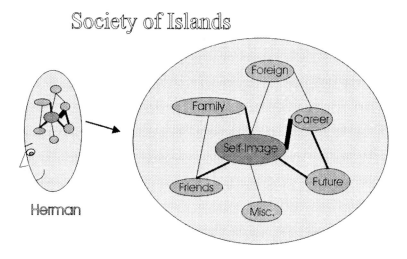

Not surprisingly residing in his hairless head and at the center of his fragmented society of minds we found his core Self-Images. Close by and strongly linked we found his images of family and friends. Even more strongly linked however are his images of his career, and still further out, of his future.

Scattered outside this inner circle lie his outer islands. We merely show a couple: first, those for foreigners—most of whom he distrusts.

Neil McK. Agnew, Ph.D. and John L. Brown, Ph.D.

He thrives on stereotypes. However since he works in an ethnic melting pot, and since business is going global he reluctantly sees 'Furyners' as linked to his career—smiling on the outside, raging on the inside. For simplicity's sake we cram all his other outer islands together into Miscellaneous: politics; religion; weight watchers; health (he's healthy as a horse so not much on this particular mind).

When we do a blow-up of his main personal islands what do we find? Not only his Dream world, not only his work world, not only his family world, not only his hunting buddies, but dead center we find a big, well defended and traditional 'macho' island. We've put down our results in Figure 3.2.

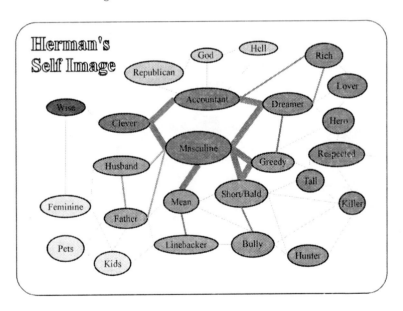

Herman does not march in the Gay Day parade! Currently his main physical self-image is 'short and bald'—strongly linked to his masculine self. A feared football linebacker in high school and college his self-image then was 'strong, hairy and tough'. In those glorious bygone days the only things he wasn't strong enough to break were his own mean habits.

Finding the Real You

CENTRAL ALLIANCES

Herman's core Selves are clear: Mr. Macho, Mr. Mean, Mr. Bully, and last but not least Mr. Short and Bald (sob!). All his other major selves link up with Macho Herman, with his Mean Self (he calls it 'tough'): "I may be short and bald but I'm one tough dude"; "When I played football they called me 'The Mean Machine'; "I wear the pants in my family" (Husband); "My kids don't dare talk back to me" (Father); "I'm not only tough, but I'm smart" (Clever); "I want MINE now" (Greedy); "Ya gotta be tough and smart to be successful in my business" (Accountant). What a sweet, cuddly little fella.

Going to pot: As he 'matured' he avoided exercise, put on the lard, and that beloved 'strong, hairy and tough' image disintegrated and split in two. One became the hated Mr. Short, Fat and Bald, and the other became Mr. Mean. The Linebacker Self is still available from an image warehouse on one of his outer islands, reappearing briefly on center stage after a few beers while watching football.

The short-bald image remains his persistent and ugly companion, coloring much of his day-to-day behavior such as Meanness, Greed and Bullying. Of course watching young children at play convinces many that these three players are bred in the bone—driving the perennial human search for selfish short-term gain. But Herman's hated physical self-image and his need to appear macho injects an extra dose of meanness into these human foibles.

One time, when he was really sozzled, he confessed he'd sent away for some powdered grizzly bear testicles—guaranteed not only as an aphrodisiac, but also containing growth hormones . . . some guys reported growing three inches . . ."then I'll be able throw away these damn elevator shoes." He heard about this magic potion on a "survival" training course using real bullets . . ." for the day law and order breaks down . . ." But don't worry, you guys are my buddies . . . I'll defend you."

On the other hand if his brutish Selves ever teamed up and established a strategic alliance, in the service of a socially desirable and heroic undertaking they could generate an awesome and admirable force. So far his strong Dreamer only engages in airy-fairy games—with heroic accomplishments way out on fantasy islands.

The clever accountant: Cleverness also holds a central position in Herman's concentric circles of islands. A clever student he memorized answers and the rules but never 'got' the big picture—his Wise Self resides isolated on an outer atoll. But being good with rules he's a reasonably successful Accountant—although he has trouble linking accounting with masculinity. You know the sort of stereotype—'yesterday I was mugged by an accountant . . . he threatened to strike me with his horn rimmed glasses.'

Nevertheless accounting enables him to meet the masculine need to 'provide' for his wife and family, live on a proper street, drive a BIG car, and afford hunting trips carrying maximum firepower.

The dreamer: Herman harbors a strong "Dreamer Self" who emerges out of the closet after his third drink: "One of these days I'm going to be one rich S.O.B"; " Also you guy's don't know it but I'll let you in on a little secret—us bald guys don't need Viagra, we manufacture our own in the old cajones and I gotta string of very satisfied partners who'll vouch for that".

This Dreamer of Herman's provides his main solutions for handling failed expectations. This fantasy weaver not only recaptures his glory linebacker days, but also briefly transforms him into Mr. Tall, Rich, and Heroic. He magically creates 'great lover' images, which periodically spill over into bedroom performances—astonishing his wife Gert. Their best sex probably occurs when they're making love to an imaginary other. Isn't that disgusting?

Poor Gert. She has the hopeless ambition of trying to please everyone.

Outer islands: Attached to his rather meager Husband and Father selves we find another little group of outer islands: his feminine side, pets, and kids. On the rare occasion when he does spend time with his children, his mean-bully Self encourages pretty rough play. Watching him teach his seven-year-old son to throw a football we heard

Finding the Real You

the tearful kid sniffle: "Can we stop having fun now Dad and I can go back in the house." The only sign of gentleness and nurturence occurs with Puddles the poodle, and occasionally on his kid's birthdays. Surprisingly, he cries when he receives one of those syrupy sentimental cards on Father's day.

At election time he becomes a staunch right winger and a cautious Born-Again-Christian. At these times he generates some pretty convincing images of a fearsome God and fiery pictures of hell. A hell mainly designed for others, but occasionally for several of his selves following wild daydreams and nightmares.

I'm outa here: Herman has pretty strong exit skills—if he's not getting more than his share he leaves, either literally and ungraciously, or pulls a quiet Walter Mitty and daydreams his way out. These fantasy escapes range from the ludicrously romantic, through the childishly heroic, to the brutally vindictive.

Herman lives very much short-term, day-to-day. "I'm not greedy but you're a long time dead so I want mine NOW". The closest he comes to generating Future Selves occurs in two places: 1) he generates household budgets which he uses to bully his wife and children into ridiculous economies; 2) he generates images of becoming tall, rich, romantic and heroic, and eventually settling ALL accountants for real and imaginary insults, by 'blowing the bastards away.'

Fortunately his aggressive fantasies remain safely ensconced on outer islands. Similarly his 'romantic self' cavorts with movie stars—the current love of his life being Julia Roberts, and includes a dog-eared picture in a secret pocket in his wallet—a picture of her being embraced by an orangutan on a trip to Borneo.

Conflicting Selves: Herman suffers the same fate as the rest of us—several of his central selves don't get along. For example, his Masculine Image and The Accountant detest each other. His Macho self sees accounting as a sissy occupation—so he handles that mismatch by playing the 'exception game': " I'm not like other accountants. I should be working with the FBI's forensic unit . . . boy would I nail em!"

Neil McK. Agnew, Ph.D. and John L. Brown, Ph.D.

Not surprisingly his short-bald-fat Self suffers rejection and snide comments from his other Selves. His Dreamer suffers burnout, not only from repeatedly reproducing the image of his linebacker days, but laboriously adding hair and another three inches in height. One of the office hackers produced a computer-generated image of Herman sporting long, blond locks a la Marilyn Monroe. After pouting for three days he asked her to do another but "Common Cindy . . . make it mannish this time".

Once in a long while his Clever self teams up with his Accountant and his Dreamer, generating a retirement scenario and producing a bit of wisdom. But these are brief undertakings, the linkages long and tenuous, so the alliance quickly disintegrates and the products, like sun dried shells, lay neglected and lifeless on distant Wise Island.

When examining a Mind Map, look for islands that have many interconnections—that's where the Real Yous and Thems hang out. It's obvious with the ones in the center, but notice the density of linkages between some of the outer islands constructed by his Dreamer, for example 'Killer'. If the connections are weak or conflicting then likely they won't lead to action. But if they're mainly positive alliances then, under special circumstances, the well-connected Killer Self could emerge on center stage and create mayhem.

Note, in particular, that not all the links or bridges to the Killer Self flow from Mr. Dreamer and his creations. Some links flow, directly or indirectly, from active Selves: Masculine; Mean; Linebacker; Bully; Short Bald; and Hunter. John and I agree to stop teasing Herman!

Conflicts and alliances—me and them: Not only do we have internal selves generating and maintaining alliances and wars with each other, but our selves join and also do battle with one or more selves belonging to others. Herman's strongest external alliances include a small group of guys who are into hunting and football. In these situations Herman's Linebacker and Hunter have a ball . . . even Killer has a few gory fantasies. At the last gridiron encounter between their

Finding the Real You

Alma Mater and their traditional football foe, Herman and his buddy Bill got arrested for engaging in a bit of a brawl with some geezers cheering for the opposition.

This little dust-up provides a nice example of how the situation in which you happen to find yourself can determine which of your Yous gets invited to 'dance'.

His strongest workplace alliances revolve around assisting the sneaky and greedy Selves of his clients avoid two things: paying taxes and an IRS audit.

At the office, his Clever Accountant Self takes center stage—most of the time. But sometimes he closes his office door, swings his feet up on the desk and becomes the Dreamer—growing rich, seducing young maidens, and leaping over tall buildings.

Herman's family life—ranging from overbearing to sentimental—produces weak alliances and wariness. All members except Puddles remain poised for flight. His weak feminine side sneaks in and out of the play but, not even Dreamer provides any supporting lines. We find only fragile selves on this side of the map—battles long over, long won. And yet. . . ?

Herman demonstrates the paradoxical character of our times: strong political views, yet only during an election; a religious 'believer' yet a doubter; a bully who still seeks his blankie and his 'mummy'. How the twig is bent so grows the Herman.

PHANTOM SELVES, PHANTOM LIMBS

To get an idea of the persistent power possessed by your different self-images consider people who have a limb amputated—a foot for example. Even though they KNOW the limb is gone they still FEEL it, it still moves, it still hurts, and it still itches. In spite of what their eyes and their mirrors tell them when not 'looking' the phantom limb prevails for years and years.

The situation we're in determines which of our various physcial self-images are 'real'. When buying shoes the amputee has no right foot, but when watching telly he feels an excruciating pain in that very same foot. Look what distasteful images emerge when you make the mistake of viewing youself with one of those three-way mirrors in a clothing store—" . . . that's not my butt . . . is it?"

While most of us don't have phantom limbs, we still harbor phantom self-images—like how we look from behind and how old we are. Notice, that although we can enter our proper age on an official form, most adults operate with a phantom age that's typically about five years younger. For example, John and I were riding on the subway and a young lady got up and offered me her seat! John thought it was hilarious but, it forced me, at least for a few hours, to desert my phantom age and painfully ratchet up ten years or so to my calendar age.

To help him maintain his phantom linebacker—twenty years out of date—Herman avoids mirrors and buying new clothes.

We all have different experiences with our various phantom selves: some quietly running the show; some waiting patiently or impatiently in the wings—the thin self perennially trying to claw their way through the fat; the bright self succeeding on rare and joyous occasions in loosening the knots of their tongue-tied spokesperson, our phantom 'leader' finally vaulting ahead of our bumbling mob.

BULLY YOUS

Among all your many Yous, phantom or 'real', which ones bully the others? Herman's center stage dominator is his Macho Self. When that one gets threatened Herman's whole network rattles. For Shiplitz his central Self resides on Big Mind Island sustained by the oooohs and aaaaahs of us lesser souls and publishers. His current Writer's Block threatens that center so his whole world trembles. When the core Selves shake a person becomes very fragile, or even dangerous.

Are you old enough to remember the folk wisdoms? Never discuss politics or religion at the table or ask a woman her age! Which translates: "Don't goose phantom selves".

Which Self did you pencil in at the center of your Mind Map at the

Finding the Real You

end of the last chapter? Some dominant selves arrived in your genes—fast metabolic rate vs slow, normal intelligence or leader of the pack.

Furthermore, some selves get extra psychological and social nourishment in childhood and so grow bigger and stronger—gender identification for example. Herman's Daddy was a Marine Sergeant in the Pacific. It remained Herman's prized image till years later when his father marched in a gay parade, later dying of Aids. Talk about phantom images rattling the cage!

ALL THE WORLD'S A STAGE

Take another look at Herman's Self Image. Think of pushing an imaginary ON button in the lower right hand corner and see the flow of information, energy and action between the islands, the shifting of lead players. Having trouble? Then merely move Herman from one situation to another: arriving home from work ("where's Puddles?"); to going over to a friends to watch football; to going hunting; to daydreaming of being tall and respected; to a child's birthday party; to the ritual Friday night sexual encounter with Gert his wife; to being bullied by his boss for losing a big client; to arriving home and finding his wife and kids have left him. All the world's a stage . . .

We chose Herman's mind to map, partly because he was readily available and with a few drinks voluble. But he also comes close to a popular stereotype . . . Yes?

MIND DEPOSIT #3

You are a dynamic society of minds, of selves, of alliances—short term, long term—of petty squabbles and enduring wars. All the world's a stage with different players taking the lead part with each shifting scene, and then exiting stage left, making way for yet another skilled or clumsy member of your wondrous cast.

51

Neil McK. Agnew, Ph.D. and John L. Brown, Ph.D.

"**Yes but** ... I never heard such garbage in my life. You guys are confusing thoughts with selves. I have lotsa thoughts but only one self. So what did ya do with that Schmuck Herman? I'll you. When he had two or more thoughts about the same thing you drew a circle around each of them and made an other island or a Self. Well, don't try that with me or you'll both be singing high notes. I will admit that this Mind Mapping stuff is not a bad way to organize my thoughts except ..."

Well yes . . . except you end up with too many islands. That's why the idea of a Society of Minds, or roles, or selves is neat. Not only can you include a lot of stuff but also simplify it down to head size. Oh, by the way, John suggested we drop over to see Shiplitz for an intellectual care package. We did—not uninteresting.

MIND MAP #3

Well you can see what's coming can't you? Time to do a first draft of your Mind Map. Bertha, if you're still there, you can make it a Thought Map.

Mind Map #3a: Go to figure 3.4 and using a pencil take a crack at identifying a few of your central selves—four or five. Then, after a night's sleep, make any revisions you want.

Finding the Real You

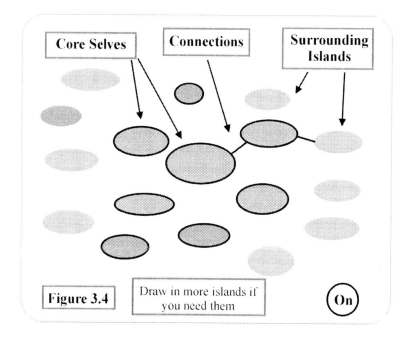

Figure 3.4 — Draw in more islands if you need them — On

Mind Map #3b: In pencil, add connections or linkages between the selves in #3a. Heavy lines between strong alliances, and light lines between weak ones.

Mind Map #3c: Still in pencil add outer Selves or islands. Next, rough in the connections. Now press the ON button and travel around your Mind Map through different familiar situations: at work, at home, in bed, in a traffic jam.

See anything interesting? See any shifts in which Real You gets to play center stage? Any particular Self making many appearances? Any major alliances? Any squabbles or wars?

Earlier we proposed that we'd find your Real Yous embedded in a network of alliances and mutual expectations. Which Real Yous are starting to make their appearance in the network of players you've just constructed?

CHAPTER 4:

LINKING AND DEFENDING ISLANDS

> "Was none who would be foremost
> To lead the dire attack;
> But those behind cried 'Forward!'
> And those before cried 'Back!'."
> —Macauly

John leads the way over to see Shiplitz who spends most of his time in his study housed in the old stable behind the house. John knocks. No answer. Knocks again. Still no answer. John hammers on the door. It opens a crack, Shiplitz peers out and whispers: "Please come at a different time for a different person." But he can't close the door with John's foot in it.

John nudges me and points. There's a little dog, a mini Dachshund. He's wearing miniature snow-shows, a tiny shirt and tie. John goes hysterical and collapses. The dog growls. Professor Shiplitz commands: "Down Epsilon."

John is wiping tears from his eyes, I tell him we should go. Still giggling he asks: "Epsilon? Why call the dog that?" The Professor

Finding the Real You

explains that in mathematics Epsilon means small number . . . which the dog certainly is . . . Called Eppy for short.

I tell the professor how much we appreciated finding out about Minksy and the Society of Minds, and can the good Professor give us any more neat stuff on how the mind works. He only shakes his great head mumbling: "You would never understand." The dog growls. "Down Eppy."

In the mirror I notice John slipping something into his pocket from Shippy's desk.

The Professor sighs and says:" Minsky had a colleague, a famous physicist who became mentally ill. All geniuses are crazy—crazy means you construct a different world than the standard one manufactured for the masses by bureaucrats, teachers, advertisers, and accountants. Anyway, psychiatrists 'fixed' Minsky's colleague—he is no longer crazy, but he no longer does good physics either. Minksy complains: "Mental health may be good for the individual but it's bad for science, bad for the country. Shippy says: "That's why I seek no treatment for my depression—the world needs my brain unconstrained by mind-suppressing drugs."

Turning to John he continues: "Ah, you may not understand Minsky but I think this may interest you. My wife wanted to have Epsilon 'fixed' so I discussed it with the vet who asked me: 'Do you want a DOG or a PET?' That settled it, Eppy still has his little round jewels. Like crazy physicists, Dogs are more trouble than Pets but a lot more interesting. You two are supposedly interested in how minds work, think about it—some minds want everything 'fixed', others are still willing to play in an 'unfixed' game."

John is puzzled and asks the Professor: 'Tell me, how does Eppy make out with the ladies . . . with the snowshoes and all.' Shiplitz is not amused. He promptly escorts us out with Eppy yapping at our heels. Having tried a bit of humour on the Professor, with sad results, I asked John to keep his wit on a short leash. Dream on!

MENTAL ISLANDS INSIDE OTHER PEOPLE'S HEADS

In the last chapter we took a peek inside Herman's head, at his islands and alliances among them. Not only do alliances form, and bullying and heroics occur among the Society of Selves inside our heads, but also between our minds and those inside the heads of others—your Mum's, your big sister's, your friend's, your boss's; your lover's. It's their core Selves that call our various selves out to play, work, laugh, bonk, cry, or run. And visa versa of course.

Not only are some of your Selves located on islands inside the heads and hearts of others, but also on islands in the 'heads' of institutions. Notice in such formal alliances the relationship is fragile. With the stroke of a computer key, or a virus induced electronic burp, poof that particular "YOU" disappears from the institutional 'mind'. If the Government computer makes an error and says you're cheating on your taxes, or you're a male, or dead—then for a whole network of other Thems you are, even if you ain't. When they misbehave computers can interrupt the music of life—let's hope they never accidently ring out the ding dong of doom.

Of course we don't have to go to computers for such examples of radical renovations or destructions. Closer to home we find booze, drugs, daydreams, or a cerebral stroke playing wondrous or devastating games—temporary or permanent—with our own internal wiring. But most day-to-day network renovations involved in normal interpersonal relations are less radical than electronic or neurological wipeouts.

MISPLACED SELVES

But notice, just as some or all of our selves can be misplaced on an institutional island, so too can misplacement occur inside the heads of significant others: the mum who refuses to move her serial killer son off 'innocent island'; the suspicious lover who reserves a permanent space for innocent You on 'cheater island'; the adoring child who places you on a pedestal on 'hero island'. For them, those Selves are all REAL.

When we encounter radically different perceptions of the same person what are we to think? Like beauty, does everything lie in the eye of the beholder? Or is it that different You's emerge and dance for different people? Recall again that mind map of your interpersonal network, the one you drew at the end of Chapter 2. In the cases of mutual selections (Bingo), one or more of your selves resided securely on someone else's central islands, and one of more of their selves occupied a treasured place on one or more of yours. You have a working alliance—maybe one-dimensional: sexual OR occupational OR social. Or maybe it's multidimensional: sexual AND occupational AND social.

While some welcome aboard all our various selves (our Mothers), and while others welcome only one or two (the University doesn't want all the Shiplitz Selves), strange to say there are those who can't tolerate even one of your Yous (Shiplitz rejects everyone who calls).

Neil McK. Agnew, Ph.D. and John L. Brown, Ph.D.

In our own heads, in the minds of others, and of institutions, we find our various Selves suspended and defined more or less consistently to fit the situation. As it changes, so too do the Selves that take center stage.

SELVES RESIDE IN THE EYE OF THE BEHOLDER

In the story four blind women describing an elephant, each one believes hers is the true picture. Similarly each family member or friend believes that their particular view represents the Real You. Hey Bertha, Hey Bert which one is the Realest You of all?

In your Chapter 2 Mind Map some of the selections were only one-way (Sob), you had a treasured place for them on one or more of your islands, but they had only an insignificant or no space for you. Or visa versa, they chose you but you had little space or time for them (Sorry). There's no way you wanted them occupying significant real estate in your Society of Islands, your Society of Minds.

Some of the business world chooses Herman the Accountant but barely tolerates Herman the ex-linebacker and his boring reminiscences of the glory days. His family tries to avoid him and he them as much as possible— they exchange brief, superficial song-and-dance routines. Only his beer buddies—his jocks and hunters—provide him with a generally accepting audience, a situation of mutual acceptance (Bingo).

The academic world chooses Shiplitz: The Writer of books. Sure, the great thinker behind the writer is appreciated, but without The Writer delivering the scholarly goods it's back to life in the intellectual backwaters—and he knows it. A non-publishing Shiplitz is no Shiplitz at all—as far as the University is concerned.

Real Yous: Think about it, which You or Yous are chosen? Which THEMS do you choose? Real ones? Ideal ones? Distorted ones? You say later: " I don't know what I saw in him? " Friends at the time said: "What do you see in her?" Who sees "straight? Them? You?

"Oh great, straight-seer, wherever you are, give us THE REAL

Finding the Real You

PICTURE, show us the Real Thems, show them the Real Me's! Well, just a minute, you can show me the Real Me's, but let's show them a composite of my better Me's, OK?"

Now of all the YOUS out there, please would only the Real Ones step off their islands and come forward and stand right here under the lights. What's that? You're all Real!

Yeah right, there's a mob of YOUS, old ones, and new ones, shrinking ones, distorted ones, emerging ones. There's a bunch of Johns over there, and over here a flock of Bruneys, but so far only a few of Shiplitz' Selves off to one side. Also, we'd like to see the cranky Shiplitz fall through the cracks but not the one who gives us neat ideas. I could do without the naive Bruney . . . well, the one who is naive about others, not the one who's lovingly naive about me.

BALANCING CONFLICTING ALLIANCES

The resiliency of our **internal**, inter-island alliances—of our networked selves— gives us our personal sense of stability, our integrity, and our character. This happy state occurs when the center island selves get along pretty well, and the ideal and warty selves are relegated to outer islands without e-mail or ferry tickets.

The strength of our **external,** inter-island alliances—networking between our central selves and the multiple selves of others—gives us a stable sense of interpersonal and social belonging. From such networks arise our sense of trust in other people and institutions: our Mum, mate, hair dresser, mechanic, maitre de, boss, doctor, broker, banker, governments—well, maybe we're getting carried away, cancel the last five.

AIN'T EASY

The minimum requirements of living are clear: maintain a working balance between personal integrity and social belonging. One of the trickiest maneuvers in life is locating and maintaining a workable

Neil McK. Agnew, Ph.D. and John L. Brown, Ph.D.

balance or trade-off between two compelling and competing needs: one, the need for stable alliances among your internal islands, the other for trusted relations with significant others. When that dynamic balance gets out of whack you suffer big time. Without personal integrity you're a vacillating wimp burdened by uncertain selves at the mercy of anyone selling instant solutions or salvation. On the other hand, without social sensitivity and membership you're a social pain in the butt or an isolate. We need access to the nurturance and support of others. Shiplitz seems to be losing such access. His two strong internal Selves are in conflict—the Big Thinker endlessly wrestling with Writer's Block. Furthermore, hardly any of his Selves get along with outsiders. Well there's always Epsilon.

The Yous representing your internal and external alliances—are a bit like the United States and it's trading partners—they are in continuous negotiations to get a viable, if not necessarily fair, exchange. So, because the integrity of the Real Yous is embedded in a tangle of internal and external alliances they must operate suspended in a dynamic network of mutual expectations. It's there, suspended in that web of expectations where we'll find your Real Yous.

If we just searched inside your head it would be like trying to understand the motion of the planets without understanding gravity. So the Real Yous must survive in the midst of the dynamic push and pull of internal and external forces. Recall Marvin Minsky and his Society of Minds? Well he also recognized the importance of personal integrity and the continuous battle to protect and maintain it.

DEFENDING YOUR ISLANDS

Minsky went further than merely proposing islands of consistency. Because we have limited mental capacity, and because our experience is filled with inconsistencies—"she loves me, she loves me not"—our fabricated islands and self-images have to be protected from the daily bombardment of exceptions to our expectations and stereotypes. When the inconsistencies gain a foothold we call it different things: stress, anxiety, panic, marriage, free enterprise, poopstorms. What do you call it?

"I'm Not Hearing You Mrs. Shiplitz"

Wendy, the Shiplitz four-year-old daughter, and her little friend Arny were playing in the sand pile. Ruth Shiplitz looked out the window to see Arny generously pouring sand over Wendy's head. Ruth read him the riot act to which Arny replied: "I'm not hearing you Mrs. Shiplitz."

Like little Arny in the sand pile we defend our islands. We raise barriers against things we don't want to hear, see or know. We automatically mount defenses against unwanted intruders into OUR space. Just when we locate a pleasant little island, just when one of our innocent pleasure-seeking selves settles in, why then the ants and bees arrive at our mental picnic. 'Whys', 'donts', 'shoulds' swarm ashore. It's no wonder when we find a consistency or short term pleasure (+-) we go for it and defend against the booger: "I'm not hearing you Mrs. Shiplitz." As a case in point our new found hero, Professor Shiplitz, can tolerate anything: except a second opinion.

Here's a simple way to get a feel for what Minsky means when he talks about defending our little 'Islands of Consistency'. Take a minute and confront one of your friends when they're having a verbal picnic and playing one of their favorite consistency tapes. For example, HE'S playing a 'dumb blonde' tape and you tell him about this really smart blonde you know. Listen and watch carefully to see how he protects his strong, simple expectation or stereotype. He may defend it with a standard, low cost defensive ploy that leaves the island in tact: "Oh she's the exception that proves the rule . . . like an honest telemarketer or politician . . . they're so rare everyone notices them." We either throw those exceptions off the island, or if we can't banish them we lock them away in the basement, in the attic, or in a shed at the far end of the sand spit.

Other defenses against inconsistencies include:

1. challenging the credibility of the message or the messenger ("to you everyone seems smart, even dumb blondes");
2. if confronted with a clear exception then escape or turn it off ("I'm not hearing you!"; "Liar, liar, pants on fire." "I'm outa here.");
3. gradually learn to avoid confrontation with inconsistencies, don't hang out with, listen to, or read sources that threaten your favorite categories or stereotypes ("I avoid him like the plague", or "I never read that left-wing rag");
4. reserve a few safe islands for novelty (going to a comedy club or secret web sites);
5. safely play with inconsistencies—particularly other people's (like 'yes butters' and critics do).

But what if the nay-sayers break through your defenses and flood in. Well in some cases no problem. You can afford to enjoy some inconsistencies if most of your selves are compatible, if most of your mental islands are allied and peaceful, or if you throw a chemical blanket to hide the mess—guzzle guzzle, sniff sniff.

THREE WHYS IN A ROW

Minsky proposes a simple way to test the adequacy of the defenses of any particular self or island: Fire a salvo of *three whys in a row*. Only the most bigoted or agile defenders of an oversimplification can gracefully or coolly handle the **3W test**. For example assault the following treasured consistency:

> "The government is bankrupting the country."
> "Why?"
> "Because they spend more than they take in."
> "Why?"
> "Because they encourage people to go on welfare.
> "Why?"

Finding the Real You

> "Because . . . because they're stupid. . . . because they're really commies at heart because . . . for God's sake I don't know why they're so stupid . . . ask a psychologist . . . a non-government psychologist."

Try the 3W test on an acquaintance (not a friend if you want to keep them). The next time you hear a nice fat generalization, or consistency, throw them three whys in succession and watch their bounded rationality sweat and squirm. But, be prepared for ill will. Nobody likes a smart-ass. A smart ass is someone who: successfully assaults one of your islands and makes you feel dumb; forces you to take a mental pratfall; sucks you into wasting time planning revenge; or hopefully teaches you to avoid that poophead in the future.

PROTECTING YOURSELF AGAINST THE TRIPLE WHAMMY

Firing off three "whys" in a row at someone is not for the faint of heart. If you're prepared to "give it" be prepared to "get it" back. If some smart-ass is throwing "whys" at one of your Selves, one of your treasured islands, here are some useful defenses.

> You: "The government is bankrupting the country!"
> Poophead: "**Why**?"
> Your ploy: "You're smarter than anyone else, you tell me.

This counterattack engages one of their treasured THEMS—their 'I'm smart' self-image—and usually takes them off the offensive and puts them on the defensive. However, if they're a sophisticated "why shooter" they don't fall for it and instead reply:

> Poophead: "No . . . no . . . I'm really curious about **why** you think the government is bankrupting us?"

Neil McK. Agnew, Ph.D. and John L. Brown, Ph.D.

>Your 2nd ploy: "**Why** would that interest you? Now you have trumped his "why" with your "why" and are hopefully out of the question-response spiral.

WHY MASTERS

But, if you have a 'Master Why' bully on your tail you may have to resort to a master escape ploy (no—not stomping off in a huff). You don't run. If you've got enough nerve you pirouette right outside the shared expectation—the shared frame of reference of providing rational sounding answers to his questions and instead "go non-rational".

How do you accomplish such a vanishing act, how do you step outside the strong box of mutual expectations? Any way that breaks his expectation. Like? Like standing up and singing "home, home on the range". Or you can get up from your chair and do a little jig and invite poophead to dance with you. Or if you've got the time you can follow John's favorite strategy and say: "That reminds me of a story" and then tell them a long but, completely unrelated tale, which they will likely listen to because they're still innocently playing inside the "question and relevant answer" frame. It's called "pulling a frame switch." While the puzzled smart-ass is trying to decipher your ploy, excuse yourself and go to the washroom.

Notice, to be able to break another person's firm expectations, you have to be able to break your own. You have to harbor at least one relatively strong self who can do silly or "non-expected" things in public. Have you? Yes you have, but you may need a bit more practice. Start practicing on a lightweight acquaintance, then fortified with a stiff drink, or a Mars Bar, take on a smart-ass.

Your defenders: Each of us has developed one or more Selves to defend against smart-ass assaults. Herman relies on Macho Man to bop the offender, or Dreamer for escapes. Shippy relies on snowshoes, isolation, and of course Eppy, his guard dog, as a last line of defense.

Finding the Real You

In which particular situations do you come under assault. Which of your Selves handles defenses and escapes?:

"My defender Self simply starts to cry and afterwards thinks of all the clever things I could have said";

"My guard dog Self turns red and tell them to 'f— off' , then later regrets it";

"My island guard doesn't get mad, she gets even . . . but come to think of it, that takes a lot of time. She thinks she may try spending that time stocking up her vulnerable islands with a supply of master counter-moves. Even though she stumbles a bit over the 'F' word, she kinda likes that 'f— off' ploy—particularly when she's in a hurry. It sure beats blushing and stuttering".

John thinks we're seeing a growth industry in big, mean island guards—like 'road rage'. Have you noticed increased island surveillance? What about political correctness? That's become a growth industry in protecting precious islands: "KEEP OFF—don't come here to picnic and drop off your garbage!" The definition of a friend is someone with whom you can share politically incorrect ideas and stories.

So in our family of minds we all need some Real Selves that help us manage the inevitable internal and external smart asses of daily life. In establishing and maintaining our internal integrity we try to choose compatible beliefs. In choosing our interpersonal network we try to choose compatible others, people who mutually and unconsciously ration the number of "whys", "don'ts", and "shoulds" they and we throw back and forth. If you want to stretch or end a relationship merely increase the flow of "whys".

If you're continuously defending your islands, or feeling dumb, then you're harboring incompatible beliefs or hanging out with the wrong folks. It's time to move. It's time 'to move' mentally, or more likely physically—recall that for most of us the 'situation' we're in controls center stage. Perpetual anxiety, nightmares, hives, sweaty palms indicate that it's probably time to relieve your overworked and probably burned out island-defenders and call in your special 'Exit

Neil McK. Agnew, Ph.D. and John L. Brown, Ph.D.

Selves' whose one line song and dance routine rings out loud and clear: "Hey, folks, I'm outa here".

IT MAY WORK WITH POOPHEAD, BUT . . .

It's a lot easier pulling an 'I'm outa here' move on someone else than pulling one on yourself. Moving out, breaking an established expectation, or pulling a "frame switch" on a smart ass or an offensive acquaintance is one thing, pulling it on yourself is quite another.

What happens if you're locked in a question-and-answer downward spiral inside your own head—if you're depressed or anxious and painfully engaged in self doubts, in a 3Why or 10 Why assault on one of your own central selves or islands? Dangerous? "He loves me, he loves me not"; "Should I or shouldn't I" or "Dear me I've got to make up my mind"; "I am not stupid . . . or am I?" "I've got to get outa here . . . but how can I?"; "Why are you doing this to yourself?" Well, you know the tune.

Let's say internal enemies sneak through your defenses and gain a foothold on one of your islands? What happens? It depends on which island. If it's one of your central treasured islands, or selves, then alarm bells ring. You get mad, or tense, or sleepless, or weepy, or pouty. You may rage, run, cry, pout, pray.

If any of these painful reactions occur it tells you, you've located a couple of incompatible "Real Yous". The simplest 'solution' is to call in your Travel Agent Self—if you've got one—and take a mental or physical trip. Hey, stop talking and start walking. Remember, it's often the situation you happen to be in at the moment that controls center stage. But more about that later, since for now we're not into self-change, rather we're trying to identify the main players.

How do we explain it when under assault you remain really cool? What if you're in a situation where you calmly consider the pros and cons of the 'landing parties' demands, and even assign them some island acreage? Then we know this is either an outer island, or one already under renovation or even demolition . . . 'Whatever you say dear.'

Finding the Real You

Also, what's it mean if in response to broken expectations you merely laugh uproariously? Interesting. Then we're not sure: are you squiffed enough to laugh at anything? Are you in a 'situation' like a comedy club or a roast—in a 'this is a joke' frame of mind—so you're not taking assaults seriously? Or, are you the kind of person who laughs instead of raging, it's a mean laugh—laugh now strike later?

In brief, if you want to identify the Real Yous or Thems, don't listen so much to their words, probe for the emotion, and look at the behavior. As dear old Granny used to say: "I can't hear what you're saying for what you're doing!"

Have you met a person who professes their undying love but can't seem to find much time to be with you? He's off earning enough money "so we can get married"; or he's got to look after his sick mother; or he's getting a divorce as soon as his kid is better; or he's got to lie low, "I'm a secret agent." Regardless of what he says, and he may be kidding himself as well as you, the clear message is: "I'm avoiding spending time with you." Hey wake up and smell the smoke: His 'avoiding' selves are running his show and yours.

CALL YOUR TRAVEL AGENT

At times like this, ring in your "I'm Outa Here" Self. You may have to call several times. You may even have to recruit several cooperating Selves. Those established networks of mutual expectations are made of sticky stuff, tough to untangle. You may even have to drag away one of your Yous kicking and screaming: ' But he's better than nothing.' No he's not . . . is he?

How are you stocked with 'exit' or 'escape' selves? Not enough? Too many? Ask a lover and divide that number by four. Then finish reading this remarkable book to get a surprising, mind-enhancing answer.

I can't hear what you're saying for what you're doing: Just as you identify the real Thems by what they do, not what they say, apply the same rule to yourself. Try not to listen to your own blather, rather watch what your various Selves DO! You can hear them natter on, oh so sincerely: "I'm really going to get more exercise, or cut back my drinking, or spend more time with the kids, or improve my computer skills, or lose some weight, or cut back on TV time." Sure you are! Just like you keep your New Year's resolutions.

But hey, some of our Selves do keep their resolutions. Some even pull off big moves mentally and even physically. How come? How can they? We'll see.

So even if an enemy or a wise guru gains a toehold on one of your central islands, even if your behavior changes temporarily, typically the occupation is soon over, the landing party disappears, or given the heave ho, or locked in the shed. That's what usually happens. But it doesn't have to. John claims he has THE ANSWER to taking charge, to finding the Real YOU. He discovered it in one of Shippy's pilfered notes—the ones that went to the laundry—and he's sure he'll remember one of these days. He does remember this much, that even he was impressed by whatever it was.

Now things are getting interesting. Now it's time to seriously start exploring how your minds really work, how your Selves build, defend, and renovate their little and big islands, how they form, stretch and break temporary and long term alliances. Even Herman makes remarkable discoveries, even Shippy rediscovers his Writer Self and banishes The Blocker to a floating island in the Everglades.

MIND DEPOSIT #4

Your minds are like a society of protected islands held together by short and long-term alliances. Some of the alliances are internal between your private personal islands or Selves. Some alliances are external between your minds and those of other individuals and institutions. Some of the alliances—resilient and multi-layered—produce your strong sense of self. When one or more of those core islands is assaulted your world trembles. On the other hand, some alliances are

Finding the Real You

superficial like a one-night stand or a one-year subscription to Time magazine. When such an alliance is threatened, no big deal.

We protect our core islands and their strong alliances. They provide, on the one hand, our sense of independence and personal integrity—like Herman's Macho Self, and on the other, our sense of belonging, of interpersonal and social integrity—like Herman's Accountant's job on the one hand and his football and hunter buds on the other.

Life consists of perennial and dynamic negotiations aimed at maintaining a happy, or at least, viable balance between isolation and wimphood. So, some of your Real Yous are embedded in a special few of your long-term interpersonal alliances. That's why we had you map your web of significant relationships on Mind Map #2.

You can locate the Real Yous, in yourself and others by various means. One method is to observe who gets the lead parts in common situations. Another is by stretching or breaking a strong expectation and seeing which Yous and Thems protest the loudest. Or alternatively you can throw a series of 'whys' at one of your own, or a colleague's generalizations, one of their Islands of consistency. When you hear yelps or see hives bursting out all over you know you're on target. For some gentle fun go to Mind Map #4 at the end of this chapter.

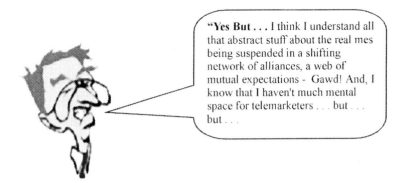

"**Yes But . . .** I think I understand all that abstract stuff about the real mes being suspended in a shifting network of alliances, a web of mutual expectations - Gawd! And, I know that I haven't much mental space for telemarketers . . . but . . . but . . .

Neil McK. Agnew, Ph.D. and John L. Brown, Ph.D.

It's alright Bert, I'll handle this. Listen up you two, this is Bertha. Bert and I have been married for 5 years and believe me he's been mostly bad news, mostly trouble. I have to keep at him all the time. But we really love each other. So where does that put your network of mutual expectations? Huh?

"WELL YES . . . Bertha you've got a point. Even though we said we're bears of small brain, each of us usually reserves at least one mind, one island, one alliance, for excitement, for variety, even for surprises and trouble . . . that's why the challenging child or independent pet is often the favorite . . . the so called spice of life. But for most of us a little spice goes a long way, otherwise all our minds start to rumble and our neurons start to smoke"—bye bye Madam War Department.

MIND MAP #4: RATTLING THE WEB

We make the outrageous claim that the Real Yous—ugh, like Herman's—lie suspended in a web of personal and inter-personal expectations. Stretch The Web in one location and it trembles throughout. In order to locate some of those Real Yous—your own and others—just rattle the web.

Everyone harbors, usually reluctantly, at least one Web-rattler. Notice what happens when one of these mental terrorists tosses a series of "whys" into one of your networks of expectations and simplifications. In a second more provocative way the web-rattler doesn't say a word . . . they merely ACT in a personally and socially unexpected or surprising manner. It's like shoving a stick into an ant heap—lotsa action!

Mind Map 4a: Shooting Whys: Don't practice on a mate but the next time an acquaintance makes a simple suggestion like going out

Finding the Real You

to eat or to a show or buying something or inviting someone over, or having a quick bonk ask them "Why". And to every answer they give, ask another "Why". Sooner or later they will tell you to stuff it in your ear. Don't listen for the rational response, listen and look for the emotion, notice how they defend their island.

How many 'whys' does it take to ring their chimes? What form does it take? Do their eyes squint, their lips thin, their voice rise, the skin color changes, or smoke come out their ears? The earlier and more emotional the response the more important the island, the more accurately your arrows have struck a tender consistency, a self-consistency. What consistency have you threatened? Next time you want to win an argument don't argue, if you've got the You for it, have them toss 'whys'.

O.K. now that you have made the necessary observations make a wee list of Tender Thems—the Thems in your social network of alliances that show an early allergic reaction to "Whys". If they're hyper-allergic to any and all whys . . . run for the hills, or keep your whys to yourself.

Yes but . . . the best laid plans . . . What if they merely respond to your needling "whys" with: " I dunno, I just feel that way." Ah Ha, bingo! You've located a Them who doesn't have to play rational mind games . . . a Them who pulls a frame switch on you . . . a Them who refers to their gut not their head bone for a decision. If they employ this frame switch frequently you've located one tough Them . . . guts are stronger and more consistent advisors than heads. For example did your choice of partner come from your head or your heart . . . or your nose? There's some evidence we choose mates by how they smell. Nonsense! But we digress—again.

Now try a 'why' assault on yourself. On second thought, not yet. In fact you may have had some difficulty finding a Self strong enough to administer the 3W test to an acquaintance—a confining web of your own expectations held you in check? So it's probably a bit too early in the game to be sticking your wiggling psychological finger inside the heads of loved ones, including yourself.

Neil McK. Agnew, Ph.D. and John L. Brown, Ph.D.

Mind Map 4b: The Wrong Side of the Bed: To get an idea of how well anchored we are in a network of mutual expectations try to stretch one, not with 'whys' but with action. Start by breaking a trivial expectation—John kissed Herman on the top of his bald head. At first his eyes misted over—we thought he was going to cry. Then he turned all red. Then the veins in his neck expanded dangerously. Then he screamed. John made it to the elevator just in time. Try the following. If you're used to sleeping with someone try to get in on the "wrong" side of the bed. First, notice whether any of your Selves feel uneasy doing it . . . if so, you've located some internal strands in your own web of expectations. Then notice what your partner does. Notice all the 'good' reasons both of you quickly generate for going back to your 'normal' locations in The Web.

Or if 'the bed' holds too sacred a place then move to a less central island, sit at the 'wrong' place at the table, or sing in a restaurant, or don't respond when the receptionist says good morning, or face the wrong way in the elevator, or offer your seat on the subway to a younger person. All simple little breeches of what you expect of yourself and what others expect of you. Trivial in the big picture, yet most of us 'feel' uneasy breaking any of them. It's usually FEELINGS, not intelligence, that notifies you when you're stretching a leash, your own or someone else's.

How easy is it for you to breach simple expectations? What do others do to bring you back to your proper place in the web? These little stretching exercises are designed to indicate that our various selves are pretty well anchored in place. To make significant moves means stretching or breaking a lot of web lines or invisible leashes. Even if external leashes are loose, even if others would give us longer leashes we rarely find out because our own internal leashes keep us 'in place.'

CHAPTER 5:

A PLACE TO STOOD

Captain of the sinking ship: "Yump Ollie, Yump!"
Ollie: "Where will I yump when there's no place to stood?"

Like Ollie all of us need places to stood—stepping stones through the day, through life.

John needs several steppy stones right now because he's in the midst of "manopause"—on shaky ground. So what does he do? He's purchased a little red sport car and races around the country patting the knees of his latest silicon enhanced trophy. I think I had mine when I was a teenager.

If you're going to discover new islands; if you're going to manage crises—menopause and manopause; if you're not going to be pushed around, and wobble like a crazy top all over the place; then your minds need a solid, safe place upon which to stood. A safe haven from which to boldly venture forth to discover the holy grail, and a safe harbor to return to for supplies and healing. So in your Society of Minds, within your network of Yous, you need a few rock solid Selves. But where do I find them? I don't want to be Stupid Solid like Herman,

Neil McK. Agnew, Ph.D. and John L. Brown, Ph.D.

I can't afford to be Sexually Solid like John, and I'm not smart enough to be Scholarly Solid like Shippy.

TURTLES ALL THE WAY DOWN

The answer to finding places to stood came on a tip from Shippy. He gave us a book by Stephen Hawking called "A Brief History of Time". Like millions of other would-be readers we didn't get by the first page. But on that page he tells a neat story. Bertrand Russell, the distinguished philosopher, is giving a public lecture about the motion of the planets around the sun and agrees to take questions from the audience. He handles them all with ease until the last one from a little old lady who says: "You know Professor Russell you've got it all wrong. The earth doesn't go spinning around out in space, everyone with any sense knows it sits securely on a giant tortoise." Russell smiles indulgently and says: " And pray madam upon what does the tortoise rest?" "You think you're very clever young man, but it's turtles all the way down!"

This Tower of Turtles supposedly going 'all the way down', gives us a hint about how healthy minds REALLY work. When someone pulls the rug out from under one of your core Selves, or knocks it off its perch with a series of 'whys', what's a sound mind to do? Apparently it just jumps down on to the next turtle in the tower. A well-anchored belief or bias has 'turtles all the way down' so it doesn't get blown away or sink from a single buffeting in rough seas.

When we tell Bruney about the turtles she says "You guys sure are generating a heap of metaphors, most of them mixed—just how are you proposing to stuff them into the small brains of all us bears?" Every once in awhile we do realize that mixed metaphors can be confusing. Like? Well like, how can we combine the "Islands of the Mind" and a "Tower of Turtles"? Mmmmh, how about each island rests on the back of a turtle. And some islands have turtles all the way down, like Herman's Macho Self; John's Sexy Self, Shippy's Big Brain Self and Bruneys bright, normal Self.

Finding the Real You

Some islands are well supported. Others are floaters—here today gone tomorrow—with only one or two unreliable turtles supporting them. The world is full of floaters, like teen fashion fads, Herman's Wise Self, Bertha's compliments, Bert's dominance, Shippy's sociability. So if someone makes turtle soup, or the supporting turtles go courting, or fishing, then gurgle, gurgle that island sinks. Does the Real You have at least one foot on an island supported by a Tower of Turtles all the way down? The answer is 'yes' as you'll soon see.

Of course, everyone at one time or another spends time on floaters. Some of them are unavoidable and tragic, for example when small children lose their mother, or a father runs off with his shrink. Some failed floaters are just part of growing up, like the high school sweetheart who dumps you for Delbert Williams just because he's tall and can dance.

Other of life's rattlers occur as you venture out on your own. For example just prior to the arrival of computers you go deeply into hock to open a typewriter sales and repair shop. Or maybe you marry Mr. Wonderful who generously gives you Aids. Maybe you loan your life savings to the phony TV evangelist; or maybe you show great common sense and avoid such dizzy flings, only to be thrown out with the trash at forty-five as part of a 'rational' corporate downsizing.

HERMAN IN A BOX

So we all spend time on floaters as well as on firmly anchored core islands. In Chapter 4 we noted that Herman, and everyone else, occupy private islands known only to our very private selves. We also harbor public islands visible to others, and some of them networked with theirs. For example look at Herman and his matrix.

Neil McK. Agnew, Ph.D. and John L. Brown, Ph.D.

	PRIVATE	SOCIAL
CORE	- Scared - Depressed - Ugly - Dreamer - Linebacker	- Accountant - Macho - Clever - Ex-Linebacker - Hunter
FLOATER	- Tall - Hero - Lover - Killer	- Husband - Father - Wise - Republican

Notice the stuff in the upper left corner, in the core/private cell. We didn't have this when we did Herm's Mind Map in Chapter 3. Those very private island/selves didn't emerge in our first interviews. They only came out several weeks later after we bought him more strong drink and hypnotized him (vino + hypnosis = veritas.). I tried to hypnotize John and he just went to sleep. He tried to hypnotize me and I broke up. But together we put Herm under.

You'll have a chance at the end of this chapter to pencil in your stuff in a matrix like Herman's. Stop and think, which are your core, private islands? How about those four or five Selves you penciled in on Mind Map #3? How many of them are safe and solid? How many rest secure on turtles going all the way down?

How many of your core islands are reliable and nourishing bases from which to smell the flowers or launch forth on voyages of discovery or pillage and return with great stories, songs and booty? How many are very private and treasured? How many are very private and not so treasured. In our last session Herm admitted that sometimes he's a klutz, then added: 'But nobody's perfect'.—and some less perfect than others as we learn all too painfully at a tender age.

Now shift perspective from inwards to outwards and have a peek at how many of your core islands are public and linked through alliances to the islands of others? How many constitute an extended family of islands—ranging from the generous and loyal support of

Finding the Real You

trusted others, to the fragile and grudging 'support' of the likes of a stingy, picky, tricky life insurance broker, or banker, or lawyer? How many of these islands will generate venture capital for voyages of discovery? Or do they just bankroll or bankrupt the status quo?

LIFE'S FLOATERS

Those floaters warrant a bit more discussion. They're like ice flows we dance upon and that add extra novelty and excitement ranging from: one night stands; to lottery tickets; to the latest instant wisdom from the Guru of the week; to temporarily and painfully taking up tennis, golf, jogging, dieting; to the fragile promises, to stock market flings, to spend more quality time with the kids; to the false starts on the jazzy computer program for your next presentation.

If you can maintain a compatible core of private islands, if you can establish compatible alliances with the core islands of others, if you can establish floaters serving as stepping stones into a nourishing future, then for Heaven's sake tell us how you did it, or what you're smoking.

Now back to earth. Do you see your various minds emerging? They're there, consisting of your private core islands, plus your supporting social networks all surrounded by floaters. Don't knock the floaters. Some will actually provide stepping-stones into the future—but ahead of time nobody knows which ones are passing fads and which emerging truths. Since we can't predict, let's focus on the Solid Central Selves, and their trusted social networks. If, right now, you were to identify at least one, solid, private self who would it be?

Herman related a poignant tale. A client being audited by the IRS blamed Herman for giving him bad advice and sued him. Herman sweat bullets during the trial but ended up paying only a token fine. But it could have been much worse—could have ruined his career. He said after the trial he went into the courthouse washroom, looked in the mirror, and speaking out loud said to himself: " You didn't turn out the way your mother wanted you to, you're short, fat, and ugly, pock-marked, and mean. But you stood up—alone—through this shit storm. I love ya, you old sonofabitch."

A painful way to locate a solid, private self! Maybe that's the only way?

SAFE PLACES

At times we all come under assault, at times feel like Olly the seaman on the sinking ship. Oh, for an island supported by turtles 'all the way down'—anchored by a foundation turtle that always loves you, warts and all!

If you want to locate the Real Yous then start looking for your safe places, your most trusted islands onto which you 'yump' when your current ship is sinking.

THROUGH A CHILD'S EYE

Keep it simple. Start with basics. We know you're grown up but to get the show on the road start by adopting a child's perspective. The child's core islands include the basic human needs: nourishment, elimination, sleep, warmth, human contact and stable rhythms. Listen for, or better, feel the sounds coming from these baby islands. What do you get? You get a lot of quiet sounds, gentle rhythms. Without lots of quiet, without the gentle human rhythms, the child soul is diminished or dies. We never outgrow the need for such core islands.

GENTLE RHTYHMS (Blankies for grownups)

We start by identifying your peaceful islands and your gentle human rhythms. To which islands do you retreat for the quiet predictable melodies of living? Certainly to sleep, but where else? To certain people, to TV, to non-human things: to a hobby, to a bottle, to food, to nature, to music, to pets: a goldfish or a cat? And of course to institutions: to a church, a corporation? To daydreams filled with imaginary friends and lovers; to enveloping novels? Maybe you find peace in the warm arms of a person of the night, or nestled in a shrink's office? These, and legions more, all serve as temporary or enduring 'safe' islands for grownups.

Don't push your search. Take a bit of time. It's like buying a new car, once you start looking you notice all kinds of different cars, all kinds of things about cars. All that stuff has been out there, you just haven't noticed it from inside your box. Likwise, once you start looking for your safe, quiet islands you'll start noticing them. Any show up so far? Have a drink, have a hot fudge sundae, watch a Sienfeld rerun, have a daydream, pet your dog, watch a sunset —it'll come to you.

BOUNCY RHYTHMS

But like kids, we need more than peace and quiet we also need noise and action. Like kids, we grown-ups wander forth from our quiet islands looking for novelty and excitement. And we find it. Some too little, some too much, and some just about right. Those 'about right' ones serve as your core action islands. Here, like the child, you find enough noise, novelty and challenge to keep you interested, but hopefully not enough to spawn nightmares and ulcers.

To which islands do you regularly travel to find 'just about right' action, noise, bounce, jive, to get your juices flowing? A jog, bridge, poker, a marathon, skiing untracked powder, single-handed round the world sailing, part-time CIA agent, working for a promotion, raising kids, starting a business, changing jobs, making a fortune, losing a fortune.... Have you ever thought of writing a book? When we're finished we'll loan you Shiplitz

Don't push it. Take a bit of time and you'll start separating the core islands from the floaters, separating the ones that fit your basic beat from passing flings, separate the safe ones from the sinkers.

Neil McK. Agnew, Ph.D. and John L. Brown, Ph.D.

TURTLES: DEEP AND TRUSTED OR SUPERFICIAL AND NERVOUS

How deep do your turtles go? How strong is your social network? Simple. The longer an island holds it's place against the tides and winds of change, the stronger the Tower of Turtles, the stronger the social net. If it's still there, not only next morning, or next week, but it's still there next year, if it's still there in ten years, twenty, thirty, well then you've built on solid foundations. Or else maybe you're in a rut? We'll get around to that last item later in the story.

You've heard that silly tale about living to a ripe old age by selecting grandparents who did the same. Idiotic yes, but a nice example of a genetic tower of turtles. Also, speaking of grandparents, if like your granddaddy, you're still voting Republican you've located another tower supporting a well-anchored political agenda. At the next clan picnic, test the stability of your place in the network by suggesting you may do a bit of island hopping—you're thinking of voting Democrat.

Or maybe you've celebrated your happy twentieth anniversary with your staunch Democratic wife. Your wife says: "Ya know Elmer, you'd vote Republican if Sadam Hussein was leading the party. To which you reply: "Ya know Roseanne, you'd vote Democrat if Monica Lewinski was leading the party . . . Hey honey, y'all want me to order in ribs?"

Or you may spend a lot of time living in a Sienfeld world—a world of floaters—then most of your islands are supported at best with one or two turtles—barely touching, let alone holding flippers—here today gone tomorrow. Here we encounter the world of retained adolescence at the mercy of passing fads . . . but makes for great TV.

In that kind of life you're consistently inconsistent. I'll dress, cut my hair, buy records, stocks, cars, gods, and vote *whichever way my group happens to be doing it now*. Come to think of it we have not only described teenagers of all ages, but also corporations that go from one management fad to another, and even to scientist's loyalty to the current hit parade theory about cancer, or the age of the universe, or the treatment of depression. So the fad-follower consistently follows the crowd—that's their consistency, that's their decision rule.

When private islands feel tippy tippy, you have a choice. You can yump to trusted networks or available floaters. How does this rule apply to you?

Stop and think, are you basically a loner or a groupie? Very few of us are real loners. If you are one you still need a place to stood. Where is it? A lot of independent loners 'stand' on rule-laden abstractions like technology, or a ritualistic career like tax inspector, or compulsively tidying the world, organizing their stamp collection, warmed by their cat or an electric blanket. Don't knock it, a safe place these days is hard to find.

So now we're starting to get a rough feel for the Real Yous. A collection of core islands: first some quiet, gentle rhythm ones from which you regularly venture forth, and to which you return for renewal and healing; and second, more noisy, bouncy ones on which you regularly work, play, and sometimes skin your knees or break your heart. Relatively stable, this core network of islands is not only linked together, but some are so solid they appear to be supported by turtles all the way down. Oh for rock solid islands—preferably ones that's aren't deserted.

Make a crude estimate? How many do you have?

MIND DEPOSIT #5

Minsky's metaphor—A Society of Minds—is initially appealing, but simple it isn't. So we start with these crude estimates of your society of islands: some core, some floaters, some private, some public; some safe, some bouncy. Like Ollie the seaman, when forced to yump all of us need a place to stood. Have you found yours? They may be your most important islands of all, but you never realize it till the ship is sinking. Where did you 'yump' the last time you: lost a pet, lost a job, lost a partner, lost a hope?

Neil McK. Agnew, Ph.D. and John L. Brown, Ph.D.

"**Yes But**...unfortunately Bertha's out at the moment but I have a few ideas. I kinda like the Tower of Turtles, sort of like self-confidence right? And the "yump Olly yump" story like where do you go when people let you down, or push you off the ship? I just realized that I usually go down in the basement to my workshop and refinish antique furniture, and have a few sips of 12 year old Bourbon with a chaser of Certs."

"Furthermore, when Bertha's feeling low she goes to bed with her cats... sometimes for a week. You know, I was starting to worry about Herman... but now I feel better since that great line of his: "I love ya, ya old SOB" I get to feel pretty low too once in while, but I think my downers are floaters, not core... yeah I'm going to write mine in as floaters... well maybe one of my downers is core...?

"**YES WELL**... thanks for talking to us Bert, and give Bertha our best. We know our manner—open-minded and humble—agitates her. We told Shiplitz about her and he said: "Praise the Lord there's someone throwing rocks at your mess-o-metaphors."

MIND MAP #5

The time has come the Walrus said... for you to pencil in your matrix

Step 5a: List your islands, core and floaters, private and social,—just like Herman did earlier in this Chapter.

Finding the Real You

	Private	Social
Core		
Floater		

Step 5b: Which ones are safe? Now underline, in pencil, which of the islands in the above matrix you feel are safe. Don't think too much—go with your gut feel. You can always change them later.

If you have trouble here are some of hints.

Hint #1: Where do you go when you're hurting or have lost your way? Do you jump to a private island or do you go knocking on the door of a trusted other among your Society of Islands?

Hint #2: The trick is to put some of your foundation turtles in a good safe place where the foul finger of fate can't goose them, and so can't create a devastating oxymoron—a turtle stampede. For example most religions put their Gods in a good safe place like Heaven—not on the mantle piece where the heathens, the children, or the movers can break them. So if as a kid you had a solid religious exposure it's still there somewhere inside and so you already have a potential safe place to go. Even if you're not practicing your religion now, when times get tough you have that hibernating haven.

Hint #3: Even if you're not, or never have been, a religious believer, never mind, a host of safe places remain. Namely, all the "isms": the unassailable "capitalism" or "socialism" of true believers; the "sexism" of radical feminism and male chauvinism, even the rigid "reductionism" and "materialism" of many scientists. What's your favorite ism of all?.

Well, of course we realize you're not a weirdo. Nevertheless, if you want your islands to be solidly safe then you've got to have a resilient "ism" somewhere among your islands. Maybe optimism, or pessimism, or humanism, or naturism, or me-first-ism, or petism. What's yours? If you're having trouble ask a friend to point one out, then pencil it in . . . then you can rub it out as soon as they've gone.

Before we reach the end of this book you will have edited this matrix pretty well to your satisfaction, including at least one safe place in each of the four cells. Of course there'll always be room for further editing, for moving islands around, even deleting some and adding new ones—life dances on. So don't lose your pencil.

CHAPTER 6:

Hey Hey IT'S THE RHYTHM NOT THE WORDS

> **"Life is just one damn dance after another."**
> —Elbert Shiplitz

Bruney's now painting the dining room. As John and I arrive she announces that Shippy needs help with his computer.

Bruney babbles on: "He says the light won't go on. He also says don't bring John!"

"Well John knows a lot more about computers than I do so John's coming—like it or not."

John says: "I could stay here and help hold the ladder."

"John, Nobody likes a smart-ass."

I wish I could remember all the clever ways to handle S-A's that we wrote about earlier. Maybe we should make handy dandy little cards for purse or wallet so people would always have neat put-downs handy. Trouble is skilled S-A's don't need cue cards. Nor do skilled S-A bounty hunters.

We go over and hammer on the door to Shippy's studio. We can hear Eppy going nuts but nobody comes. I peek in the window and see Shippy at his desk wearing earphones and scribbling on a pad. He's writing! John tries the door, it opens. Eppy clatters out barking. We zip in and slam the door. Eppy is out.

John goes over and examines the computer, bends down, plugs it in—the 'screen lights up'. He takes off Shippy's earphones: "Shippy old trout, Epsilon pulled out the plug. Furthermore, he's been chewing on the cord. A few more chews and you can have him in a bun for lunch."

Tears come to Shippy's eyes: "Please don't talk that way, Epsilon is my little treasure." Even John is touched and let's a scratching, whining Eppy back in the room.

The Professor takes off the little dog's snowshoes and cradling him like a baby croons while the little dog laps at Shippy's face. Quietly weeping Shippy says: "Outside of my work Epsilon is my world, and when the work is going poorly he is my lifeline—my only real alliance. A true friend is someone who goes to bed when you go to bed, gets up when you get up, is always happy to see you no matter how miserable you've been. Will people do that? Will cats do that? NO! Only dogs do that. That's the perfect alliance for a solitary genius like me."

He wipes his eyes. "Yes, there's Ruth and the children, and they put up with me. But we just don't seem to dance to the same beat. I'm sorry for talking this way but you frightened me. We will permanently unplug the computer and I will go back to the pencil."

For once John is at a loss for words. Finally he says: "No need for that Professor, we'll just rig up a high plug-in up here out of Eppy's reach."

It looks like the Professor and John may have the beginnings of a beautiful friendship—a Bingo? Time will tell. If Shippy calls you anything—which he usually doesn't—he uses your last name. He says it saves brain space. The only person he calls by a first name is John. He calls him Harold.

By the way, did you notice that the Professor used the term 'alliance' twice? It was when he was talking about his dog. Was that a

Finding the Real You

coincidence or has Bruney been showing him some of our stuff? That's a switch!

John: "Professor, why keep the earphones on while you're writing?"

Shippy replies: " Well Harold, it's because music helps my little gray cells all dance to the same tune, helps my many minds—even the ones on far out islands—sing or at least hum the same song. The music provides a rhythm for the words to follow—it's my new cure for writer's block. In fact I believe that life is a matter of finding the right rhythms. In fact that idea may help you boys in your work. Let me get you some books."

As he shuffles over to the far wall to search, John pilfers some notes off the desk saying: " Little books Professor, little books. You got anything in Reader's Digest."

Giving us an armful of textbooks Shippy says: "Thank you boys for making that thing work . . . you needn't stay . . . make sure you close the door tight after you." He puts on his earphones and starts pecking away on 'that thing', paying no more attention to us and not noticing his missing notes.

Shippy's 'back'—no longer lost in his own vast mental space. Once again happily suspended in his very own network of alliances, not of people but of ideas and one little dog.

We went back to my place, opened a couple of beer and pogosticked through a few of Shippy's books—and his notes. We desperately need 'a place to stood' for this chapter. Luckily, on one of the notes, we came across the following neat quote by Einstein:

"The significant problems we have cannot be solved at the same level of thinking we were at when we created them."

NINE DOT PUZZLE

Shippy had also included a really nice little example of what Uncle Albert meant—try it.

Neil McK. Agnew, Ph.D. and John L. Brown, Ph.D.

The Nine Dot Puzzle :   Join the nine dots with 4 straight lines without lifting your pen off the paper

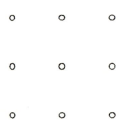

Solution: To solve the puzzle you have to draw three of the lines beyond the boundaries of the imaginary square

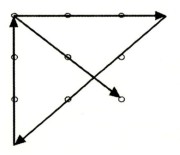

When people who can't get it see the solution they say: "Hey you didn't say we could go outside the square." To which you reply: "What square? And furthermore I didn't say you couldn't. Your mind built the square, and it imposed the limits. As Albert says, to solve problems ya gotta shift levels or perspectives"

    Didn't get it? Neither did I, nor Harold, oops, John. Like Einstein said, to solve a puzzle you have to shift your level of thinking, you have to somehow escape from the mental box of your own making.

    Give it to your friends to test their capacity to shift their level of thinking, to test their mental agility in escaping from their own drastically confining 'mental prisons'.

    This little puzzle provides an excellent model of what's meant by a 'frame of reference'—a mental frame up. In this instance the confining 'square' that you unconsciously constructed—by mentally filling in the empty space between the dots—became a restricting per-

Finding the Real You

ceptual prison of your own making. And although bringing order to your world it also made solving the puzzle impossible. The price of order is inflexibility. The price of flexibility is uncertainty. That's why most of the time we go for order—it's cheaper and less stressful—most of the time.

The square you constructed out of a few observational dots is what? An Island of Consistency—mentally real, but really imaginary. When you encounter one of life's problems, typically composed of more space than dots, then you must rely on your imagination, or your bias, or your beliefs to fill in the gaps. That's why different people come up with different solutions to the same puzzles—the solution depends on who holds the pencil.

LIFE'S DOTTY PUZZLES

Shippy had scribbled on the bottom page of the nine-dot-puzzle: "The universe has an infinity of evolving dots and potentially connecting lines. Even a remarkable brain like Einstein's was only big enough to map a tiny slice—which will have to be continuously redrawn to accommodate emerging dots. The researchers provide the dots, the great theorists, like Einstein and Hawking, draw in their particular lines. Different theorists link different dots . . . that's why scientists fight among themselves."

So don't feel too badly when you find that like Uncle Albert you can only map a few islands of your world, and in the process keep wearing out erasers, or continuously arguing about the dumb dots or dumb lines in other peoples maps.

Life keeps us busy, continuously joining the dots, forever drawing imaginary lines linking tiny bits of evidence. Living involves building mental squares or frame-ups, building Islands of Consistency; building mental bridges over the spaces between them; building mental skyways out across the unknown; of trying to discover and uncover new dots to help fill in gaps in the present and provide stepping stones into the future.

Neil McK. Agnew, Ph.D. and John L. Brown, Ph.D.

Most of life is space or gaps between observational and imaginary dots: what is she REALLY thinking? What do I REALLY want? What are they ACTUALLY going to do? What did he REALLY say or do? What are my kids going to be when they REALLY grow up? What am I going to be when I grow up? What's this pain in my gut connected to? Where's the market headed? How long will I live?

What dots or islands do I connect to find the REAL ME? What dots do I connect to find the REAL YOU? I've seen the one's your mother connected, I'm not sure yet which one's I'll connect, but I do know they'll certainly be different than hers!

Not only do different people draw different maps, but so too do you on different occasions, in different situations, in different moods. At times you draw 'reality' with compulsively straight lines and 'square' shapes—producing tight little islands. At other times you loosen up, using what-the-hell zig-zagging lines joining almost all the dots you can see and think of. Sometimes when you're 'high' on success, or sex, or booze, or drugs you can produce The BIG PICTURE where everything fits nicely together—at least 'til tomorrow morning.

Living involves navigating a heap of unknown space, locating and linking dots (real or hopeful), locating and linking islands. We try to fill in the spaces by constructing mental boxes, islands of consistency supported by towers of turtles, linked by trusted alliances. We human beans have been building space platforms and bridges between them for millennia—long before NASA was even dreamed of.

Our images of ourselves, of others, particularly of the future, are all dotty puzzles. We're forever drawing linking lines trying for consistency, avoiding wayward dots. Institutions favor simple squares and straight lines—no surprises please. Lovers like surprises—for awhile. Then even they start trying to fit their mates into a tidy 'square' . . . what were once cute—mobile dots—become a pain in the brain. Then when dots misbehave and step out of their connecting lines we try to bully them back in place, or erase them from our map and re-establish a comfortable consistency.

As long as things are working—great—we're happy inside our

Finding the Real You

protected Islands of Consistency, inside our little mental boxes. Sure, little surprises are OK, even enjoyed—the kind that healthy pets produce. But when things start to really rattle we want to reinforce the box. There's the rub, we've failed to include doors or escape hatches in our boxes. Just as such frame ups keep the puzzle down to mind size and keep the noise out, so too do they become our prisons.

We'll be providing ways of enlarging or even escaping from these prisons, of creatively dealing with life's poop storms by shifting your perspective, or by sneaking, deaking, or leaping outside your personally constructed and confining frames of reference. When we finally recognize this irony and the necessity of shifting our level of thinking—Einstein is so happy he jitterbugs on heavenly atoms—even without snowshoes.

RING MY CHIMES

No wonder we can't solve many of our problems. No wonder we repeatedly become born-again helpless. Most of our life is spent working within protective but drastically confining Mental Frame ups. You ask: "Come on, cut the hyperbole—what's a 'drastically confining mental frame up?'" Answer: the biggest self-con is that we wrongly assume that the important part of our mind consists of words and sentences. Sure, minds produce words and sentences but the words ride on rhythms, just like song lyrics ride on the melody. Remember Shippy and his earphones? By changing his rhythm he escaped his writer's block, his mental prison. How? By hitching rides on Mozart's music.

Notice what happens when you take away the melody from a song—the words lose their way—like cats they drift off in all directions at once. Or take away the rhythm and you produce a numbing word string—like boring professors and monotone talkers. Without rhythm you go to sleep, eventually you die.

Without a rich repertoire of rhythms you make bad love, bad dancing, bad speeches, bad conversation, bad thinking, bad working, bad feeling. You produce a dull, or noisy mess.

Neil McK. Agnew, Ph.D. and John L. Brown, Ph.D.

You don't ring people's chimes, or your own, with words. Ya ring their chimes with rhythm—with rhythm decorated with words. So for a moment forget about the decorations, forget about the lyrics.

BABIES DANCE

Did you know that infants a few days old mimic, with their body movements, the rhythm of the language being spoken around them? In other words they learn the rhythm of the language long before they learn the words. Week old infants are rhythm detectors and mimickers.

At birth, babies arrive with the potential to learn the rhythm of any of the world's six thousand languages. So if they're born in China they learn the rhythms of a Chinese language, and later decorate these rhythms with Chinese words. But if they're born in the Bronx guess what? And, if they're born in the Bronx to Chinese parents, glory be, they learn the rhythms of both those preposterously complex melodies, and later add the relevant vocabularies.

But of course, as any adult knows whose tried to learn a new language, this magic capacity for universal language learning doesn't last. When growing up we gradually lose that easy facility to learn new complex rhythms—we may learn some of the decorations, some of the word runs, but produce strange jerky, accented strings of words. We have trouble understanding native speakers who 'sing' too fast. It's like trying to dance with someone who's listening to a different tune even though it's the same music, or march through life with someone who hears a different drummer—you're only in step for very brief periods . . . every tenth beat. You're missing most of each other's song, most of their music. If you see life as one 'dance' after another, well then . . . the kids who inherit and pick up the most rhythms 'win'—physical rhythms (Wayne Gretsky, Michael Jordan, Jim Carey); musical rhythms (Mozart, Louie Armstrong); language rhythms (Shakespeare, Dylan Thomas); perceptual rhythms (Picasso, Loyd Wright); abstract rhythms (Einstein, Stephen Hawking, Shiplitz).

Finding the Real You

CHILDREN DANCE

Bruney does a syndicated column—sort of 'science for the citizen'. She told us about an anthropologist who took hidden camera movies of kids playing in a schoolyard. Turns out they were all moving to the same rhythm. In this particular situation the rhythm was being 'set' by one very active little girl. Unwittingly, she was serving as the drummer or conductor of the playground 'ballet'. Kids are rhythm machines.

"No no" says Bruney, "not machines, rather mobile members of one dance troop after another. Different kids pick up and respond to different beats, but they all dance. The situation determines which ones are prima donnas, which members of the chorus line, which on the sidelines tapping their foot or beating on a drum or a nerd. Everyone 'dances' all the time, whether you're a Nureyev aleaping, or an autistic child arocking, or one of us at a meeting swinging a foot, or two of us gracefully or clumsily making love. All God's children got rhythm, some shared, some unique—that's what life's all about!"

When Bruney goes back to pecking out her column—pretty jerky rhythm that—we talk about grown-ups doing one damn dance after another, at home (the morning gavotte, the evening waltz) at work (the musical chairs of small business, the ponderous march of large corporations), at play (the slow cadence of baseball, the frenetic jive of ice hockey). And all this time we've been worshipping the words instead of beaming in on the beat.

THE BEAT

The verbal decorations are neat—as long as they go with the beat. In the back of our minds we know that and sometimes say: "Now say it with feeling"; or "They're a phony!" So maybe the really big 'nine-dot' challenge of life is to escape out of the 'word box' by shifting to the much larger 'dance box'. So let's try to move from word island, where we waste our time trying to get along with ourselves and others by yatta yatting, to dance island where we go with the flow, groove to the beat.

Neil McK. Agnew, Ph.D. and John L. Brown, Ph.D.

Bruney knows this intuitively as well as intellectually—she not only talks a good game, she plays one too. She claims I'm a fast beat person. That's why I don't put on weight, even when I'm sitting, I fidget, burning it up. That's why I'm always trying to get the family to 'hurry up'. That's why I kick the tractor when it won't start—a tractor at rest dances to a very slow drummer.

Sometimes I suspect Bruney puts tranquilizers in my corn flakes, particularly on weekends when I'm going to be home—saves wear and tear on the kids, Bruney, and the garden tractor. Last weekend, while working with the tractor, I tried Shippy's trick of wearing a Walkman. I put in a slow beat tape—a lazy waltz. This slowed down my Rpm's so my rhythm and the tractor's were more or less in sync. Wonder of wonders, I only kicked the dumb thing once—lightly.

John's more of a slow beat person. When he works out at the gym he prefers peace and quiet for contemplation while he thinks about getting the hunk of iron off the rack and keeping it above his chest. The clash of booming heavy metal that the more muscled devotees prefer gets John off to the steam room early.

WHAT ABOUT YOU?

Do you see yourself as generally a fast or slow beater? For example take our two neighbors across the street. The one drifts home from work and deflates down into his rocker and leisurely strokes his old cat. The other neighbor zooms into the driveway, nips through the door, and dives down on her hands and knees to frolic with her zippy kittens. Yes, we realize this is an oversimplified example to make a point. But does it help you see yourself 'beat wise' . . . fast, medium, slow?

Do you have a pretty good ear for the rhythm of your core selves, for the major music of close others, for the cadence of the culture? Or are you a toe stomper like Herman?

Certainly fast beat people often burn up so much juice they need intermittent periods of "I vant to be alone!" So we all dance fast and slow at times. But generally speaking do you see yourself as a fast or slow beater—a waltzer or a jitterbugger—just what kind of bugger are you? And what about your mate?

Typically, we choose mates with generally faster or slower Rpm's than our own—that way we extend the duo's rhythm range, extend the number of situations we can dance in. What's the rhythm range for you and your mate? Do you both groove to the same beat? If not what happens? Are you faster or slower? How do you slow them down? How do they speed you up? When do you dance off in your separate ways?

PUT ANOTHER NICKLE IN

Fortunately you're not restricted to one rhythm, all of us have a repertoire of beats so we can swing to lots of different tunes—alone, and even intimately with a few others. Crudely put we're like an old fashioned Nickelodeon—put another nickel in and one of our selves sings the selected song, does the chosen dance. So who puts the nickel in?

Well, sometimes one of your minds (basic rhythms) puts a nickel into one of your other minds—hey, says the bladder to the urinary sphincter, here's a nickel play the tinkle tinkle, wee wee tune. In older folks the tune takes longer to get started and tinkles on and on. Shippy's wife Ruth tells him there are three stages to aging: first he forgets his telephone number; second he forgets to pull his zipper up; third, he forgets to pull it down! Apparently our various selves retire at different rates, during the day, during a lifetime.

Have you ever heard one of your upper rational minds saying to one of the lower emotional minds, ya know man your records stuck on that anxiety jazz—get off it. Poor old rational minds believe in words not rhythm nickels, so they spray words all over emotional selves: "Hey man this is silly, relax, you're worrying about nothing—so the boss didn't say good morning, and the secretary did Helen's stuff before yours, and your parking space has been moved. I'm sure there's a nice simple explanation." Yeah right, replies sweaty palms and keeps right on dripping.

PILLS WORK LIKE NICKLES

Finally, running out of words, one of the frustrated rational selves takes the lower mind to a shrink who tosses in pills—that cost a lot of nickels—and 'Voila', they chemically turn down the frequency and the volume of the anxiety tune—for a while. So? So don't waste words on emotional minds.

Of course, in calmer moments one of your wise outer island selves knows you don't have to rely on pills either. It knows that a nice hot bath, soft music, and warm milk with a shot of rum in it, will do as well or better, and without the hangover or side effects of the pharmaceutical opera. Except sometimes it's more convenient to pop pills or slurp booze than have a hot bath—especially at work or lunch. We need more offices and restaurants with hot tubs.

Anyway, the most effective way to change an unsatisfactory tune—boring, anxious, angry, or painful—is of course by knocking it off your charts with a stronger tune. You do that, obviously, not by throwing unmelodic or weak rhythm words at it, but by overriding the current repulsive rhythm with a stronger melodious beat.

In brief, to change a pukey personal opera, ya don't feed nickels into one of your talk machines, ya feed them into one of your rhythm machines. You'll know whether or not you've found the right machine. If you have, then your breathing and pulse rate change. When they do, the lyrics will change automatically. Remember, the lyrics ride on the music, not the other way around.

THE POINT?

The central point of all this yadda yadda is what? That the Real Yous are not a collection of words and sentences but a wondrous repertoire of rhythms, or symphonies, or operas. If you want to meet

Finding the Real You

the Real Yous don't be distracted by the lyrics, listen to the underlying music: fast and slow; high frequency and low frequency; melodic and cacophonic, long and short.

For example, most of the time Herman's selves march to a slow steady beat—his overweight Macho Thug, his Accountant, his Dreamer. But when watching football games, and for the odd raunchy or violent daydream, a lean, mean fast Rpm Herman emerges, captures center stage, and jitters the bug. We get a clear picture of all this stuff in the next chapter when John liberates a treasure trove of notes from Shippy's desk.

Bertha Butter drops in to complain about the escalating number of Real Yous. "You guys are producing Real Yous faster than a machine pops corn. I'm OK but those bears of small brain must have them leaking out of their ears. Get real!"

Ah yes . . . well . . . we'll have to do something about that very soon. John's keeping a record of all these promises we have to take care of.

WHO CONDUCTS YOUR PERSONAL ORCHESTRA?

Each of our selves triggers different rhythms in our other selves (eating, sleeping, menstrual, sexual, etc.) but so do "outsiders" including friends, family, co-workers, experts (shrinks), institutions, tractors, . . . even rocks which triggers the stubbed toes song: "OUCH OH . . . @ # % * $!"

In fact the music we play, and the lyrics that ride along on them, rely very, very, heavily on outside conductors and scores. Without stimulation and orchestration by outside rhythms, your minds gradually start leaking. You know this from personal experience when you sleep—that particular form of mind leakage is called dreaming.

We can get mind leakage while awake as demonstrated by daydreaming but particularly with stimulus deprivation studies. Here for a few hours you languish in a special tank where all stimuli are reduced to a minimum: sound, touch, smell, and sight. What happens? You start to hallucinate. Your minds need external rhythmic

Neil McK. Agnew, Ph.D. and John L. Brown, Ph.D.

stimulation or they start to dribble into each other. Daydreaming in a quiet place produces similar effects. Isolated and brainwashed prisoners experience a devastating leakage in spades.

REPERTOIRE OF RHYTHMS

In brief, which particular music our minds play, and the lyrical accompaniment, depends not only on the size of our natural and acquired rhythm repertoire, but depends particularly on the rhythmic score being played around us. In institutional settings we are like members of an orchestra—the music we play follows, more or less, the institutional score and the rhythmic direction of particular conductors.

At a more personal level, life is just one glorious routine or painful dance after another. The Real Yous are those familiar dances. To start getting a handle on the size of your repertoire of rhythms you must identify your major dance partners—personal and institutional. Are there lots or just a few? You will have identified many of them earlier in your Mind Maps. Some of us have many partners but do the same jig with all of them—the short two step. Some have only a few partners so have the time and energy to enjoy longer and more sophisticated dances. And for some, they find their main partner under their hat.

Some genetic disabilities, neurological accidents, and impoverished early environments can all lead to a limited repertoire of melodies or minds—a restricted rhythmic range or reach. Or we may have lots of quick, superficial two step partners, plus a special one or two with whom we do a variety of dances: the slow, languorous love waltzes; the quick, exciting, jive of argument; the highly variable fun dances of play; the slow, long marches of work. Here we see someone with a large and rich repertoire of mind rhythms—someone dancing life to the full.

You may not dance much with people but still have compatible partners to swing and sway with: your cats, your C.D. collection, your

Finding the Real You

African violets, the vacuum cleaner, and of course the TV and so maintain integrity among your minds.

Alternatively, your Minds may spend most of their time dancing with each other, and like great poets, composers, or theorists create the rhythms and melodies that the rest of us follow. And maybe worship.

HOPE SPRINGS ETERNAL

But notice that our view of life as one "dancing partner" after another provides hope. The scope of your current world—the boxes you can dance into and out of—is defined by the current range and depth of your repertoire of minds, by the partners we've danced with so far. As long as you have the juice to try new partners: jobs; hobbies; people; places; as long as you're willing to try, then rich, deeply satisfying music may emerge—melodies you never knew you had cycling around deep inside just waiting to be lured into action on center stage. You've got rhythms in store that neither you nor the world has even dreamed of . . . yet.

There's an important hint about living there: "if you have the juice to try new partners . . ." (and we're not talking one night stands—we're talking partners in the figurative or general sense) then your potential repertoire of rhythms, of minds, is wide open. So if you're interested in discovering hidden selves then the place to start is by increasing your juice, your energy level; your basic beat. How?

INCREASING YOUR BASIC BEAT

Somewhere in your Society of Selves reside juice generators or merchants. Maybe as core, Center Stage Selves. In which case you're already jiving all over the place. You don't need more juice, you need an internal or external bully to stop you from riding off in all directions at once.

However, if your juice generator resides on an outer island with no transportation, then they need travel money.

Neil McK. Agnew, Ph.D. and John L. Brown, Ph.D.

A wise friend tells the tale of an immigrant arriving in New York already convinced the streets were paved with gold. He wrote home explaining that, unfortunately, in order to dig up the gold you need a shovel—he didn't have enough money to buy a shovel. He lacked 'shovel money'.

In honor of the poor immigrant our friend crafted a lapel pin in the form of a golden shovel. The glowing pin of course became a conversation piece providing him with the opportunity for elaborating the importance of shovel money, of startup resources in any venture, whether in the form of venture capital, a helpful friend, a resourceful self. All these juice generators provide a form of leverage—transforming a little into a lot.

One way for you to strengthen your basic beat is to take whatever extra juice you now have—even if only a teensy weensy amount—and leverage it into producing more juice. For example? Winston Churchill used fifteen-minute catnaps . . . he had a Nap Self with enough travel money to gain regular access to center stage. Less obvious juice generators include dancing by yourself for fifteen minutes to a Walkman, or a bit of good sex, either of which can generate extra energy, optimism and confidence. Look for leverage, where a little yields a lot.

But whether your basic beat is currently too fast or too slow, don't despair—there's hope. Somewhere, on one of your islands resides a You with a solution.

For their integrity and coordinated functioning our minds depend upon basic integrating rhythms—just as an orchestra depends on the coordinating rhythms provided by the conductor and the percussion instruments. Without such integrating beats your minds, like the instruments of an orchestra, get out of sync and the music becomes noise: mental noise; emotional noise; and physical noise called illness.

Finding the Real You

SET POINTS

All systems have magic set points where everything runs in sync. In the case of ships it depends on the Rpm's of the engine. Set it too high, everything on the ship starts to rattle. Set it too low and everything still rattles. Set it just right and 'Voila', all the individual rattlers join the party and dance to the same integrating beat.

You too have magic set points. You may not know how to get there, but you know when it happens—you know when you've "got it all together". Correction, we should say you may not know how to get there 'naturally'. Some of your selves certainly know how to get there with chemical help: with stuff that turns up your Rpms like caffeine, speed, acid, or turns them down like booze or tranquilizers.

And of course, like ships, you have more than one integrating set point depending on the state of life's seas—whether they're calm or rough. Being more complex than ships, and having to dance with changing and novel rhythms, you need a host of functional set points depending on the situation: dancing with a tractor or a cranky boss or temperamental lover, or a surprising illness. Life is just one damn Rolling Stones concert and Mozart concerto after another. No wonder some of your selves still rattle, no wonder you haven't located all you're magic set points—yet.

MASTER SET POINTS

Not surprisingly there are set points and set points. To start with we're after your master or 'home set point'. That's the one where you get it ALL back together: the rejuvenating, refueling, life-sustaining magic set point. Which Yous, on which islands, pull this off? As Herman says: "Damned if I know."

Most of us get 'reset' with a good deep sleep. How powerful is your 'go-to-bed now' Self? Stronger than your 'Late show TV-watching' Self? How about your 'nice-hot-bath' Self? Some get their various selves swaying together by slowing down their breathing through

Neil McK. Agnew, Ph.D. and John L. Brown, Ph.D.

meditation, listening to music, or the ocean waves, or a walk in the woods, or a paddle on the pond. Whatever works for you. Or it may be gin, hot fudge sundaes or pills—short-term gain for . . . short-term gain . . . We do what we gotta do.

LOCAL SET POINTS

Besides master set points we have local set points for 'work' and 'play'. Have you noticed others searching for their short term or local set points? Watch a World Series pitcher just before he throws with the bases loaded. Watch public speakers just before they start to talk, or observe an agile family member generating an excuse. They all try to shut down the rattles, try to get it 'back together'—at least temporarily.

A popular means of trying to get your minds united momentarily is to take a deep breath and let it out slowly. Doing this repeatedly is of course the basis of all meditation techniques. Other tricks involve following some ritual—again watch big league pitchers and batters for the infinite variety of set point searches—they all involve a little dance of some kind and the rhythms never vary. Speaking of searches for local set points, how about sexual foreplay? Bim, bam, thank you mam! And from what uncivilized outer island did you arrive?

You have selves that do little dances and postures to adjust your Rpms as well, for tuning your breathing and heart rate to the rhythm of the situation. Can you think of a very popular one? How about tuning your shoulder and neck muscles so tight they almost hum. That's a way of telling the rest of your orchestra to tune up tight too, to get ready to play the flight or fight concerto. Shivering, laughing, crying, are all primitive non-verbal ways of tuning our Rpm's.

We'll work on generating 'sweet points' in specific situations later. For now, try identifying the selves that tune your master or home set point—the calm, peaceful one where hardly anything rattles. If you have trouble ask a bud to help you. Believe us, you have them, even though they're probably not working as often or as well as they might

Finding the Real You

be. Or maybe they're working in the short run but also shortening your life unnecessarily. Why not climb into a nice big hot tub and listen to your rattling selves gradually rumble down, sigh, and shmuffle . . . shmuffle . . .

MIND DEPOSIT #6

Einstein says to solve major problems you must escape from the frame of reference in which it was created to another. To make such a big breakout you need a You who's an escape artist. Herman has his Dreamer—better than nothing but not good enough. One of Shippy's selves discovered he could escape from the Writer's Block Box by hitching a ride on Mozart's music.

Somewhere you have a core Self that recognizes that your Yous don't consist of boxes of words but rather of a repertoire of rhythms. And furthermore, with the renewed confidence gained from Shippy's soon to be revealed Secret Formula, we will discover your Wise Self who will start bullying some of your other Yous into listening to the basic beats, to the rhythms, not just the words. Then we and you are on our way!

On your way WHERE you ask? Well on your way to realizing that to enter and play in a particular box or situation you ride a rhythm. To escape and enter a different box you ride a different rhythm. Like Mary's little lambs the lyrics will follow, dragging their tales behind them. Get it? Tales not tails. O.K. so we're not Shakespeare.

Hey, hey. Hear and ride the beat. That's where the set points are— the situational, local-in-a-box ones, as well as your universal set points that reduce your inter-box rattles and let the sweet music of living flow. Maybe there's even hope for Herman? There is as we will soon see.

WELL YES . . ."Tell Bert to take a deep breath . . . tell him to swing and sway . . . the natural way. Bert old trout, now that you've got the beat here's the lyrics: 'You take us too literally. Look up the word 'figurative' in your dictionary. Whether you know it or not you are one magnificent symphony after another with your breathing as conductor.

Bert, don't worry about 'literally' singing and dancing. Every day, in every way, you swing and sway, pulse, flutter, vibrate, undulate, wiggle, waggle, and boogie woogie. In the next chapter we'll prove it. There we reintroduce you to the soon to be famous "Shiplitz Formula". Old Shiplitz may be a bit weird but he got 'THE FORMULA' right. Don't tell Bertha but once you get it you'll be a new man . . . more than she can imagine or manage.

MIND MAP # 6

This step is like a lottery: invest a little, win a lot. Except unlike a lottery this is a sure thing.

Mind Map 6a: Put into three groupings the following situations in which you are: 1) Calm (low heart rate, slow breathing, low rattle); 2) Focussed (medium heart rate, medium breathing, interesting rattle); 3) Tense (high heart rate, fast breathing, high rattle). Here's an example:

Group 1 (Calm): hot bath; soft music; gentle book; waking from good sleep, easy time with trusted other; after good sex; leisurely walk. In brief, big, slow, integrating, rejuvenating, and harmonizing rhythms that restore emotional and intellectual resources.

Group 2 (Focussed): during sex; favorite hobby; challenging work; civilized argument, new places and people; great meal-book-movie-play-surfing net; jogging-dancing-swimming. In brief, faster, exciting, integrating and energizing rhythms that pleasantly stretch emotional and intellectual resources but stay within your basic limits.

Group 3 (Up tight): bad sex; impossible work; high uncertainty; high risk; major loss or illness, unraveling personal relations, untrustworthy or hostile institutions. In brief, fast, jerky, rattle rhythms that deplete emotional and intellectual resources.

Now generate your list :
    Group 1 (Calm)

Finding the Real You

Group 2 (Focussed)
Group 3 (Up tight)

If you have difficulty then review step #1 (Ch.1) and Step #2 (Ch.2) for ideas. Focus on short-term Yous (+-), and rejected Yous and rejecting Thems. These Yous spend a lot of time 'beating fast'. While long term gainers, and mutual choice Yous spend more time riding moderate and slower beats. Some of your positive payoffs (++,-+) probably belong in Group 1 and 2, along with your mutual choice or "Bingo" interpersonal relations. Whereas, your negative payoffs (—), and interpersonal mismatches (Sobs and Oh Yeahs) probably belong in Group 3. Does it work that way for you?

Mind Map 6b. Beat bullies: Which of your Selves bully others into changing their beats? Shippy's music-playing Self? Herman's Dreamer and his Beer-drinking Selves? Bruney's Ladder-climbing Self? John's Note-stealing Self? All Bertha's Selves! Hardly any of Bert's.

List four of your own Bullies:

Two that bully inside Selves:
1. _____
2. _____

Two that Bully outside Thems:
1. _____
2. _____

CHAPTER 7:

THE SHIPLITZ FORMULA

> "If a man does not keep pace with his companions, perhaps it is because he hears a different drummer. Let him step to the music he hears. However measured or far away."
> —Thoreau

I get home to find Shippy's wife Ruth and Bruney with their heads together giggling. Bruney leaves carrying a can of paint and our stepladder. Mmmm?

John is away in California giving a paper on 'Mediating property settlements in divorce cases'-held in the Napa Valley. Mmmm? Bruney is off to Bermuda to a conference of Science Writers. You know how many golf courses there are in Bermuda? Mmmm? I suspect Ruth has agreed to come to the rescue if things fall apart during the three days the kids and I are on our own.

But before Bruney leaves she gives me the above quote from Thoreau with instructions to 'sanitize' it for multiple gender consumption. Must remember to do that.

Only one fly in the ointment, Herman's wife Gert conned Bruney, and Bruney conned me, into inviting Herman over Saturday afternoon to subtly demonstrate to him that fathers can actually take responsibility—sort of. I'm nervous about this. We'll see.

Saturday morning, after a negotiated breakfast of belgian waffles and ice cream, the kids do the dishes and then invite over a couple of friends while I get time to scribble a few words of my own creation before Herman's arrival.

JACK POT

John has successfully 'liberated' a few scribbled fragments from Shippy's desk, with excellent results. He's now perfected this devious but profitable habit. Still, his latest heist will make us famous and should make you healthy, stealthy and wise.

We're kind of smug because it so neatly and elegantly summarizes what Shippy set us up to say in the last chapter: Namely, in looking for the Real Yous don't just identify the lyrics . . . listen to the music. In brief, Professor Shiplitz has maneuvered our escape from that mental prison, where restrictive nouns —conceptual corsets—rule the day, into a larger world where verbs and rhythms are the name of the game.

He agrees that nouns are necessary to simplify experience, to identify many of your Real Yous, just as we did in earlier chapters. Nouns help us categorize your activities and the major players inside and outside your head. Nouns provide the raw material of your solid islands of consistency supported by towers of reliable turtles, linked by strong bridging alliances. We need nouns.

But we need more. We need to breathe life into those corseted islands of consistency. To add meaning and motion to the Yous we find there, and to solve the major dotty puzzles of life, we must be able to deake out of our self-made frame-ups. We are going in search of your rhythms and to do that we need—The Formula.

Neil McK. Agnew, Ph.D. and John L. Brown, Ph.D.

THE SHIPLITZ FORMULA

Thoreau had the basic idea about marching to the drummer you hear; Shippy generated The Formula. While it's simple, it's also potent, even dangerous. Remember, Einstein's formula, $E=MC^2$? It's simple and powerful but like everything powerful, it's potentially risky, producing not only nuclear energy but also the meltdown at Cherynoble and the atom bomb. So while you will learn how to harness some of the power of THE FORMULA, be careful! Here it is.

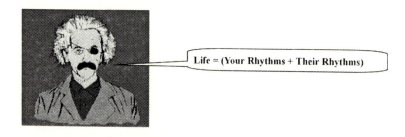

Life = (Your Rhythms + Their Rhythms)

In brief, the formula says all life consists of one dance after another. Your life consists of an endless flow where your physical and psychological rhythms dance —gracefully or clumsily—with the physical and psychological rhythms around you: people, television, cars, and tornadoes.

The Formula was written with an addition sign on purpose. It shows that if you only have your own rhythms, you still have a life. But what a life. It's the life of a hermit. But if you are without any rhythms of your own, it's the life of a puppet, at the whim of any puppet master you meet. So, how do you balance, "Your Rhythms" with "Their Rhythms?"

Since Shippy's been wearing his Walkman he seems almost normal—the musical rhythms it feeds in helps tune his brain, reduces the rattles. He only laces on his snowshoes in the evening. Now he's tolerated back at the University two days a week to give lectures.

Finding the Real You

AN OLD FAMILIAR SONG

Ordinary people see and hear lots of things. Geniuses are exposed to the same stuff, only they see through the noise and discover or create compelling underlying patterns.

Ruth told Bruney that Shiplitz got the idea for his formula one morning in his pre-snowshoe days while driving in to work. As he pulled away from a stoplight he heard the radio of a passing car playing the first few notes of a song, a song he hadn't heard for years. And yet, with only those five or six notes to go on, the whole song unfolded: melody, words and all. Not only did the tune and lyrics flow forward automatically but also the song called forth a flood of detailed memories and rich feelings.

At various times throughout the morning Shiplitz found himself humming the tune. One of the secretaries heard him and said "My golly, I haven't heard that in donkey's years—does that ever bring back memories." She blushed and started to hum along. Just as the few notes from the car radio triggered his stored rhythm, so his bit of humming triggered hers—same song but different memories and emotions.

According to Shippy, we're just a bag of rhythms. And of course all environmental signals (raindrops, snowflakes, northern lights) consist of rhythms in the form of physical frequencies: sounds, sights, touch. All it takes is a fragment of one of those familiar frequencies to trigger your stored version and its associated brain waves and psychological baggage.

A UNIFIED THEORY OF EVERTHING

That night as he started drifting off to sleep it came to Shippy in a flash, "That's it. That's the way the brain works . . . that's the way the world works . . . not only do electrons dance, so do brain cells, ideas, feelings. I've just discovered a unified theory of EVERTHING—everything rides on Rhythms!"

Neil McK. Agnew, Ph.D. and John L. Brown, Ph.D.

Everything rides on rhythms: our thoughts, our feelings, and our actions. All you need is the first few beats of a familiar rhythm—whether inherited or learned—and automatically the pattern of those first few beats trigger full blown sounds, sights, and feelings. And unless it's a new one or a weak one, once it starts it's almost impossible to stop—like a haunting melody ("raindrops keep falling on my head", just can't shake that one). As a familiar rhythm starts to flow, it in turn triggers thoughts, memories, feelings and actions associated with it.

The only way you interrupt one flowing rhythm is with a stronger one. That's why throwing mere words at feelings, or New Year's resolutions at habits, rarely works.

Have you noticed when you're in a foreign country you keep seeing people you think you know? That's an example of how a few familiar fragments trigger the feeling of familiarity. The Shiplitz Formula also helps explain why we have immediate reactions—positive or negative—to people we meet for the first time. It's because they trigger fragments of familiar rhythms—sights, sounds, smells—of people we know: parents; sibs; friends; teachers; bosses; bullies; lovers; or TV stars. And the old familiar rhythms from the past and their associated feelings play in your head and heart, even though those feelings may be inappropriate, even though friends say: "I don't see what you see in him," or "Why are you mad at her, you don't even know her?"

Just as a few notes from a passing radio can trigger a rich and continuing stream of memories, so too can the first few beats of other rhythms in our environment-particularly those generated by people. These trigger associated flows of images, actions, and feelings—particularly feelings. Some are positive (good loving), some negative (bad loving), some conflicting like trying to simultaneously sing two different songs, or to perform two different dances, or when making love to coordinate the rhythms of a present lover and fantasized one. Or like laughing on the outside and crying on the inside.

Before he was banished from teaching, in the middle of one of Shippy's lectures something or somebody would trigger The Urge—

Finding the Real You

the overwhelming compulsion to put on his snowshoes. If he detects it early enough, before it really starts to flow, he can escape by whipping on his earphones and playing a few bars of Mozart, or Elvis' version of 'You Ain't Nothing But a Hound Dog'. Otherwise one of his research assistants has to take over the lecture while another guides Shippy to his office and steadies his trembling hands as he consumes two mugs of warm milk laced with rum from a thermos Ruth has prepared.

He's working with a bio-engineer on developing an implanted brain pacer, like a heart pacer. It will be programmed to identify and override his snowshoe vibes and other inappropriate rhythms. He says most people won't need such a radical solution. He says neither John nor I have to worry —only people with very powerful and conflicting brain waves need such potent dampers and integrators.

RHYTHMS: SHORT AND LONG, WEAK AND STRONG

Some of our triggered rhythms generate a rich and vivid flow of memories, feelings, and actions—almost creating a sense of total recall—of being there. While others generate only fragmented associations, like vague feelings of familiarity. Sort of like the tip of the tongue phenomenon.

Furthermore, when the few notes from the car radio start the rhythm flowing, once triggered, it hangs on and on. It often pulses just below the surface for the rest of the day, popping into consciousness and taking control of the brain when there is a lull in the day's stronger rhythmic flows.

Ergo! Shiplitz concluded that you can think of your brain as consisting of rhythm trains carrying psychological passengers—memories, thoughts, feelings, actions. The familiar tunes wait for the main switch's green light so they can highball down the main track of your mind. While other weaker and less familiar tune-trains stand patiently by on various sidetracks waiting for their go-notes, their flow-notes.

Neil McK. Agnew, Ph.D. and John L. Brown, Ph.D.

Some of those triggering go-notes come from outside: a passing car radio, a lover's touch, a child's cry, a boss's grumble, an alarm clock's squeal. Others come from inside like a stomach rumble, a recycling thought, a lusty urge, a bad dream, a tumor's stomping pain.

"BINGO"!!! cries Shiplitz. Rhythms are it! We travel into the past on rhythms, and when they weaken, the memories riding on them fragment, scatter and fade. But notice, the memories and various functions can often be recovered through music, a tune, a song, a beat as demonstrated in the treatment of stutterers, Alzheimers patients, disabled athletes, and even previously dysfunctional lovers now merrily bonk away to CDs they both love.

Shippy's wife disclosed to Bruney how Shippy used his formula to reignite their sex life . . . which had petered out—so to speak. They experimented with different music till they tried Ravel's Bolero which gradually builds to a crescendo, to a climax. With that rhythm available to both of them they made love like teenagers, like rabbits! Ruth says it took so much out of Shippy that completely exhausted, he gave up writing for three days. So now he rations himeself to once a month till he finishes his current book.

TIME TRAVEL

We travel back into the past on rhythms—physical and psychological beats—triggered by fragments of familiar sounds, sights, smells. Likewise we travel into the future on rhythms embedded in plans, hopes, and dreams. But as we age the future shrinks, those rhythms shorten and can't carry the plans and hopes very far. As the future shrinks the past provides the only long rhythms available. That's why many old folks spend so much time travelling back in time on the strong, long beats of early memories.

Lucky seniors extend their futures in various ways. Some enter an endless future riding on a strong religious or spiritual faith; or living on 'borrowed time' through profound identification with their children and grandchildren; or robustly romping toward a compelling

Finding the Real You

yet distant goal like writing a family history; or perhaps compulsively practicing an established hobby—growing prize African violets, collecting stamps, or pictures of Marilyn Munroe or James Dean.

We know an eighty year old colleague who rises at six each morning to work on her memoirs—not for publication—but to share her accumulated wisdoms with her grandchildren. She opens her memoirs with a quote from T.S. Elliot: "time present and time past are both perhaps present in time future, and time future contained in time past." (T.S. Elliot, 1934, Burnt Norton.)

Certainly in her writing she busily travels back and forth between the past and the future. She's only on volume three with more volumes to come than she has years because as she writes she keeps discovering or creating new 'truths'. As her strong rhythm train moves through time it keeps rolling out an infinite supply of new track into the future. That woman will LIVE until she dies.

When future cadences are strong and long we dance into that unfolding future with high confidence. Of course, the young and the healthy possess that kind of basic beat, on which all their rhythms blithely ride, stretching beyond the horizons of time. Such a secure and basic beat provides a foundational rhythm for an endless variety of dances, 'Just play the tunes dude and we'll do the dance.' Sure, there may be "rattle" times but an infinite future travels ahead out of sight, out of mind. Have you ever tried to talk to the young about insurance or pension plans? Yeah right!

What happens, even if you're relatively young and your basic beat is weak? When your future is uncertain? We get out of step. We have no strong rhythms to follow. Like many elderly people even the young may regress, may falter, procrastinate, or dependently ride on the rhythms of others. If we can't relocate strong rhythms of our own we may become the perennial back seat drivers of life, complaining loudly or in safe, whiney asides, about the ride, the route, and the driver—but it's the only transportation we can afford at the time.

What happens when we have strong but not long rhythms? Then we lurch from dance to dance. We're like the poor rider who wildly

Neil McK. Agnew, Ph.D. and John L. Brown, Ph.D.

zigzags through life. Or worse, leaps on a passing horse and rides off in all directions at once.

When we told Bruney about all this she said: "Yeah, kind of like some people's lives seem to be a series of disconnected short stories, whereas others seem to be able to weave their short stories together into a fascinating novel. Or, in melodic terms, some people sing one unrelated ditty after another while others produce a compelling life-long opera—happy or soap—or better still a magnificent symphony. What happens when, at any age, we sense our basic beat is at risk? What happens when the beat on which all our dances rely falters or fails? What happens when threats to survival, real or imagined, interrupt our current short story or our novel and force us to ponder the end of our life dance, ponder an empty bag of beats? A profound question, but one we'll postpone to the final and optimistic chapter containing a very Strange Attractor.

SOLVING THE BIGGEST PUZZLE OF ALL

All kinds of multi-dot puzzles can be understood and solved once Shiplitz realized the profound role rhythms play in guiding and controlling our minds. If rhythms run our minds then tricks or potions that help control and integrate conflicting rhythms become a source of magic.

Remember the point about tuning the ship's engine up or down to find just the right Rpm's so things stop rattling? Well, according to Shiplitz that's the name of the Big Game! We spend our lives unwittingly trying to tune our Rpm's to particular situations so fewer things rattle. The reason we often do it so poorly is the lyrics distract us. When you can ignore the lyrics you have a better chance of detecting the beat. It's so easy to be seduced by words that we miss the underlying message. Granny liked to say: "I can't hear what you're saying for what you're doing!" For what you're dancing.

If, as Herr Doctor Professor Shiplitz claims, rhythms dominate our minds then ANYTHING that helps change those rhythms can

Finding the Real You

also change our minds, our feelings, our behavior. For that kind of power, for that brand of magic we'll make deals with the Devil, and do. Like what? Like getting hooked on uppers. We'll go for anything that speeds up our Rpms, like caffeine, nicotine, bennies, fast music, speed, alliances with 'fast' people or cars.

But remember how to stop rattles in the ship? We do it not only by turning the Rpms up, but also down—whatever works. So some of us go for downers, anything that slows down our Rpms, like sedatives, soft music, sleep, routine, quiet, warm drinks, booze, alliances with 'slow' people, jobs, things. Things? Yes, 'things'—stuff that's 'dead", that have no minds to change, safe things that you can push around, you know like collector's items, working with wood, or cloth, or bricks, or steel, or numbers or words or logic.

Of course while each of us has a general preference for fast or slow partners, nevertheless we can stretch that preference, we change our beat when absolutely necessary, for a short time. O.K. so sometimes it takes a transition maneuver—counting to ten and/or taking a tranquilizer or a drink, or even going on a retreat to execute a jump off a fast train and climb aboard a slow one. Conversely, it may take a loud, strong beat, or pep pills, to get you moving fast enough to leap aboard a speeding, fast Rpm express.

What's your dream holiday? A quiet tropical beach and a good book? Or is it the snow flying in your face as you ski through untracked powder in the backcountry of the Rockies? Have you noticed how many couples prefer different holidays? She wants action, he want's peace, or visa versa. While some of our rhythms overlap with those of our mates, some don't. Such differences provide advantages. First, they help ensure some independence. Bruney loves golf. For me it's TOO SLOW. Furthermore, why pay for a failure experience—I can get all of those I want for free.

Second, through overlapping rhythms we provide interpersonal anchors, and through differences we extend our paired or group range or repertoire of rhythms through building alliances with people who can dance to a different drummer. Between them the pair has an

Neil McK. Agnew, Ph.D. and John L. Brown, Ph.D.

increased range of competence, can explore directly and vicariously a larger lifespace.

There's the phone! It's Herman saying he can't make it this afternoon—he'll come for dinner.

YOU'RE SMARTER THAN YOU THINK

Shiplitz feels he's solved a universal puzzle, which is 'Why do people keep acting so stupid, when they know better, when they know that what they're doing is dumb, really dumb?' The answer: because just 'knowing' that something is dumb is a weak rhythm. Such a whimp insight puffing away on a sidetrack does not stop the through train anymore than sincere self-instruction stops an ugly worry or a familiar tune from recycling through your head.

The philosopher William James proposed that we do what we must and call it by the best name we know. Shiplitz figured out what it is that we 'must' do. We MUST find a basic beat that carries us out of a personally unsatisfactory 'rattling' present. If the only train we can find to carry us away NOW from our current rattles happens to be long-term stupid, happens to be bound for Dead End Gulch, so be it—c'est la vie. We just gotta reduce the worst of the daily rattle somehow, someway—and rationalize it as best we can.

As Shiplitz says: "If you're trying to figure what makes someone tick or rattle, don't listen to their lyrics—the rationalizations—listen to their beat—fast or slow, strong or weak, long or short, smooth or rough, integrated or fragmented." In particular, listen for their escape rhythms—the fast or slow trains they catch to escape the rattles in a bracketed or boxed situation of their own making—or maybe you helped them? Hello Bertha. Hello Bert.

So what's the answer to the puzzling behavior of the speed freaks, the risk takers, the bungey jumpers; race car drivers; stock plungers; acid heads; illicit sex hounds; horror story addicts; oval office zippers; wealthy shop lifters? The answer to those dotty puzzles is simple, they're merely tuning up their Rpms so some personally annoying or

Finding the Real You

intolerable thoughts and feelings stop rattling. RIGHT NOW! For Herman it's bullying and guns—that's how he tunes his Rpms up.

Similarly, when you puzzle over the slugs, the risk avoiders, the rule followers, the couch potatoes, the tranquilizer takers, the boozers, the gorgers, the hand washers, relax. The answer is they're merely tuning down their Rpms so some personally intolerable thoughts and feelings stop rattling. RIGHT NOW! For Shippy it was snowshoes, now it's a Walkman—that's how he tunes his Rpms down.

In brief, the speedsters and the slugs have both found ways to replace a currently unbearable rhythm, or rhythm conflicts, with a bearable one. It ain't perfect, but according to Shiplitz it's the name of the game, it's the dance of life. Remember how we tune out the ship's rattles by turning the Rpms up or down—whatever works, NOW.

TRADE-OFFS

We know what you're thinking. What happens when you can't find the right Rpms? When annoying or even intolerable rattles remain? It's raining, you've got the flu and you're working to a deadline on your income tax return? Fate deals you another busted flush? The chicks come home to roost? Ye' 'sinners' get your comeuppance? When what goes around, finally does come around? You fly too close to the sun and like Icarus, your wax wings melt?

Well be of good cheer, there's some good news. All of us still have a few rhythmic tricks in our repertoire, some damage control Rpms hidden away in the back of our Rhythm Closet. Like what? Well like running away for an hour, a year, a lifetime, to a movie, a "mummy", a cause, a shrink or a guru, an addiction, a 'religion', a peaceful cemetery?

Our self-righteous conscience sings out loud and clear: "But all this stuff you're doing is so short sighted. It's so dumb to pay such a high price in exchange for a bit of short-term peace and quiet! Can't you see that in the long run YOU ARE GOING TO PAY—BIG TIME". Be careful Mr. and Mrs. Conscience before you ride too high on the self-righteous train. It looks like that's the way Real Yous, probably including yours, are wired. As the whiney little voice inside reminds us: it's easier to see dumbness in others, or from a safe distance. Nobody can afford to be too virtuous on this one: everyday in everyway all of us make THE TRADEOFF: short-term gain for long-term pain. Ask any Tom, Dick, Marnie or Mary. Ask the movie stars and the sports heroes who require a little ritual dance or chemical tune-up, or two, or three before taking center stage.

How do your Yous work the trade off? With an aching head sustained by a swollen liver, with a big career and a shriveled family, with a lot of hangers on and no friends. Or do you have the formula so you can manage peacefully with a pond just about the right size for your 'frogs' and an early warning system to pick up the hum of hawk wings?

There's a knock at the door—it must be Herman, early? No, it's Bertha Butter and she's rattlin. "Listen up. You characters have been spewing out REAL YOUS faster than Orville Redenbacher pops corn. I lost count of how many, but a lot more than will fit into the heads of the small-brained bears you keep yappin about. I told ya' way back at the beginning that your many minds Schtik was going to get you into trouble." She slams the door shut and ankles off down the driveway.

Bertha's got a point. Fortunately for us the Shiplitz Formula saves the day.

USING THE SHIPLITZ FORMULA

As Bertha says: 'When are you guys going to turn the damn thing on and make The Formula work?'

Life = (Your Rhythms Dancing with Their Rhythms)

First notice the brackets. Remember we said that situations usually control who gets center stage. Well the brackets define the situation you're in—in a mood, in a restaurant, in a meeting, in a bed (alone or with company—friendly or otherwise), locked in a dotty

Finding the Real You

puzzle. Brackets are the frames—the psychological cookie cutters—carving up life's moving picture into mind-size bites. The *bracketing situation* could be a passing glance lasting a few seconds, a fleeting dance. Or the bracketed rhythms may cover years, reflecting the pulsing flow of career or marriage, providing stage time for almost all your Yous.

Whether short, or long, weak or strong, the dominant rhythms may come from the particular You in control at the moment. It may be the You controlling the rhythms of 'things' (computers, tractors), or of people (children). Conversely your rhythms may be dominated and driven by the Selves of others, by traffic jams, computer glitches, mates, children, bullies, bosses, lovers, lightning, or a wildly bouncing truck wheel heading your way.

Bruney's now helping Shippy translate some of his scientific mumbo-jumbo into people prose. Before she left for Bermuda she saved John's pilfering soul by giving us a peek at an updated version of THE FORMULA:

LIFE = F^3 (Your Rhythms + Their Rhythms)

F^3! Where the Hell did F^3 come from? Just when we get the brackets decoded we get a new twist thrown at us. Well apparently F^3 stands for **"Fate's Fickle Finger"**. Remember lightning and anarchistic truck tires? In any situation the best-laid plans remain at the mercy of the unplannable, like the oncoming driver's heart attack, the lightning strike, the computer glitch, a surprising corporate downsizing, a child's death. It isn't that we're completely unaware of these possibilities. It's just that we can't afford to always include them inside our daily brackets or we'd go nuts.

So we bunch all Fate's Fingers together and leave them outside the brackets, outside of our limited attention in a bag called F^3. And that's where they stay until a smart-ass opens it for you, or an insurance agent calls, or you need an explanation for something 'that went terribly wrong'.

Neil McK. Agnew, Ph.D. and John L. Brown, Ph.D.

There you have it. The Shiplitz formula of life. Bertha, wherever you are THE FORMULA will help us find the predominant Yous in, and across, situations. We start by focusing on the brackets because where you draw your brackets, and where they are drawn for you, determines which Yous and Thems are dancing between the walls of that particular stage.

BRACKETING

Starting with a simple example, we bracket a common greeting situation, a few seconds where you exchange rhythm fragments ("Hello", "Hi", smiles, nods) as you walk down the hall to your office, or arrive home. Trivial? Well just try not participating in that little dance. You'll soon realize these short jigs are integral parts of a larger dance—Yours and Theirs. An integral part of the ongoing rhythm of living. So in a sense the brackets, like nouns, are a form of mental economy, and serve as little integrating jigs in the multi-layered flow of life.

The bracketed situation may last no more than seconds or a few minutes. Remember how just three or four notes on the passing car radio triggered the whole song and its baggage of memories and feelings. Or the bracketed situation may last a few hours where a given rhythm, like that old song, cycles up and down in your consciousness. Like a host of other rhythms it remains just below the surface whenever stronger rhythms subside it flows in, dragging memories and feelings behind it.

Notice too, just as the passing car radio triggered the unfolding nostalgic flow in Shippy, he in turn triggered it in the secretary. So where do we start the brackets for this rhythmic process? With the passing car radio? With the disc jockey who played it? With the composer who wrote it? And when will it stop flowing? Apparently never, like Bing Crosby's White Christmas or Beethoven's Fifth?

Our brackets are inherited and learned mental cookie cutters designed to maintain rhythmic order, to avoid being overwhelmed by

Finding the Real You

the knowledge that rhythms, like rivers, flow endlessly and seamlessly from the past into the future, surfacing and submerging. And many of our brackets continuously recycle like the morning office ritual, like the 'arrive home' ritual or the December, 'White Christmas' ritual.

Of course what you and we are seeking are those down deep, long term rhythms upon which all the medium and short term ones dance or ride. So we're looking for a hierarchy of rhythms. At the very bottom is **your** life's basic beat. If it's strong and long there are no DEAD END brackets in sight—as is the case with the young, or the healthy, or the profoundly spiritual.

But as a result of real or imaginary threats to your 'survival' the dead end brackets suddenly roll in from the future. Then what happens? Well, when you or someone, or something blocks the main route into the future then traffic starts jamming up behind. The brackets of all the other rhythms compress and you start living "one minute or one day at a time," you stop buying green bananas.

On a positive note what wonderful things happen when you or someone or something expands your brackets: you get a new job; fall in love; have a baby? Wow—the future belongs to you!

A TOWER OF RHYTHMS

In the figure below we provide a crude map of a hierarchy or tower of rhythms with all the short and medium cadences riding along in perfect order on the deep basic beat. Now we realize that life isn't that neat and tidy. Rather, some short and medium rhythms flow backwards, in circles, get out of sync, or drift off on their own performing weird dances that dismay all your other selves. But we need to start simple and later turn the mavericks loose.

Neil McK. Agnew, Ph.D. and John L. Brown, Ph.D.

Tower of Rhythms with foundation beat, flowing uninterupted into Future, on which a host of other short and medium rhythms ride.

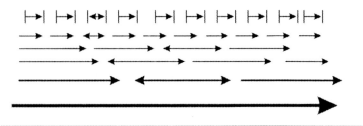

Legend examples:

⊢▶⊣ Brush your teeth	◀——▶ Uncertain Rhythms - arrows at both ends
—▶ Drive to work or to doctor	
———▶ Month long project (e.g., Paint House or wind up an affair.)	
—————▶ Year long project (e.g., take a course, have a child, etc.)	
——————▶ Years (e.g., Marriage/Children/Career)	
————————▶ "Forever" - Your Basic Beat Life Line	

Tower of Rhythms with foundation beat encountering **dead end** so providing collapsed and weakened base beat now capable of supporting only highly restricted or conflicted short rhythms - "one minute, hour, or day at a time." A highly uncertain future (percieved or real) has similar effect leading to short disconnected rhythms - "rope of sand."

Dead End (present threat to Physical or Psychological survival), **or perceived Uncertain Future**

For now we'll assume you're blessed with a strong basic beat with no mental, physical, or spiritual "dead ends" blocking out your horizons. So we can start identifying some of your characteristic rhythms that ride on that primal beat. Our final goal is to locate some of your long-term rhythms, to identify brackets with extended time frames—big box stuff.

Getting a university degree, or writing a novel, or taking early retirement—all three involve long term goals. But if not tied to a strong, long-term beat they all disintegrate into a series of false starts. A person without a basic beat, without long integrating rhythms is like an orchestra without a musical score or a conductor. The players lose their way and drift out of sync. Here's one of Shippy's notes that attached itself to John's hand:

> **Integrating Rhythms:** Fridtjof Nansen, Norwegian Arctic explorer, provides a clear example of our human need for hope strongly linked to daily routines as integrating rhythms. These linked time/space brackets serve to coordinate 'our' dances and 'their' dances. Following is a quote from his journal as the Arctic winter passes before him:
>
> "Everything around is blankness, and my brain is blank. I look at the home pictures and am moved by them in a curious, dull way . . . I have no inclination to read, nor to draw, nor to do anything else whatever. Folly! No, I will go to bed, though I am not sleepy . . . Yes, man's life is nothing but a succession of moods, half memory and half hope."
> (Clipped from: The Economist, December 19, 1998)

Mind Deposit # 7

Well there it is!

Life = F^3 (Your Rhythms Dancing with Their Rhythms)

A simple little formula soon to be as famous as Einstein's. Not only is it simple but it also solves Bertha Butter's problem of too many Yous. There are many Real Yous, as we saw in earlier chapters. But at the base, how you do Life's Dance and who you strut your stuff with will depend, not only on the bracketed situation, but on the main long term drummers that you dance with—internal drummers and external drummers . . . ones that play the long gigs, the life long gigs.

Neil McK. Agnew, Ph.D. and John L. Brown, Ph.D.

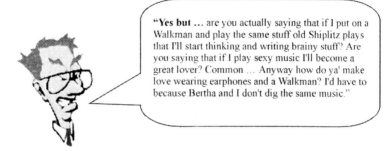

"**Yes but** ... are you actually saying that if I put on a Walkman and play the same stuff old Shiplitz plays that I'll start thinking and writing brainy stuff? Are you saying that if I play sexy music I'll become a great lover? Common ... Anyway how do ya' make love wearing earphones and a Walkman? I'd have to because Bertha and I don't dig the same music."

Well yes . . . you've sort of got the general idea. You might not have the same ideas as Shippy but all of a sudden you'd start gaining access to your unconscious warehouse of different ideas and different emotions. Give it a try the next time you work on a project or try to solve a multi-dot conundrum. Different rhythms call different Yous onto center stage, giving you a chance to use more of your mind power. After all what is boredom? The same You two-stepping to the same two-beat rhythm, without end.

And Bert, concerning making love, we admit you've got a point about the distracting effect of wearing a Walkman. But what about secretly experimenting with 'drum music'—you may actually find a beat that some of your's and Bertha's raunchy Selves can march to . . . move to . . . swing to . . . well you know . . . dance to—leading to a kind of a sexual 'sweet point'. John says he finds a Martini and any music ranging from marching bands through Beethovens 5th to chopsticks does the trick. Well the first few times anyway. Then you can just change the brand of gin and/or the CD.

And finally Bert, in the next chapter we tell you how to identify some of your Bracket-breaking Selves, ones who specialize in 'breaking the chains that bind', well at least scratching the paint off. Don't tell Bertha.

Finding the Real You

MIND MAP #7: YOUR YOUS AND THE FORMULA

Now you get a chance to try out The Formula on some of your Yous.

Map 7a Play it again Sam: To reacquaint yourself with the power that music has to 'drive' feelings and memories, play several old familiar tunes. Notice how your mood and thoughts shift with each piece. Notice how the tune brackets your experience, how it determines which Selves—Yours and Theirs get center stage. Keep experimenting till you find a set point.

But notice, it's not only musical frequencies that drive behavior, so too do the rhythms of smell (fresh baked bread), touch (a warm, gentle hand), and taste (chocolate); not to mention those of visual images. (old photos, or clothes). Or merely try changing your posture (straight and tall or slumped) and feel your Rpms shift. And along with that shift, thoughts and feelings change too.

Map 7b Pick a goal: Next look at the Hierarchy of Rhythms again. Take a pencil and on a clean page draw an end bracket with a date, indicating your most compelling long-term goal, deadline or end bracket. Pencil in that particular goal that looms largest on your horizon, that bullies your other goals, that pushes them around, or will if you go after it.

In calendar time it may be short (where will I jump when there's no place to stood) or long (retirement, Florida and golf). But it's as long as you can mentally 'afford' at the moment. It may be: to get one decent sleep, or to get a drink as soon as possible; or maybe like Herman it's the Monday night football game—sort of living week-to-week; the college prom; or in six weeks to complete your radiation therapy and start getting your hair back; to graduate or get a promotion or a new car in one year; or to get married or to have a child or finish your novel in two years; to change jobs or houses in five years; to have the kids finish college and then you can move to the country in ten years; to take early retirement in 20 years?

Whatever you penciled in, does it have a strong or weak rhythm driving it? Are there integrated medium and short-term goals and rhythms strongly linked to it? Or is it kind of free floating like a kid's balloon? Soon to disappear in the clouds, or deflate to nothing. Is it a short story, or a lifelong novel? We'll come back to this life-shaping theme later in the book.

Map 7c Breaking the chain: A well-ordered life consists of a long, integrated chain of bracketed dances. To get an idea of the driving power of even one tiny link—of one well-bracketed situation—to trigger and control your rhythms try the following experiment. The next time you're traveling the chain and arrive at work, or arrive home, or pass someone you know, try to break the chain—don't join in the ritual-greeting dance. Don't say or do anything. No "Hi's," no "good morning," no comments "awful weather" . . ."lousy traffic," . . . no nods, no waves . . . Just walk on by. Here you are not buying into the rhythm defining brackets, even if your significant other does so. You are saying, damn the brackets, I'm picking my own stage, my own dance.

We know, we know . . . such behavior seems so trivial. Nevertheless, we want to make the point that your behavior is more highly programmed than you think, and that it is chained—break one little link and some of your Selves and their Thems start to rattle.

We suspect you'll get an unforgettable lesson on just how much your rhythms—even in supposedly trivial bracketed situations—are driven by the situational dance. You will also learn how your failure to join even such a trivial ritual dance profoundly affects the internal and external network. How it rattles the web. How did you feel not joining in on the little greeting dance? How did you enjoy lunching by yourself, or did you actually meet a whole new group of dancing partners? As Shippy says, that's what life's all about: a chain of packaged situations involving Your Rhythms dancing with Their Rhythms.

Map 7d Stretching the brackets: Of course deviant souls—like Shiplitz—break traditional chains regularly. They not only pick the dance but redraw their brackets as well. If they're successful,

Finding the Real You

they're called 'creative' and receive awards (Nobel?). If not, they're avoided or locked up. But back to you.

If you had the self-confidence—the underlying strong long beat—to try step 7c, congratulations! We hope you quickly explained what you were up to and that you will be allowed to rejoin the greeting jig next time round. And get your old place back at the lunch table. If you still want it, that is.

Now you're ready for stronger stuff. Try stretching the brackets. We suggest you start modestly, close to home. Tell the family you think they should take an extra half-hour for dinner so you can have some family conversation. How does that go over, especially with the children? If you don't like that one, try changing the hours of bedtime, an hour earlier or later. How does that affect your social life, your sex life, your dream life?

If you had fun with these examples you might get a little more daring and venture outside the home. If you're not doing so already suggest at the office that you are going to do more work from home. What do you think would be the results from such stretching of your and of their brackets? Rationally, all of the above are possible, maybe wise, and even legal.

So because what you're doing is 'rational' and 'legal' and maybe wise, you have nothing to worry about. Right? Notice how you feel doing it? Nervous? Excited? That may tell you something about the strength of your Risk-taking Yous. Notice how they react. Do you end up—sqwuitty-sqwack—comfortably back inside the old bracket?

This little experiment is an example of how we ritualize our flow for the sake of mental and behavioral economy. It's an example of how those consistent rituals have strong turtles down below working day and night to protect the integrity of The Chain, the consistency of the islands, the reliability of the bridges linking them, the stability of the chain. It took Shiplitz the deviant, the chain rattler and breaker, to recognize how important linked rhythms are in maintaining personal sanity and social sustenance.

CHAPTER 8:

YOUR RHYTHMS DANCING WITH THEIR RHYTHMS

> "Will you, won't you, will you, won't you, will you join the dance?"
> —Louis Carrol

If you set clear goals, and if you carefully plan your route, and if you really follow through, then, like Herman, you're day dreaming. But seriously, I plan to get my various worlds in order (setting up a firm budget, cleaning out the basement, organizing my computer files, and helping mother find a condo and sell her house)—as soon as Bruney returns and stiffens my frail resolve.

Speaking of 'will you, won't you, join the dance,' so far Herman has avoided joining our little family bump and jig. Maybe he feels our rhythms may stomp on the toes of his rhythms.

It's thirty-eight hours and forty-three minutes since Bruney left for Bermuda. Not that the kids have given me a bad time . . . it's just I'm not used to being bracketed together with them for such an intensive period. We keep bumping into each other, literally and figuratively.

Finding the Real You

Sunday morning breakfast—BLT sandwiches with Canadian bacon—Max, ignoring loud protests from his sister Kate, is about to share his latest acquisition from his voluminous Joke Book. But 'sooprise', at that very moment Herman arrives. Wisely declining a sandwich he accepts coffee, pulls up a chair at the kitchen table, turns it around, sits with his arms on the back, and has a look on his face that says: "O.K., so show me the ideal American family in action."

Goody, goody, just what I need.

Me: "So . . . Max was just about to tell us a joke. Go ahead Max."
Kate: "Oh Gawd!"
Max: "Well, you see this man goes to his doctor and tells him that his sister thinks she's a chicken. The doctor says: 'My gosh we'll have to lock her up.' And the man says 'If you do that where will we get our eggs?'"
Kate: "Oh Gawd!"
Herman (dead pan):"Got any more of those have you Max?"
Max: "Sure, I've got a whole book of em."
Me: "Great you can take Uncle Herman up to your room and read them together."
Kate: "What about my art work?"
Me: "Ah! Right. Kate has some drawings she did for a school project. Let's have a look."
Kate (holds up her production exclaiming): "Da Dah!"
It's a drawing of our family—the heads are easily recognizable, clever caricatures—but we're stark naked with ALL the details accurately portrayed.
Kate: "Well, what do you think?"
Herman: "Great . . . great. Can I borrow it?"
Me: "No you can't borrow it. Kate needs it for school."
Kate: "No it's O.K. I've already shown it at school."
Me: " Max take Uncle Herman up and read him ALL your jokes. Kate and I have . . . well we'll clean up down here."

Neil McK. Agnew, Ph.D. and John L. Brown, Ph.D.

Now I know why, at the last Parent's Night, Kate's blushing teacher blurted out: "I feel I know you so well!" Obviously, you can 'dance ' with someone even if you're not there. Dancing? Is dancing the right word? At times it feels more like professional wrestling. I certainly can't dance with Herman, I can't find an Rpm that stops the rattles—no set point in sight. Come to think of it, with Bruney away, the kids and I seem to be dancing to numbers most of the time—the flow just ain't there —not the way it is when she's home.

Monday. Hallelujah! Bruney's back. John's back. I'm dancin, I'm dancin—the world's flowin, sweet set points everywhere. Well, at least until I show John the scribbling I've been doing while he was away. His only comment: "Let's go steal some good stuff from Shippy."

After much door pounding and shouting Shippy let us in. Eppy tears a small strip from the cuff of my pant leg—because of his snowshoes, he can't get at John who has hopped up on a chair.

We ask Shippy how come the dog is still wearing his clumsy footwear when Shippy's not. Shippy says it's because the dog refuses to wear earphones, so he hasn't got access to the rhythms that makes the holes between the atoms disappear.

We're all yelling because Shiplitz is still wearing his headset—he's trying to keep us out of his peaceful brackets. For him we're nothing but rattles—I even caught him nervously edging toward his snowshoes, now mounted on the wall.

John goes over to Shippy, lifts one earphone and hollers: "We won't go away till you give us some more neat stuff about rhythms." Shippy sighed, took off his headset, took down his snowshoes, and while cradling them in his lap made us promise to leave in precisely fifteen minutes. Then he talked!

WORLD (-1), WORLD (1), WORLD (2)

Shiplitz claims that not only is each of us a bag-o-beats or rhythms—but there are two bags, two kinds of Yous: Bag 1 Yous (reporters) and

Finding the Real You

Bag 2 Yous (editors). See Bertha, we're actually starting to simplify things.

He says the reporters—the Bag 1 Yous (B1s)—resonate to brief rhythms in the flow of experience and attach lyrics to them. Thus, they spend their time collecting and creating bits and pieces of news about The World—about big R REALITY. But because information about The World is filtered and transformed by the senses and minds of the reporters, and because they only pick up fragments of 'reality' as it flows by, we can never get a complete and clear picture of REALITY.

WORLD (-1)

Shippy calls that inaccessible reality World (–1). It's the world that exists after you subtract all the transformations performed on it by our senses, beliefs, and human biases—by our B1reporters and B2 editors. Since we can't 'get at it' in a form stripped free of our current biological, cultural and scientific distortions. He says: "Forget about it, SUBTRACT that idea of 'reality' from your mind". For you, me and even for the scientists, it doesn't exist.

Apparently, even for scientists, 'knowledge' is based on tiny samples filtered through, and transformed by, their fancy instruments and current theories. Shippy says you can get the idea if you run a clean piece of paper through a Xerox with nothing to be copied. You will still see some 'stuff'—specs, dots, smudges—on your copy of 'nothing.'

All sources of information, all instruments—like reporters, like your eyeglasses and fax machines make a contribution or deposit— poop on—our pictures of Reality. As astronomers oh-so-conscientiously study their photos of the universe, some of those specs, some of those distant planets are merely lens deposits, or even fly shit.

Notice how 'reality' changes it's spots every time a new scientific school of thought emerges. We get a new view through the flawed and smudged lenses of their flavor of the month, high tech toys and always biased minds—Theory A Vs Theory B: you should have a mammogram vs no you shouldn't; you should take beta carotine vs no you shouldn't; and have you ever wondered how they keep on finding yet another 'smallest particle'—when will they discover the word 'smaller' and stop kidding us and themselves?

NO CONCLUSIONS

Shippy is not merely commenting on minor smudges and fly specs, on otherwise clear pictures of The World. He claims the really big manufacturers of reality are not so much the B1 reporters filing their brief and isolated news reports or pictures. The mammoth Reality Makers —the editors, the theorists, the advertisers—decide which bits and pieces of the already flawed news are to be included, and more important excluded, and then they weave them into a tapestry to reflect their particular picture of the world.

As one of Shippy's buddies, a Nobel Laureate, said: 'No conclusions without premises'. It's the assumptions of our cultural, scientific and personal editors that manufacture our reality. Concerning the big picture, apparently as we speak, one of Einstein's key assumptions, namely that matter is distributed evenly throughout the universe, is being challenged—pardon us, but what about all the lumps like earth, the sun, the galaxies? Bruney says you've got to be 'way out' to buy Einstein's assumption. Get it? The further you move away from something the less lumpy it becomes, till from 'way out' it becomes a spec and then disappears. If Albert's challengers win popular scientific support then we get a New Universe—just like that.

Even if nerds like us can't understand what the scientific fuss is all about, we can get the point. For example, consider a person's view of their loved one, early and late in the relationship. During the honeymoon warts are beauty marks, farts are cute little fluffies, ignorance is innocence, childishness is charming, dead-beat in-laws are quaint . . . So, says Shippy. Reality like beauty lies in the eye, but mostly in the mind or the assumptions of the beholder, scientist or citizen.

Finding the Real You

We all select and shape the news to fit our editorial perspective. Sure, we can often agree about trivial stuff. For example, a reporter working for a Republican newspaper, and another working for a Democratic paper can both agree that Bush spoke for 22 minutes. But disagree radically about what he really said.

Anyway, even if we can't get direct access to World (-1) we still create and live challenging lives in two other worlds that are within our sensory and mental reach. Shippy calls them World (1) and World (2).

WORLD (1)

World 1 consists of all the little jigs and fragments of news provided by our B1 reporters. Our news hounds resonate with passing rhythms of experience that fall within our five basic brackets—our senses. In different cultures those bracketed rhythms have different lyrics riding on them. World (1) represents the flow of those lyrics. Like a hectic newsroom, this world is inundated with an endless stream of bits and pieces of incomplete and often conflicting news bites: It's cloudy . . . but the weatherman says it won't rain; he kissed me . . . but he didn't phone back; she got a raise . . . but I didn't; my gut hurts . . . was it the water . . . the raw fish . . . the booze . . . the flu. . . ? And on it goes.

Shiplitz rants about this mob of B1 messengers all trying to crowd into the narrow confines of our mind. This rabble of the senses must be ordered into meaning and purpose, the rabble requires an interpreter and organizer, an EDITOR.

WORLD (2)

In order to 'make mental sense' of the flood of inputs that our physical senses deliver we need interpreters, we need Editors. That's where your Bag 2 Yous come in—they are masters at locating or inventing patterns in the flood of fragments, masters at sensing or creat-

Neil McK. Agnew, Ph.D. and John L. Brown, Ph.D.

ing long term rhythms, of manufacturing consistency. They link together selected bits of news, sometimes consciously but mostly unconsciously, picking and choosing which of the reporter's jigs to include and which to ignore.

Our B2 editors most important job is filling in major gaps and Voila, they not only construct Islands of Consistency but build bridges linking them together—at quiet times providing an illusion of one mind. Through this continual editing and re-editing, your B2s attempt to construct a rhythmic symphony, a stable network of expectations—a meaningful world. According to Shippy this world—World 2—becomes your current and continuing REALITY.

So, says Shiplitz, showing us the door: 'World 1 consists of transformed fragments, bracketed samples of World (–1), and World 2 consists of edited Islands of Consistency built from those sensory transformations and distortions, from the songs and dances of your frenetic B1 reporters.'

We tiptoe out leaving Eppy sleeping peacefully under Shippy's desk—maybe dreaming of snow.

We agreed that we don't like Shippy's view of the World—sorry Worlds, but may you be blessed, may your many islands float on trusted turtles, swimming to coordinated rhythms, carrying you into a safe and nourishing future. Or even if you're like the rest of us, splashing about madly and crying for a life raft, may the water be warm and the sharks attracted to your neighbors.

We trudge back to my house for a large sip of Rpm stabilizer. Bruney is blazing away on the computer—wearing earphones.

I ask John whether he has constructed any Islands of Consistency from what Shippy told us. He said he had one a few minutes ago, but it fell apart when he stumbled against the door jam. Some islands are like the pictures in a kaleidoscope—they're clear as long as you don't move.

So I ask: 'What about a turtle? Do we have a trusted turtle to carry our island into the future?' John says: 'Of course we have a

Finding the Real You

turtle. Our turtle is to write a book that makes a lot of money. All we need now is the island to build on that turtle, all we need is to locate some consistency in our scramble of notes, hunches, ideas, scribbles. So far all we have is a mob of notes as Bertha and Bill Butter gleefully point out.'

John points out that Bruney knows how to construct beautiful islands of consistency from a mess of notes. Yes, Bruney knows how to make the words jig into lovely sentences, and the sentences waltz into compelling articles. Maybe we could get her to use her mental music to write our lyrics. Of course we'd make her a fourth author—after us and Shiplitz.

We explain to Bruney what we have in mind. She replies: "I don't think so. There's a difference between looking for order in a cluttered newsroom and tidying up after a mental hurricane. Ya know boys, your idea of 'growing' a bestseller seems to consist of throwing mental manure to the winds. Good luck."

Well, it was worth a try. Back to tossing our word salad.

As you know, if you've got more than one B2 editor working on a story—each dancing to a different tune and so selecting different lyrics, then it hurts inside your head: Editor A: "She loves me, otherwise, we wouldn't be having such wonderful sex!"

Editor B: "Yeah, right, then how come she won't move in with you?"

Oh for an Island of Consistency! Oh for a bridge to a peaceful plot. Hey you turtles common, get with it, we need a solid place to stood.

WORLD MAPS

If Shiplitz can make up formulas on which to stood so can we. We made up this one:

**B2 Mind Maps =
B2 Editor Bias (B1 Reporter Stories + Available Mind Space)**

Neil McK. Agnew, Ph.D. and John L. Brown, Ph.D.

Bertha, are you still there? If so, this neat formula breaks the code, shows how your's and Bert's brains really work. Well, come to think of it you usually provide the B2 Editor Bias for both of you . . . Bert must have a lot of unused Mind Space . . . he must have a lot of potential?

So now we're homing in on the really Real Yous: 1) Your B2 Editors construct maps of your world using: 2) stories from favorite B1 reporters; and 3) available mind space. John says you and Bert are short supplied on number 3. He's just joking . . .

You build your Islands of Consistency—B2 edited World Maps—of femininity, masculinity, a lover, etc. from what your B1 reporters tell you about men, women and what happens next door, plus the Mind Space you have at hand for the task. All of course edited according to the bias you have about women, men and your neighbors.

MANY WORLDS—ONE WORLD?

Hey, hey, Bertha, one of your B2 Editors holds the persistent bias that there is One You and One World. Whereas, our editorial bias is that there are Many Yous and Many Worlds. So ever since Chapter 1 we've been arguing that line. Our B1s and B2s have been trying to feed you stories and maps for The MANY box. And of course your B1s and B2s have been feeding back 'Yes buts . . .'—stories and arguments for The ONE box.

We must admit you're not alone, everyone, sometimes even John and I, try to dance, —albeit clumsily—in the ONE YOU, ONE WORLD, box. Herman's fictional ONE You is Mr. Macho; Shippy's is Herr Doctor Professor Genius, John's is Smart, Tall, Handsome and Sexy, while mine is simply Humble, Curious and Open Minded.

Now the popular 'One You' editorial dance has one big advantage over the 'Many Yous' dances—it seems to save precious brain

Finding the Real You

space, but only if we ignore the garbage it accumulates. Furthermore, it helps generate nice simple lyrics or fatuous 'wisdoms' like: 'To thine own self be true, thou cans't not then be false to anyone.' Notice, that advice assumes you know who 'thine own self' is at the time.

In contrast, the bigger 'Many Yous' box generates less garbage but produces a larger repertoire of dance steps and more interesting lyrics—challenging wisdoms like: 'to thine own SELVES be true . . . ' So you trade off a lot of garbage for a bit more complexity, and entertain such challenging cocktail conversations as: "And pray tell me Herman, which particular self are you being true to this evening, or at this moment . . . and which self is acting as Senior Editor this week?" Now, how might Herman reply?

Ah, Herman's editors know a lot of bad words!

So? So reluctantly we admit Bert and Bertha have a point. To be mentally affordable most of our 'wisdoms' or selves have to be simple, simple. You only make a wisdom more complex if the old one really isn't working, resulting in your mental house being so crowded with junk there's no place left for your minds to sit down.

You've either got to do a lot of spring-cleaning and throw out a bunch of obsolete mental and emotional stuff or break outa the box.

BREAKING UP, BREAKING OUT

When people talk about 'breaking up' a relationship or a marriage they're using the right word ' BREAKING'. Similarly when you break up with one of your Editors-in-Chief it's the same thing. You're painfully breaking up, even blowing up, some favorite boxes, some familiar consistencies and their connecting bridges. And in the process scaring the hell out of neighboring islands and their aging turtles.

And then what have you got? A lot of flotsam and jetsam, a limited construction budget, and a desperate need for places to stood. When you, or someone else, like a trusted lover, sets off bombs in the middle of your Society of Selves, blows holes in your network of unquestioned expectations, then you lose some minds, some islands, and also the bridges connecting them to your other selves and those of significant others. No wonder serious New Years Resolutions seldom work, we can't afford all the destruction and reconstruction they involve.

When you break out of a box, when you fire a senior editor, blow up an island, scare off a turtle, well you're stretching or breaking a bunch of linkages, a heap of strong expectations. Then you desperately NEED to re-establish order, build some replacement consistencies. In order to do so most of us go out squitty-squack and 'buy' a replacement that 'fits' the old hole That's why divorced people keep marrying the same 'kind' of person—one that more or less fits in with their remaining expectations, and those of friends and family. Such apparent idiocy disturbs fewer Islands of Consistency and doesn't scare off so many trusted turtles supporting the remaining islands.

To avoid falling out of your head when islands and bridges get blown up you need to build new ones. But as good old Ludi Wittgenstein quipped: "When you tie-up loose ends, stand on tippy toes and try to see what the other ends are attached too—what do you find . . . love and trust and pixie dust . . . or a slow burning fuse disappearing into a pretty package? "

OCCUPIED TERRITORY

The reason it's so tough to 'break up' an established relationship or an editorial bias is because your brain space is pretty well filled with evolved and compatible song and dance routines and networked turtles. So whatever the editorial bias—Herman's dumb Macho image or the One You, One World simplification—it involves hard won Islands of Consistency, and their linking bridges, on and across which we habitually perform our familiar song and dance routines.

Yes, we confess. When trying to break up the 'waltz of the ONE', or even cut it, our brains hurt. Like you, we were brung up on the One You, One World 'truth'. Breaking it up brings brain pain. In fact what we suspect we're doing is leaving most of our islands and bridges intact, and constructing the MANY Yous, MANY Worlds box in our mental back yard. So when we're not working on this book we sneak back into the more mentally affordable, if junk-cluttered Box of ONE.

Bertha, maybe you could think of your REAL You as your Editor-in-Chief with lots of assistant Editors and then. . . ?

No?

Like all editors, your B2s develop points of view in handling the news reports that flow to them second-hand from their B1 reporters. So the B2s of a radical feminist may bracket in and bracket out different parts of the story than the B2s of a born-again Christian housewife, and those of a Wild 'n Wooly Biker would be stranger yet.

Our own reality consists of a flow of edited rhythms, of surfacing and submerging beats, and their linked lyrics. So what parts or islands of World 1 and World 2 knowledge, what consistencies, what supporting tower of turtles, can you trust?

TRUSTED EVIDENCE: 'OBJECTIVE' WORLD (1) RHYTHMS

We trust two kinds of evidence: Selected World 1 rhythms we call 'objective' evidence; and selected World 2 rhythms we'll call editorial 'convictions' or 'truth', and which our enemies call 'ignorance' or 'bias'.

Rhythms that trigger strong beats in your B1 reporters typically arise from contact with strongly bracketed rhythms we call objects. Like? Well, like strong beats that 'kick' our B1 reporters where their nerves are and get them twanging—like rocks on bare toes, skunks on clear nasal passages, scalding water on bare skin, fire alarms on ears. All detected physical signals—whether light, sound, smell, or touch—consist of rhythms (physical frequencies). Some within our sensory reach trigger Rpms in our neurological systems, that wake up

B1 reporters and get them scribbling. Some of those signals even arrive well bracketed, like skunk stink, other rhythms arrive with fuzzy brackets like whispers and baby burps.

Bruney overheard us talking and suggested a good example of what we're nattering about, is the game called Rumor. You remember? Sitting in a circle, one person starts the game by whispering a short message to the person on their right, who in turn whispers it to their neighbor until it arrives back at it's source. The originator then reads out both the original message and the unwittingly transformed one that resulted from its passage around the circle of B1 receivers and B2 editors. The unwitting transformations and distortions performed on the original message are astonishing. In a nutshell that's how Bertha's, Bert's and Herman's minds work. Not ours. Not yours. But theirs.

Bruney insisted, as a reward for giving us that example, that we take a few minutes encouraging Max to learn how to dance. She had Kate teaching him the two-step.

Why teach him so young, he's only eight? Bruney says every mother has the responsibility to make sure her sons know how to dance. She owes it to The Sisterhood. When a man knows how to dance it provides at least one occasion when he and his partner know what he's going to do next. Mmmmmh? John's taking dancing lessons and his teacher Sabrina says Bruney is into wishful thinking—no one will ever know what a man will do next.

Anyway, John and I bullied Max into taking his dance medicine amidst a flood of 'Oh Gawds' from Kate. Then as our reward we bullied Bruney into giving us some good stuff about how people edit their flow of experience. She replied: "Isn't bracketing similar to 'nouning', to putting corsets around stuff that's really in flux, things like atoms, people, kittens and the future?"

Finding the Real You

VERBERS AND NOUNERS

How you cut up your experience into mind sized bites, how you draw brackets around the endless flow of life's rhythms reveals some of your Real Yous. If life is a continuous and seamless flow, as Shiplitz says, then we help make it fit into our brain by freezing parts of the flow, by constructing Islands of Consistency.

We must carve up or chunk the flow of sensations into manageable time and space bound objects and events. We package and ritualize much of the endless stream. We draw a circle around part of the flow, freeze it into a nine to five habit and call it 'work'. Or we compulsively and unsuccessfully try to squeeze it into a robotic ritual and call it golf, or chunk it into a person and call it 'Bertha' or 'Bert' or 'Herman'.

We take a buzz of verbs and, for mental convenience, transform them into nouns. The experts claim that every cell in our body has dandruff and is completely replaced once a year. So you get a brand new physical YOU every twelve months or so. So who is the Real You. Obviously not the body's bits and pieces since they're always changing. You is a verb, masquerading as a noun.

This 'nouning' of the verby world goes on all the time. For example take a whirlpool under a waterfall. Every minute fresh water whirls in to replace the old. So what's the same? Not the parts. It's the whirl. It's the rhythm. It's the bracketing. The parts are along for the ride.

Where's the consistency? It's in the 'whirl' of the pool, it's in Bertha's, Bert's or Herman's repertoire of rhythms. According to crazy Shiplitz, those rhythms are the real Herman, not the physical stuff in the shirt and pants. Take away the coordinated rhythm and you take away Herman's memories, thoughts, and feelings. His actions fragment and ultimately disappear. In gentle forms we call it 'sleep', in more severe forms we call it 'dead drunk', or 'coma' or 'death' even though the meat is still there occupying the shirt and the pants.

But our rhythms are strong stuff. Many of them 'live' on in the minds and hearts of loved ones and others long after the physical stuff, including the shirt and pants, have lost their brackets, have relaxed into dust.

But let's not kill off poor Herman. We need to talk a bit more about his durable rhythms.

Herman can change some of his bits and pieces, change some of his baggage, learn to talk a better game. But not necessarily learn to play or dance one. Not unless he ignores the words and works on locating and tuning the appropriate rhythms. It's like teaching a kid to apologize to granny—'now say it with feeling' which means 'get the rhythm right'. Getting Herman to apologize for anything is hard enough, but getting him to do it with feeling? Forget it . . . at least for now. You can fake the words, it's harder to fake the feelings that reflect the basic beat. Psychopaths can fake feelings in the short run, but eventually the lack of the basic beat exposes them—that's why they have to keep moving on to the next trusting soul.

THE LOGIC OF STONES VS THE LOGIC OF WATER

The logic of stones is simple and slow, it deals with nouns, with self-contained things that when you lay them down, they stay where you put them:

1 stone + 2 stones = 3 stones

Accountants, engineers, most mathematicians, administrators, bankers, and aunt Mattie like the logic of stones. A place for everything and everything in it's place. If something doesn't have hard boundaries they stuff it in a corset. If the rhythm is complex they transform it into a march or a ritual. They love rules.

The logic of water is complex and fast, it deals with irrepressible verbs, with stuff that ebbs and flows and melts together:

Finding the Real You

1 drop + 2 drops = a bigger drop
1 river + 3 rivers = a flood

Criminal lawyers, entrepreneurs, poets, lovers, fast water rafters, Uncle Chet, and kittens like the logic of water—hey, hey, let's play. If something is corseted they cut the strings, if it's a march they turn it into a tango. They love breaking rules.

The logic of stones is for Nouners and freezers—for those who play by the rules. Whereas, the logic of water is for Verbers and melters—For those who play by their guts.

Surprisingly, even though they frustrate each other, Nouners and Verbers seek each other out and typically work or live together. Whereas, two strong Nouners cause sparks, even flames, through frictioning each other's brackets, conversely two Verbers will just get lost. But a Nouner provides a Verber with some structure, whereas a Verber provides a Nouner with some flexibility. So together they can do more dances, in more places, at more times.

Of course each of us is a mixture of Verb YOUS and Noun YOUS, but as a first rough cut watcha think—are most of your predominant Yous, Nouners and freezers whose goal is: 'a place for everything and everything in its place', or are most of your strong Yous, Verbers or melters: 'I know it's here somewhere..'

TRANSFORMING VERBS INTO NOUNS

How you transform verbs into nouns and nouns into verbs helps us locate some Real Yous. If you like sharp brackets, clear beginnings and endings for most of your activities then some of your very strong Selves are verb to noun transformers, are 'Nouners'.

How can you tell? Here are some of the ways: 1) people can set their clocks by you; 2) if you're going to do something like paint a room, or take a trip, even write a book you usually plan it carefully, set dates, line up materials, follow through; 3) even with

Neil McK. Agnew, Ph.D. and John L. Brown, Ph.D.

long term projects like career, marriage, retirement, you tend to make a list, follow a plan. You know, or think you know, where you want to be, or should be, next week, next month, next year. You're a 'nouner' if you thought the millennium was a big deal.

Sure, some of your nouns keep leaking into verbs—like golf strokes and daydreams—keep escaping from their mental corsets, but your various Selves and your cardiovascular system strain hard, rounding them back into 'where they belong'.

Oddly enough there are people who never saw a noun they really liked—particularly yours. If some of your strong Selves prefer flexible or readily movable brackets, like fuzzy beginnings and endings, then those Selves are noun-to-verb transformers, are 'Verbers', and can drive' Nouners' to distraction.

Here is how you can identify Verbers: 1) people cannot set their clocks by you; 2) if you're going to do something you often do it in fits and starts, if at all; 3) you don't follow a road map through life –you zigzag—although after a crises you resolve to noun like crazy. But most of the time you kind of muddle through, sort of wander into the future following whims and paths of least resistance. For you tomorrow will come when it comes. You just can't understand all the fuss about the millennium—just another arbitrary noun. Even the Nouners can't agree on where the brackets start—one second after midnight year 2000 or 2001.

Nevertheless, even though we know in the back of our minds that life's a flow, our reporters and editors spend a lot of their time 'Nouning', bracketing the flow of what leads to what—'experts say massive doses of Vitamin C can block the flow to cancer.' But once in a while even devout nouners face up to the fact that life is a running battle with gravity from the time the infant laboriously stands up, til the time the old folks reluctantly lie down.

Some reporters, particularly investigative reporters and critical editors, spend some time stretching or demolishing brackets, releasing the flow: 'Researcher says Vitamin C may prevent cancer in some people, if started early enough, if combined with

Finding the Real You

Vitamin E, but watch out, it may be a powerful laxative, you may go with the flow!'

If you think of your bag of B2s as editors receiving stories from their bag of B1 news reporters you will understand old Shiplitz's basic idea—probably better than he does. So what? So to find the Real Yous—which way back in the beginning of this book is what we promised to do—we should focus on your *star* B1 reporters and your *senior* B2 editors.

Hint: Most of them are 'Nouners'. We need to cookie-cut the flow to fit inside our brain. If you're currently a bit short of free brain space concentrate on finding the really Real Yous among your senior editors, among your most powerful Nouners.

B2 EDITORS MANUFACTURE REALITY

In a high technology information age our poor overloaded B1's rely increasingly on prepackaged lyrics. They're increasingly exposed to flooding rivers of second, third, and fourth hand reports: reports from parents, peers, teachers, experts pouring in over the airwaves and Internet. By the time one of your own B2s gets a story from one of his or her B1s, its been filtered through, who knows, how many other myopic B1s and biased B2s. How many times has the story been edited before it is seen on CNN or read in a major newspaper? So most of our B2 editors are occupied drawing World 2 mental maps consisting of editings, of editings, of editings.

How long since your B1 senses had direct contact with relatively unedited, unpackaged, unprocessed "nature"? How long since you were so close to the ground you actually smelled unfertilized grass, or got earth, rather than dirt, under your nails, or watched wild fox cubs at play, or inhaled unpolluted air? As Robbie Burns put it:

'Gie me ae spark o' Nature's fire
That's a the learning I desire'.

Neil McK. Agnew, Ph.D. and John L. Brown, Ph.D.

When was the last time you felt that spark of nature's fire rather than got it prepackaged, perfumed, or laced with all the sincerity of an insurance agent sending you a birthday card. Finding time for a 'walk in the woods', or smelling the proverbial flowers is more than vacuous advice, it's a way of triggering primitive rhythms, rhythms bred in the bone, rhythms tied to the tides, marching to the moon, sashaying with the seasons—sweet yet primitive set points for the species. To do so provides a respite, a nourshing holiday away from the artificial and fragmenting jigs of the cultural and corporate song and dance routines.

As Shippy persists in saying: 'The world we call Reality, our own World 1, is mainly of our own making, it's manufactured. We spend more time looking into the cyclopean eyes of our computers and television sets than into the hearts of our loved ones' (Shippy should talk). The roads we drive on, the planes we fly in, the food we eat, the teeth we consume it with, the artificial exercise we take, most of the smells we radiate are increasingly manufactured, packaged, or bracketed.

And as we speak, the boogers are synthesizing and packaging our pheromones—our sex smells. Them be potent rhythms that will bully our beats. We won't have to rely on seductive music and sweet talk anymore. Just a squirt of synthetic lust musk on the potato chips and away we go!

So when Shiplitz talks about 'your rhythms dancing with their rhythms' he's also suggesting that most of those rhythms are manufactured, artificially bracketed and corseted. Most of nature, including humans, has been tamed, culturally programmed. So most of our dances must be pretty predictable? Well, yes and no. When Bruney's away my world becomes less predictable.

If we believe Shippy, we should be able to identify most of your Yous, most of your dancers and dances, and most of their Thems as well. But not all! Some of the most interesting Yous, and Thems, some of the down deep Turtles are harder to find. As we'll discover later in the story.

Finding the Real You

RHYTHMS: FAST, MEDIUM AND SLOW

Remember the Shiplitz Formula:

Life = (Your Rhythms Dancing with Their Rhythms)

Earlier in this chapter in a rare flash of insight we recognized that people who aren't as smart as Shippy—like us—needed a simpler formula. Since we're more familiar with the words and lyrics that ride on rhythms, we rewrote the formula using familiar words as follows:

B2 Mind Maps = B2 Editor Bias (B1 Reporter Stories + Available Mind Space)

For example, what's the basic reality or rhythm of a newspaper? It's editorial policy. Reporters come and go, but its 'liberal' or 'conservative' policy usually persists. It's usually predictable which political party a paper will support. How it will slant or spin the news. If you want to get to know the Real Yous or Real Thems don't pay too much attention to the song and dance routines of their B1 reporters. Instead, listen for the patterns of editorial commentary, listen for the long-term rhythms, the symphony of their beliefs and the mood of their operas.

In terms of lyrics, is your editorial policy generally optimistic or pessimistic? Individualistic or social? Passive or aggressive? Hot or cold? Detailed or general? In terms of basic rhythms are yours short or long, fast or slow, weak or strong?

Herr Docktor Professor Shiplitz claims you select and reject others, and they you, not so much on the basis of their surface lyrics and B1 verbal news reports but more on the basis of something deeper, their Rpms, their range of rhythms. We're so busy consciously listening to their sound bites that only unconsciously do we eventually detect the underlying beat, the tune, the music. We don't know it but we select intimate others more on the basis of their smell, their skin texture and temperature, than by what they say. That's why we get confused. They and we can horse around with words, but not with

Neil McK. Agnew, Ph.D. and John L. Brown, Ph.D.

each other's basic rhythm, unless you're a consummate actor. But even actors burn out muckin about with their core rhythms.

For a minute think of yourself as a Bag-o-Beats, some fast, some medium, some slow. Your bag may contain mostly fast beats, mine mostly slow ones. Ah'ha! We're getting close to some really 'Real Yous' now—close to your foundations, to your deep turtles and the rhythms they swim too. Bertha! Bert! Hear this! All your thoughts, feelings, memories, words, actions ride on your particular profile of beats: fast, medium and slow.

As the prairie poetess, Rita Stinchcomb, so wisely warbled in the Gopher Gazette:

"Know me . . . know my verbs . . . know my nouns . . . but above all KNOW MY BEATS."

According to Shippy there are three types of people and you're one of those three. You could be a 'Speedster' with a bag mainly full of fast beats, with a few medium and slow ones thrown in. Or, You could be at the other extreme, a 'Laidback', a bag of mainly slow beats, with a few medium and fast ones for good measure. Finally, You could be a happy 'Middler'. A bag of mostly medium beats, with a few fast ones and slow ones holding down either end.

Finding the Real You

Bag-O-Beats Profiles

Figure 8.1

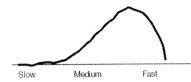

Speed Freak : Profile is shifted to the fast end. Has the capacity for a few slow beat, and some medium beat dances but most systems - metabolising, thinking, feeling, acting - typcially operate on fast.

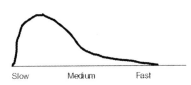

Slow Poke: Profile is shifted to the slow end. Has capacity for a few fast and some medium beat dances but most systems typically operate on slow.

Middle most : Profile mainly centred on medium. Has capacity for a few fast and slow dances but most systems typically operate on medium.

Mix and Match: For short term activities any of the three profiles can dance with the other. For example, slow pokes have a few speedy dances in their repertoire, and the speed freaks have a few slow ones in theirs. They can trot them out for brief encounters. Such temporary mismatches can produce either a pleasant novelty effect, or repeated frustrating calls to "speed up" or "slow down." Similarly, for brief periods, or under special circumstances, two speed freaks can jive, or two slow pokes can waltz. But such specialisation, such a limited range of RPM's, restricts their futures.

Since all experience - memories, thinking, feeling, behaving - rides on rhythms, restricting your repertoire to any one profile limits your experience, limits your life. While genetics and early experience dictate your preferred RPM rate, you can extend it, but teaming up with others who help trigger and tune your less preferred rates. In so doing they give you access to experiences normally beyond the reach of your rhythm profile. If your fast or slow you've probably mated with a medium, and periodically whether you want to or not , due to family or employment connections, you're forced to have the odd clumsy jig with opposites.

In order to experience a full life you need access to a wide range of rhythms.

For starters look at Figure 8.1 and pick one of the three profiles that you think best reflects your rhythmic foundations. Sure, everyone beats fast, medium, and slow at times, but what's your preferred or usual rate? Are you a relaxed, comfy slipper-clad stamp collector, or a spandex-encased racer? Is your resting heart rate 55 or 80? Don't know? Take your resting pulse rate, or ask a friend.

RHYTHMS, STRENGTH AND DURATION

But notice, not only can beats be fast or slow, they can also be strong or weak. So a fast dancer with a strong beat will lead another fast dancer with a weaker beat. It's called leadership, bullying, will, worship, etc.

Also, notice not only can beats be fast or slow, strong or weak, they can last merely a minute—bim bam thank you ma'am—or they can beat on . . . and on . . . and on . . . It's called pig-headed persistence, commitment, tenacity, even love.

In the next chapter we look at *long, strong, slow rhythms.* Shippy claims that it's such foundations that provide the basic beat—the drummer that keeps the band members coordinated. It's the long strong rhythms that give you a secure sense of future, that provide a resilient foundation on which to build a rich repertoire of linked, shorter dances.

You take zillions of short trips on short rhythms: trips to the bathroom; to the office; to the beach; to the hairdresser; to the pub; to the football game; to the love nest, even to the doctor. But the only thing linking them together may be your calendar. How many lives are held together by a ruddy calendar? And how many by the long symphony of hope and purpose? Bertha . . . sounds like a MASTER YOU?

Our human search for long, strong rhythms may come in many forms, ranging from: strong genes by selecting long-life grandparents; to becoming a health freak; to joining an ethereal sect whose motto is: "God wouldn't have provided tobacco if SHE didn't want us to smoke—in fact I just know SHE smokes, and provides a favored cough free place in heaven for puffers." But more of long, strong dances in the next chapter. Now back to basics.

Shiplitz solved THE cosmic nine-dot puzzle. Following Einstein's

Finding the Real You

advice Shippy shifted his level of thinking, and maybe ours. He claims that we now have a new and powerful way of engaging the perennial puzzle: Who am I? Presumably we can go beyond our lyrics and identify the music we ride on, go beyond the baggage, and see the rhythm trains that carry them.

But of course we can't forget the baggage. We've been taught it and memorized it too well. Listening carefully to the lyrics and examining it's logic is what we've been programmed to do. But by looking through the Shiplitz lens maybe we can see life's baggage in a new way.

BAGGAGE

You say: "All well and good to yammer on about bag-o-beats and rhythm trains but, how in the hell do I relate it to my everyday experience?" Dirty question. One obvious answer involves selective deafness—don't listen to the song, try to change the music, modify the beat. That's what coaches mean when they say we have to stop the other team's momentum. We have to break their rhythm.

For instance let's say you're a 'speedster' and you want to slow down your train, want to get off and smell the flowers. Or maybe you're a too cool, laid-back dude who wants to rev up your Rpms. Well, whichever, you've been tuning your natural Rpm unwittingly for years, like every time you have a cup of speedup (coffee) or a glass of slowdown (booze). Now you can start doing it wittingly! Like? Well, for example, like Shippy with his earphones—tuning his Rpms with music, just music no lyrics.

Even without earphones maybe you can stop throwing so many words at yourself and others. For brief periods sneak outside the lyric box. Close your eyes and try to feel the swing and sway of your train: breathe slower and deeper, turn off the sound while watching TV, stretch and stand as tall as you can, crawl around on your hands and knees, lay naked with a lover but refrain from sex. What happens? You enter new worlds. Once you get a feel for the new music then you can start considering the baggage.

What kind of baggage do fast or slow rhythm trains carry? First consider emotional baggage.

Fast trains can carry excitement or anxiety. Instead of throwing words at the anxiety, slow down the train. Slow trains can carry tranquility or sadness. Instead of throwing words at the sadness, speed up the train.

When you're having an argument with someone—a dance where you tread on each other's toes—stop throwing words at yourself or them, stop repeating your lyrics louder and louder. Change the rhythm. Slow down the train. Remember all that stuff about taking a deep breath, or counting to ten—both are primitive but wise pre-Shiplitzian folk wisdoms—beat changers.

You say: 'Yeah, easier said than done. Ever tried to stand in front of, or push a train. Your own or someone else's?' When we posed your question to Shippy he said: 'No, of course you don't stand in front of an oncoming express, and don't try to push a freight train. Instead, bribe the engineer. As we noted above you already do that, have been doing it unconsciously for years. To speed up your train you feed the engineer some coffee, some nicotine, some Mars's bars, some fast music, some power aerobics, some jazz, some promises and hope about what's waiting at the end of the line.

To slow down your train feed the engineer some warm milk, some booze, some pasta, some slow music, some waltzing, some meditation, a neck massage or even some gentle sex. And hope it's a long, long track.

MIND DEPOSIT #8

As good ol' Shiplitz keeps scribbling in the margins: ' The rhythm is the message. The lyrics at best are decorations or at worst lies. If you want to change the message change the beat.'

So be it, but in our search for the Real You we must decide whether the basic You is a fast or slow beater. So consult your senior B2 editors and ask them this question: 'On the basis of watching ALL your B1

Finding the Real You

reporters race or crawl about, and after reading the stories they file, do your Yous come across as mostly fast or mostly slow beaters?' Do you like to glide to a waltz or pulsate to a Latin beat?

While you're at it, ask them what or who most bullies your beats? Ask who or what—insiders or outsiders—triggers your rhythms and brackets the beggars? Who or what is it, family, job, mate, kids, chemical cocktails, TV, illness, or other things? Later in the book we'll see if your B2's have any power over your life or whether all they do is sit, like couch potatoes, and watch reporters come and go and edit endless news reports? In brief, are your B2's more like armchair quarterbacks or more like coaches, or bosses?

"**YES BUT...** Jeez you guys are at it again. Nouning and freezing all over the place. One time you're telling us we're all a mix of fast and slow rhythms. Another time you're telling that our environments, both physical and social, trigger our rhythms. According to that, we're at the mercy of whatever situation we land in. Then you're telling us how to control our rhythms with caffeine, warm milk, and sex. Finally you're telling us long, strong rhythms are best, so carefully choose our grandparents, or failing that drink carrot juice, buy a treadmill, and join a transmigration of souls sect. Come on, get your act together, you've only got two or three chapters to go"

WELL YES . . . but remember all this Shiplitz stuff is new. Even he's still working out what it all means. So think how hard it is for ordinary brains like ours to get it straight. Actually, John told him several times that he was contradicting himself, and copping out on answers.

Well Shippy never even blinked, just reminded us about what ol Abe Lincoln said about a sermon he'd just heard: ' It was too neat and tidy. Wrestling with important questions is like fighting bees—protect yourself on one side and they strike from another'. Shippy added, any new thing of consequence requires trial and error explorations, like engaging a new job, lover, or violin'. He probably would have found some common ground with Joseph Conrad who's pen produced: "It is not the clear-sighted who rule the world. Great achievements are accomplished in a blessed warm mental fog."

Bertha interrupts: " Yeah you guys are not only wrapped in a warm mental fog you're stuck in verbal goop".

Bertha, just relax and listen to what else Shippy said: "When you run into an apparently insoluble puzzle first try to 'unnoun' it, sneak outside it's brackets and 'verb around' a bit. But you can't do that for long or you end up getting lost. So after a bit of exploring you'll find yourself building new nouns, constructing new brackets—or more likely sliding back inside the comfortable old ones. It's called life".

But as Bruney says, if you come up with a set of nouns that work for everything, you're probably drunk, or in love, or a politician, or a TV huckster selling Heaven to frightened old folks to con them out of their pension checks. Or are you comfortably back in your ONE WORLD, ONE MIND space?

O.K. John says it's time to move to the next chapter, to 'unnoun' and 'verb around' a bit, to unfreeze the overly simple fast-slow brackets, to ride around and corral some of the more interesting, multi-layered Yous.

Finding the Real You

MIND MAP #8

Step 8a) First, consider whether you spend most of your waking time operating at high, medium, or low Rpms. What's your preferred rate of thinking, talking, walking, loving? If you want some help, imagine you are behind the wheel of a car—how fast are you going? Now think of yourself walking, talking, thinking, making love—how fast are you going?

Mark it with an X: Fast___; Medium___; Slow____.
How about your mate, partner, or colleague? Fast___; Medium___; Slow____.
Which one of you tries to speed up or slow down the other? You __: Partner __ .

Step 8b) Next, get one of your B2 editors to review the 'news reports' you filed in previous Mind Maps. For example, check the Mind Maps at the end of Chapters 1, 2, and 3.

Are they mainly short-term payoff activities (TV, booze, drugs)?
Yes:____; No:____.
Are they mainly fast or slow? Fast:____; Slow:___.
Do you have any long-term payoff stuff? No:____Yes:____. (e.g., trusted mate or friend, cause, spiritual commitment?)
What's your resting heart rate when you first wake up in the morning?
Under 60:____; 60-70:____.; 70-80:___
Keep a record of resting heart rate for a week to get a more reliable estimate.
One Week Average:_____.

Step 8c) Remember Shiplitz claims: "If you want to change the message change the beat." So who or what controls your beat? What insiders or outsiders most bully your beats, speeds them up or slows them down? Brackets them? Think of examples of short term bullies like a toothache or finger nails scraping across a blackboard, medium term bullies like your lover or job, long term bullies like marriage and children, a corporate position, an addiction or a "calling"?

Examples of short-term bullies—do they speed you up or slow you down?
1) New heart throb. Speed up X Slow down:___.
Baggage: Sweaty Palms; *Lyrics*: 'What'll I wear'; 'What'll I say'; 'You remind me of an old girl friend . . . I mean . . . I'm sure you're different . . . smarter.'

Examples of medium term bullies:
1) First job. Speed up X. Slow down:___.
Baggage: Excitement/energy. *Lyrics*: 'I'm on my way'; 'I goofed'; 'Oh I get it'; 'Let me show you the ropes.'

Examples of long term bullies:
1) No promotion. Speed up:___. Slow down X
Baggage: Depression. *Lyrics*: That's the thanks I get. 'What do I tell Louis?' 'Will we have enough to retire?'

Step 8d) Your turn
1. Examples of short-term bullies:
Speed up:___. Slow down:___. Lyrics:_____
Baggage: _____
2. Examples of medium term bullies:
Speed up:___. Slow down:___. Lyrics:_____
Baggage: _____
3. Examples of long term bullies:
Speed up:___. Slow down:___. Lyrics:_____
Baggage: _____

CHAPTER 9:

YOUR DANCE CARD

"To dance attendance on their lordships' pleasure."
—Shakespeare

Ruth, Shippy's wife, phoned Bruney. Crises! She's in tears, not only because he's back on snowshoes, but insists she and the children join Eppy in wearing them too. She pleads with Bruney to send over 'the boys'—John and me. She says even though our visits upset him they seem to get his mind off atoms and snowshoes.

So away we go to 'dance attendance' on his Lordship's pleasure. On the way we puzzle over how any of our dances can help Shippy. How can agitating him have a normalizing effect on the old goat? John thinks it's because in getting him mad we increase his Rpms and so presto, also change his lyrics, his thoughts. Maybe we change his 'set point' so that different things rattle. Instead of worrying about falling through the space between atoms he now worries about how long we'll stay and when we'll come back. Also, we probably make him appreciate how smart he is and so he returns to practicing his geniuses.

John tries the door. It's unlocked. Always the gentleman he steps back and let's me go first. Instantly, a yapping Eppy comes clattering

Neil McK. Agnew, Ph.D. and John L. Brown, Ph.D.

after me trying to add to his collection of pant cuffs. John sweeps a big dictionary off Shippys desk and drops it on the back of one of the pups snowshoes anchoring him in place.

The little beast whines plaintively but Shippy pays him no mind. In truth, the professor looks ill. He's wearing his snowshoes but no earphones. His hair, beard and clothes are even scruffier than usual . . . and he's starting to smell a bit ripe.

Here we see an example of 'verbing' getting out of control. Shippy needs nouns. Shippy needs brackets to help contain his hair, his beard, his aroma, but most of all to noun his leaky mind. When he's scribbling a formula on the blackboard, or designing an atom bomb, it's OK to think of surfaces as made of dancing atoms separated by great spaces. But hey, to start seeing all those holes when you're going downstairs, to the bathroom, or shopping—common!

We tell him so. Surprisingly it has absolutely no effect. He remains with his eyes closed, slumped in his chair. John goes behind him and starts humming 'rock a bye baby in the tree top when the wind blows the cradle will rock.' As he hums, he also gently massages Shippy's shoulders. Shippy whirls around and punches John in the stomach. Whoosh goes John. Yap, yap, goes Eppy. Giggle, giggle, goes me.

Shippy is clattering after John screaming 'Don't you touch me. Don't you ever touch me . . . ' Eventually the yapping, the clattering, the screaming subside. Shippy takes off his snowshoes, releases Eppy, puts on his earphones, turns on his computer, and tells us to leave. We do.

I ask John what on earth he was trying to do? He says: 'Well our theory says that to change a person's lyrics, feelings, or thinking all you have to do is change their rhythm—increase or decrease their Rpms. So I tried to lower Shippy's beat rate with the lullaby and the massage. It worked!'

Well of course we should have known if someone's already down in the dumps their Rpms are too low so you shouldn't try to lower them still further. Rather you'd try to raise them—which unwittingly

Finding the Real You

John did. Did he ever. I ask him how long he thinks Shippy's productive rhythm will last? John says it doesn't matter. When he slows down all we have to do is go over and give Shippy's engineer another massage to speed up his train. That'll stop the rattles. John added: 'By the way, the next time it's your turn to give the aroma-rich old goat a back rub'.

I suggested we go back and see if Shippy was appreciative enough to give us some good stuff for this chapter. John said: "Don't' waste your time. Anyway we don't need to. When we first went, while he was sitting in a funk with his eyes closed, some of his recent notes snuck into my pocket.

Back to the office for some profitable plagiarism.

YOUR DANCE CARD

When Shiplitz first told us about his formula (**Life = Your Rhythms Dancing with Their Rhythms**) he also made a promise. He promised he'd show us how to MAP OUR DANCE CARD. Once you know how, you can map your life. Get to know the Real Yous. Get to know the Real Thems. He promised, but he never delivered. It turns out that the notes John 'liberated' consist of Shippy's first draft of that good stuff. John says if we get off our butts we can publish it before Shiplitz ever does! I point out the obvious, namely that Shiplitz will sue us. John points out the even more obvious, that Shippy only reads books written by BIG brains so he'll never know.

SHAKESPEARE GOT IT RIGHT

Shippy says Shakespeare knew what he was doing when he scribbled 'dancing to their lordships pleasure'. Except in our lingo it would read 'dancing to a bully's pleasure'—Inside Bullies and Outside Bullies, Inside Selves and Outside Selves.

Neil McK. Agnew, Ph.D. and John L. Brown, Ph.D.

Figure 9.1 **Shippy's Dance Card**

Their Dances	Your Dances			
	1	or 2	or 3	or 4
1) Hear bad voices	Give in - listen	Argue back	Take Eppy for walk	Put on earphones
2) Boys drop in	Give in - listen	Get mad and argue	Give them a couple of books - anything	Prepare notes for them to steal
3) Eppy is mad at me	Give in - listen	Give him a kick	Take him for walk	Give him special liverwurst
4) Ruth feels horny	Give in ...	Fake migraine	Wear snowshoes	Have a good old riggy-jig
5) See holes in floor	Put on snowshoes	Put snowshoes on Eppy	Don't go ANYWHERE!	Wear Earphones - Mozart

His notes contained a bunch of diagrams scribbled on squared paper—all depicting 'Their Dances' down the left hand side, and 'Your Dances' across the top. He used himself as an example in Figure 9.1 (Shippy's Dance Card).

Well that gives us a peek at a bit of Shippy's current dance card—it's kinda sad. Except that section where he says: 'Prepare notes for the boys to steal.' The old booger.

But I don't think he meant us to steal these—they're too personal. I think maybe we should try to sneak them back before he misses them. John says: 'No way—not after the old kook had the nerve to actually believe I coveted his ugly bod.'

How do your B2 editors interpret Shippy's dance card? As we pour over these bits of news from his B1 reporters we observe several things. First, notice on the left hand side of the card, of the five 'Their Dances' he lists, two of them are Inside Selves: #1 Self delivering bad voices inside his head; and #5 Self seeing big holes between the atoms. The other three are Outsiders: the boys (John and me); his dog Eppy; and his wife Ruth.

Notice also the kinds of dances he does in response. His most frequent jig is #1—'give in and listen'. Not very admirable or creative—although it involves low Rpms, low energy. Maybe that's why he 'vants to be alone.' Because he is so short of social skills. He's good at working with symbols and ideas, but not with people.

Finding the Real You

Furthermore, maybe he's basically a slow beat person, maybe that's where he locates his Master Set Points, so most of his dances involve low Rpms. But not all of them. He also has some faster aggressive ones in his Bag-O-Beats. Dances involving His Selves pushing and controlling Their Selves (arguing, getting mad, kicking the dog, and of course punching and chasing John). Also, faking a migraine and wearing his snowshoes to bed is unfriendly—passive aggressive but a form of Bullying nonetheless because it pushes other people around, pushes them out of his space.

His snowshoe shuffle seems like a dance of last resort, it's another form of giving up, slowing down, and isolating himself. On the other hand, wearing his earphones to help gain control of his rhythms, and making up notes for us to steal, are both examples of dealing with his rattles—inside and outside—more realistically, a form of creative dancing.

So here we have examples of Shippy's repertoire of rhythms. We don't have enough to draw a complete beat profile to conclude whether he is primarily a slow or medium or fast beater. Well, I think from what we've seen he's not a 'speedster'.

But our combined B1 reporters have delivered only small fragments of Shippy's behavior to our editors. Nevertheless, we conclude it's not surprising he leads a pretty solitary life—not many warm interpersonal or even standard social gigs in his bag—either on the dance card he drew or in our dealings with him. No wonder he likes ideas. Ideas are safely bound and bracketed in books. He can decide when to let a few of them out, push them around, and put them back in a good safe place—between the covers. Maybe that's why he suffers from writers block—if you turn ideas loose you lose control, they can come back to haunt you.

But wait a minute. Some of his stuff is brilliant. He hobnobs with the Big Minds, and has created some highly respected stuff. So in his repertoire he's got some dances we haven't seen and not displayed on this card. Where are they?

Neil McK. Agnew, Ph.D. and John L. Brown, Ph.D.

THE IDEAL DANCE CARD

John says, 'never mind' what some dotty professor does. What about something 'real' people can understand. For example what would be the Ideal? Something we can measure ourselves against like Martha Stewart, or Tom Cruise?

We retire to the neighborhood 'health club' to drink about the problem. It gave me an excuse to duck out on some duty jobs Bruney had tacked on the family bulletin board. And it gave John a chance to try out some recently acquired cigars a comely acquaintance had brought back from Cuba. After a bit the 'Ideal Card' came to us and we transcribed it from the napkin:

Their Rhythms	FIGURE 9.2: THE IDEAL DANCE CARD Your Rhythms				
	Dance A (Play)	Dance B (Work)	Dance C (Sex)	Dance D (Sleep)	Dance E (Alone)
Dance A (Play)	X				
Dance B (Work)		X			
Dance C (Sex)			X		
Dance D (Sleep)				X	
Dance E (Alone)					X

Now we realize this is a Mickey Mouse example but bear with us. Why is it ideal? Because whatever rhythms one of their Selves, or one your Selves throw at you, one of your Selves can respond appropriately—can follow or take the lead. If they do a waltz, you can do a waltz. If they want to boogie to a latin beat and throw a salsa at you, you're right in step. If they wanna play, you know all the 'games'. If they wanna get serious and work . . . hey, can you ever work. If they wanna bonk, you can bonk with the best of them— even without Viagra .

In an IDEAL dance card one of your Selves can always swing with whatever rhythm one of your other Selves, or their Selves, originates .

Finding the Real You

If one of your Yous feels down in the dumps and starts moanin the 'poor me' blues, starts shufflin the funeral march, one of your other Yous joins in, maybe even subtley taking over the lead and changing the rhythm so it turns into a rollicking wake. If one of your Yous is into a high anxiety shake and rattle jig then one of your other Yous joins in and maybe tunes down the Rpms with soft music, warm milk with a gentle rum echo, plus a hot bath. With an Ideal Dance Card, somewhere in your group of Yous is one who, when life starts grindin or rattlin your teeth, can locate a sweet set point.

For example when Shippy's Mean Self says 'bad things' about him, instead of holing up with snowshoes he plays Mozart. Offers or demands to dance inundate us—life is one damn or dandy dance after another—from inside, from outside, from heads and hearts, from family and friends, from bullys and bosses; from hot lust to icily frigid to flacidly impotent, from cars that won't start to cabs that won't stop, from youthful jazz to retirement shuffle.

Will you . . . won't you . . . join the dance? Of course you will—you have no choice! But not with an IDEAL dance card . . . nobody does. No matter how healthy, wealthy and wise they seem, some of their Selves and the Selves of others are rattling their teeth. Like the rest of us they're still looking for sweet or sweeter set points.

John has second thoughts about even discussing the Ideal Dance Card because it's so unrealistic, because you'd need a humungous, unimaginable repertoire of rhythms in order to swing to all the dances generated in the unfolding worlds of experience. He finally agrees that the ideal card may be useful to help explain the dance card idea but it's time to get down to some 'real world' stuff. So, in its place, with a 'leetle' bit of help from Shippy's notes, we generate a 'Pretty Damn Good' dance card.

Neil McK. Agnew, Ph.D. and John L. Brown, Ph.D.

PRETTY DAMN GOOD DANCE CARD

Dr. Shiplitz claims we all practice four basic types of dances, that there are four types of Yous available to dance with the various Thems who step or leap onto your dance floor as shown below:

Type 1 Yous doing Standard steps;

Type 2 Yous doing Escape and Avoidance jigs;

Type 3 Yous Bullying/Leading other Yous and Thems; and

Type 4 Yous Exploring and Learning new steps, and even stroking your soul.

Pretty Damn Good Dance Card

Their Rhythms	Your Rhythms							
	A	B	C					
Type 1				Standard	Steps			
Dance A	X							
Dance B		X						
Dance C			X					
Etc.								
Type 2				Escape	Avoid	Steps		
Dance H	X			X				
Dance I		X	X		X			
Etc.								
Type 3						Bully	Lead	Steps
Dance L		X		X		X		
Dance M	X						X	
Etc.								
Type 4							Explore	Learn
Dance Q	X				X		X	X
Dance R		X						X
Etc.								

Finding the Real You

TYPE 1: STANDARD DANCE STEPS

In the case of Type 1 steps, if They do a waltz one of your Selves can do a waltz. If it is a work day, you know where to dance from 9 to 5. If it is family time you know when to shuffle off to practice—music, ballet, football. Most of us have a wondrous supply of Type 1 dances in our repertoire where we can match and resonate to the rhythms thrown at us from inside or outside sources. That's why we survive, even thrive, dancing to the variety of everyday life. Embedded in our genes and enhanced by learning we jig, jive and swing along with nary a thought given to the automatic beat of our biology, the familiar cadence of our culture, and the personal music buried deep in our soul—'doin what comes naturally'.

The Type 1 or 'standard' dances in our repertoire fill most of our dance card. They represent our habitual dances. They represent the dances we are most likely to perform no matter what rhythms are thrown at us from the left hand column. We tend to respond with Type 1 Standard Steps even when it would be wiser to perform a Type 2 Escape/Avoidance jig; or a Type 3 Bully/Leader tango; or a Type 4 Explore/Learn mambo.

So maybe we don't perform an ideal Dance Card we're still pretty damn good. We don't notice the variety of dances we perform so effortlessly and automatically so we rarely appreciate what master dancers we are. Well, we don't notice till one or more of our standard dances falter or fail. Like when we're sick or old and our biological beats can't keep up. Or when the cultural cadence pulls a switcheriooooo and leaves us behind, or a lover beats us to the punch and leaves first, or a string of catastrophes sends arrows deep into our soul and we're left with no place to stood. If we still have an island to stand on, the only turtle left is likely on life support with a spear in its heart.

However, most of the time there's no need to pay any conscious mind to our standard dance steps. But experts trying to design robots pay them lots of mind—just try getting a two-legged robot to 'dance' with the undulations of uneven terrain. Or try teaching it the rhythms of language or the cadence of conversation. Stuff that's no sweat for the average 2 year old—rhythms bred in the bone and honed in the home. To possess a child's B1 reporters and B2 editors, well robots would die for—and do, for lack of them. Shippy says our current robots can only survive in very small worlds on tiny dance floors dancing with rigid partners. Don't hold your breath waiting for experts to teach these jerky roids the ballets of love, hope, and faith.

While we don't appreciate the multitude of dances we do well and do automatically (those that fill most of our card) we certainly notice when out on the floor our toes get stomped on, or our dignity diminished by clumsy shuffles or a pratfall. When our standard Type 1 dance steps are inadequate, when we're invited or, even commanded to resonate to a rhythm we can't get, dislike or even hate, then hopefully one or more of our damage control Selves spring into action. It's the business of these Selves to protect and repair our network of consistencies, and hopefully even extend it and grow our soul.

These damage control and self-development Selves may be: Type 2 dance steps (Escape and Avoidance); or Type 3 steps (Bully or Lead); or even Type 4 steps (Explore and Learn).

TYPE 2: ESCAPE AND AVOIDANCE DANCES

If ya don't wanna do it? If ya can't do it? What ya gonna do? You already have a pretty good feel for the answer cause you've encountered that kind of rattle lots of times. You usually reach into your Bag-O-Beats for an 'I'm outa here' jig. Or even better, you've already learned to perform the Avoidance Waltz called 'I'm not going near there in the first place'.

These dances deserve an honorable place in your repertoire. Unfortunately, they've received bad press having been labeled the dances of slackers and cowards. Ridiculous! Well, maybe some people get carried away, but for the rest of us they're not only time savers but also life savers.

Finding the Real You

Being 'bears of small brain' we just can't do or learn all the jigs demanded by nature, the bureaucrats, our families, our pets, and the experts on 'healthy living' and firm buns. Ya ain't gonna survive, let alone thrive if ya cain't say NO! If you can't say it loud and clear then every Tom, Dick and Mavis will be trying to get into your head, your bank account, even, we hesitate to say, your pants. Possessing and performing the 'NO' jig in it's various forms comes hard for most us. Not socially correct. What makes it even more difficult is inheriting the sweaty uncertainty and smelly guilt that nay saying frequently entails.

Remember, your dance card is already almost full with Type 1 standard dances—embedded in your genes, your culture and your soul. You must either 'oh so carefully ration' the tiny and precious white space—sorry clear space-left over or else. Or else what? Or else you're a martyr or wimp trying to serve many masters and serving none too well, including yourself. What do you do as the relationship turns poisonous or the boss turns cruel and comes after you?

In his notes Shippy scribbled: 'The name of the Life Game is not to do everything right, but to do the RIGHT things.' So we tell Herman; 'Herman, old trout, in the small space left on your dance card be damn careful that only very very high priority dances are included.' Herman says: 'Yeah right, like killing pheasants and drinking Single Malt Scotch—no ice.' It's hard to get one up on that man.

But while you may quibble with his priorities you have to admit our Herman is an escape artist. Just the other night John and I were over at his place watching Monday night football and sipping a little whisky. The game ended and we started to watch the late night movie—Dial M for Murder.

A few minutes into the show Herman stood up, put away the Scotch bottle saying: 'Don't know about you guys, but I'm going to bed.' Now that's a clear example of performing a neat escape jig —not very polite, but very effective, and as far as we can gather dragging no guilt in it's wake—not for Herman.

Also, his Dreamer Self has a goodly supply of escape or exit jigs as well. Whenever his Bald, Fat Self ends up over-exposed on life's dance floor, Herman's Day Dreamer can usually lead him to another stage where his college days Svelte Self swings with erotically ripe groupies.

In addition to his effective escape jigs, Herman has well honed, if inelegant avoidance waltzes as well. Like? Well, like not keeping appointments, not answering the phone, not spending time with his wife and family. Herman has learned to escape or avoid most inside and outside rattles—for now. He's good at it, very good. But he fills the salvaged space with such junk.

Shippy too has escaped from, and avoids, many standard cultural cadences like the responsibilities of being husband, father and professor. But he escapes, not to watch football, kill dewy eyed creatures and booze up. Instead he uses his clear space trying to discover and deliver great 'Truths'. Not only do Ruth, his kids and the University pay a high price but he does too. Escaping from one dance floor means you've still got to dance somewhere—you're always dancing—it may involve trying to lead and bully others, or laboriously exploring and learning new steps that may generate fewer rattles— or maybe more, plus brain blocks?

After talking about Herman and Shippy, John said: 'Have you ever noticed that bad husbands usually have good wives?' Mmmmmm?

Those blessed with a generous supply of Type 1 dances can effortlessly handle most of the predictable rhythms the inside and outside worlds throw at us. If you are also agile or devious enough to escape from, or avoid, the major rattling resonance's of Type 2 dances, and in doing so generate some clear space, you have a glorious opportunity to develop and practice two other dances: Type 3 —Leading and Bullying Jigs; and Type 4—Exploring and Learning, and maybe even soul enhancement. First, consider Leading and Bullying.

Finding the Real You

TYPE 3: BULLYING AND LEADING DANCES

Shippy thinks Bully dances are bred in the bone. Other experts believe they're honed at home, in back alleys, or business schools. Take your choice, or mix and match. The important point for us being that one way or another Bullies/Leaders get the rest of us to give in to their push and shove or to follow their lead.

If you possess strong Bully Jigs or Leader Waltzes in your Bag-O-Beats then they appear in the left-hand column of the dance card. These Selves generate a resonance which the rest of our Selves and some of Their selves dance to. John and I argue about whether the main purpose of these Type 3 Steps is to clear space or capitalize on space made available by the Escape and Avoidance jigs.

What do you do when one of Them wants it done, 'Their way'? Does one of your bullies take over and say, 'no way', we do it 'My way'?

We asked Herman, who is the best example of a bully we know, to provide us with an example: "Me a bully . . . you've gottta be kidding . . . I'm a pussy cat. Why just last week I promised to take the kids to the circus . . . unfortunately one of them spilled my drink so I cancelled the circus and made them clean up the yard instead . . . my wife keeps saying take it easy, they're just kids . . . but I have to over-rule her . . . they gotta learn to be responsible . . . how the twig is twisted so grow the roots."

Herman continued: "Ya know you guys are snoops, standing back, not getting your hands dirty, watching the world go by, looking down your snoots at the rest of us.

Well let me tell you what the great writer Goethe had to say. He said: 'Men ought to know that in the theater of life it is only for Gods and angels to be spectators', and for your information you guys don't fall within either of those brackets."

Well, well . . . more to our Herman than meets the eye.

But still speaking of bullies, which of your B1 reporters dominate the others? Which ones push the others aside and get their stories in first? For example, the ones from your head or from your heart? The

Neil McK. Agnew, Ph.D. and John L. Brown, Ph.D.

ones who focus on what people say or those who concentrate on what they do—the ones who 'can't hear what you're saying for what you're doing'.

If you don't want to think of them as Bullies, think of them as the Leaders of your News Team. Shippy is certainly a 'head over heart man' most of the time—except for Eppy. Whereas Herman's the reverse—he goes with his gut feelings. Both guys get into long term trouble because of biased reporting—but what are 'bears of small brain' to do?

But a more important question remains, which of your B2 editors rule the roost, which ones bully or lead the other editors—Yours and Theirs in interpreting the news. For Herman, no matter what his B1s report, his senior Editor asks one question, looks for one answer: 'What's best for Herman RIGHT NOW?'. If his gut news is positive, his editor says 'get me more, more, more'. Conversely, if the news is negative his favorite editor has a variety of favorite jigs including: smack or tranquilize the reporter; don't get mad get even; get outa there, avoid this situation in future, etc.

Shippy's most senior B2 Editor is a high level 'consistency maker'. From the vast array of scholarly news reports his B1s deliver, this editor selects, rejects, and shapes them to construct a pattern—one that passes his tests of masterly consistency, one that solves problems other scholars haven't solved. But when he can't locate or construct the master consistency or when other scholars rain on his parade, most of his Selves get depressed and pessimistic, his reporters and editors go on strike—he blocks.

Shippy says John and I are lucky. He says: "Our senior editor is simple, naïve Optimism. No matter what news our reporters deliver this Editor of ours, this Bully/Leader transforms shit into silver—at least in your own eyes". I know what John is thinking. I hope he doesn't say it . . .

Unfortunately for Shiplitz, lurking in the wings of his brain is a powerful pessimistic editor, patiently waiting for the first signs of trouble—an idea rejected, or a criticism from a respected senior

Finding the Real You

scholar, or Eppy getting sick—and this bleak bastard shoves his way on stage, takes over, and leads everyone in the funeral march. Shippy prays for an optimistic second-in-command to help him ignore or declaw bad news. Since he hasn't got an optimistic Self inside his head we suggest he hire one. Sadly he's tried, but they all resign— 'my Pessimist bullies them'.

Bruney's particularly good at tranquilizing his terrors.

Come to think of it, Bruney seems to have the best combination of Dance steps of anyone we know. She's healthy and grew up in a happy home in a calm neighborhood so she has a reasonably complete repertoire of effective Type 1 standard Steps. Consequently, she doesn't have any BIG emotional scars or biological demons to escape from or avoid—except us, her family. Furthermore, she's got us pretty well charmed and tamed—Bullied and Led?—so there's a reasonably good division of labor—well, come to think of it she manages the overload and the crises. Also, the family respects—most of the time . . . some of the time—her private space when she's working, exploring and learning, for the weekly column she writes.

Mmmmmmhh. How does she manage?

Anyway, apparently our Bully and Leader Selves take over when our other Selves stumble and fall. Sometimes it's one of our internal senior editors that takes command during a crises or during a lifetime. However, if no internal editor can gain control— fails to bully or lead our disorganized crew—we turn over our dance card, or parts of it, to an external senior editor. These external bullies or leaders may be personal (kids, pets, parents, friends, mates), or things (musical instruments, TVs, computers, booze, drugs), or institutional (colleagues, bosses, 'experts' including TV hucksters and Self-Help authors, clergy, distant bureaucrats, politicians, con-artists, dictators— like Hitler or Stalin). Anyone, anything that helps some of your Selves: reduce their rattles, find a more tolerable set point, find a safer place to stood, or helps you do an ego jive, or releases some of your darker selves to do a Bully's Ballet.

Neil McK. Agnew, Ph.D. and John L. Brown, Ph.D.

But all is not lost, as you know your bag-o-beats contains yet another resource: Exploring and Learning.

TYPE 4 DANCES—EXPLORING AND LEARNING

By possessing an adequate repertoire of Standard steps, and by supplementing those with some effective Escape/Avoidance, or Bully/Leader jigs we can gain a bit of clear space on one of life's dance floors. We can fritter that freedom away by merely repeating familiar steps—by doing a bit more of what comes easy. But there is an another alternative. We can try out a bit of exploring, a bit of snooping about into some of our internal or external worlds—like you're doing right now with the aid of this remarkable book.

Exploring involves snooping around inside or outside one of your boxes, one or more of your Islands of Consistency. Even a bit of snooping will uncover some surprises, some previously unnoticed inconsistency. When you're operating in a bit of clear space such surprises emerge, not as they ordinarily do as rattles to be banished or buried, but rather arise as interesting novelties to be viewed, touched, tasted, talked about. To a certain extent you're practicing a bit of childlike curiosity. As they say: 'you stop and smell the flowers' . . . or if you're a little Herman pull wings off flies.

Not only are you exploring but you're learning—kind of a passive learning. In doing so your internal or external world is never the same—a slice of it is transformed. But in addition to such passive learning some of us acquire open space for more active acquisition of skills or knowledge. Sometimes we do it gently by taking formal language training at night so we can bargain in the street market on our upcoming tour of Mexico. Sometimes by fine-tuning current dance steps so we are on top of the latest software innovation, even if the old application meets our needs. At other times a few among us will throw caution to the winds and seek a more radical change as we risk the gut churning effect of a career transition, or move across, or out of the country. Trying out Type 4 dance steps allows us to move onto new dance floors and swing and sway with more internal and external dance partners. It may also get us into dances where we are more in tune with the new Thems than the ones that step on our toes now.

Herman uses his free space, acquired from shamelessly neglecting his wife and kids, to fine-tune his shooting skills, and by taking trips to Scotland to travel 'The Whisky Trail'. John and I use our free space heroically acquired by neglecting to sleep, to explore Shippy's brains, to learn how to use Microsoft Office 2000, and making wine.

But how about you? Perhaps a course in Chinese cooking, belly dancing, beating the market, constructing beautiful candelabras from old soup cans, finding the Real You? How much of your energy is available to explore new spaces. Does the Real You have a little room for such adventure?

HOW GOOD IS YOUR BAG-O-BEATS?

So you've got this Bag-O-Beats, this repertoire of rhythms. How adequate is your dance card? Do you feel that Type 1 Standard Steps are handling most of the predictable rhythms thrown your way by your Internal Selves and External Thems? And furthermore, do you feel that your Type 2 Escape/Avoidance jigs, and your Type 3 Bullies and Leaders pretty well handle the exceptions. The major rattles. And after all that still leaves you enough room for some soul stroking, fine-tuning and expanding your Bag-O-Beats?

Or, is the world gettin to you? Are you forever fighting bees, don't got enough fingers for the hole-popping dikes? Sounds rough. Have you tried a glass of warm milk and a cookie? No? Well we'll ask Shippy. He says: "It's obvious. Look at their dance card. They have two choices: 1) either cut back the left hand column and so reduce some of the rattling demands; or 2) increase the top row and expand Your Rhythm repertoire of dance steps."

John asks how does that happen? Shippy shakes his head: 'What have I been telling you? Cut back the left column of your card. Reduce the number of demands to dance. Use whatever escape and avoidance steps you've got. Convene any internal or external Bullies you can and turn them loose. Just get away from some of those left-side demanders. You counter their bullies with your bullies. You delegate responsibilities—rattling rhythms—like crazy. Pass on some of the demands and let others share the load. Just because some of your second-in-commanders do it different than you doesn't mean its wrong. And even if they screw up, it will give you a bit of breathing room. Better that than have smoke pouring out of your ears.

Remember, one of the common characteristics of alcoholics, and other 'high flyers', is perfectionism. One of the first lessons they have to learn is to start resigning from being a know-it-all. They have to start fine-tuning their Escape and Avoidance jigs, just like anyone else who's got more rattles than they can manage.

Once you cut the left hand column of your card down to fit the size of your rhythm repertoire, you may even find enough clear space to have a bath, kiss a friend even have peak experiences: sexual, conceptual, social, spiritual. Shippy says: "Conceptual orgasms beat sex every time—well almost every time."

MIND DEPOSIT # 9

Well, well . . . we think even Bertha will be pleased with the Dance Cards. In your heads you each have 4 types of Dance Master—at least four Real Yous. The Senior dance boss controls your Type 1 Standard dances—your biological beats, strong habits, and cultural cadences. Since these are all automatic you don't have to worry about them—well not until one or more of them breaks down. When that happens, or when a novel situation demands a jig you can't or won't do, then you call in one of your other three Dance Masters.

The Step 2 Master may provide you with an ESCAPE JIG so you merely sashay out of the rattling scene, hey I'm outa here, mentally or physically—sorry, not feeling well today, think I'll just pull the blanket up over my head; 'hello' Auntie Alice, guess what, I'm coming to visit you up in Fairbanks. Or they may have seen the noisy beats com-

Finding the Real You

ing and provided you with an AVOIDANCE WALTZ. Hey, hey detour _ go and have a nice visit with your mother. I feel a cold coming on and don't want to spread the germs . . . or maybe it's just I'm allergic to something. . . ?"

The Step 3 Controller may provide you with a Bully Beat which frightens away the nuisance noise, or buries it leaving a bit of clear stage. Or the Master may provide a Leader Leaping whose bounding vaults so impresses the intruders they cease their random walk and fall in line, exiting stage left—dragging their rattles behind them and leaving you in charge of the status quo!

Speaking of smooth bullying: "I'll tell you what you're allergic too, you're allergic to my mother." "Don't you dare say anything like that again. If you feel that way you can ruddy well stay with your mother . . . her great cooking . . . her perfect ironing . . . you don't love me anyway . . . sob . . . sob" "Ah honey don't say that. I'm sorry . . . I love your cooking. Listen I'll postpone my visit and we'll go out for a nice dinner." Not bad. They both win. She bullies him and he avoids her cooking.

At last, if given half a chance, your Step 4 Learning Master sweeps in with the energy to enable you to casually snoop about smelling the roses, running barefoot through the grass, tasting sweet air, smelling skin, stroking a bit of soul. Or maybe you use the mind space to acquire the novel beat of new knowledge, or listen to the enduring music of wisdom, or for the very first time hear the faint strains of your soul's sweet symphony. Or at least cut 3 strokes off your game.

But the Learning Master can't do it without some help from you. You have to provide the time and space to get things kick-started. Only then can the Learning Master swing into action. If you're being rattled out of your head, radical applications of Escape and Avoidance will be the order of the day. You know that throwing an alcoholic or chemical blanket over the mess works for awhile. But you also know what you get? When you take off the blanket . . . a bigger mess!

Don't neglect available outside help: family, friends, even dare we say 'Gurus'—well gurus in training.

Neil McK. Agnew, Ph.D. and John L. Brown, Ph.D.

"**YES BUT...** Well that's a bit better. What's that Bertha? Oh... Bertha says it still stinks. You got 96% of our mind chock-a-block with Type 1 Standard Steps we do automatically like ruddy robots ... and just a minute ... and Bertha says you got another 2% of our mind occupied by cowards, escape artists and shirkers ... and just a minute ... Bertha says you only give us 1% for putting dummies in their place or leading em to water ... and... just a minute ... Bertha says that at best only leaves 1% for appreciating the finer things in life and for learning ... Bertha says BULL SHAVING ... she says anybody that can't organize all the clear space they want ... deserves to be confined ... ... get it ... ha ha. And furthermore, all that Bertha says are my thoughts exactly!"

WELL YES . . . John says to tell Bertha to . . . wait a minute. No, don't tell her that. Instead tell her we've got something very special just for her in the next chapter and a real prize in the last one. Ya got that Bert?

MIND MAP #9 THE THEM-YOU DANCE MATRIX

Shiplitz says life is just one damn dance after another. He invented the Them-You matrix to help keep track. Remember The Dance Card. Also remember that one of your very important Selves is called Avoidance and possesses a repertoire of jigs all designed to avoid or escape rattles? Some are pretty low quality like a heap of TV watching; some dangerous like big drugs and buckets of booze; some not bad like going for a walk instead of finishing the assignment; some very wise, like avoiding or escaping debilitating relationships—persistence and loyalty is not always a virtue.

Finding the Real You

Step 9A: Go to Map One from chapter 1 and pick out a (+) and a (—) payoff dance. Now list the most frequent avoidance dances you do to bypass the negative rattle.

1. (-+) situation _____
D1: _____
D2:_____
2. (—) situation_____
D3:_____
D4:_____

Step 9B: Go to Map Two from Chapter Two and pick out two relationships: one, where you avoid someone else, and a second where someone else avoids you:

1. You try to avoid/reduce relationship with:_____ by doing dance:
D5:_____
D6:_____
2. _____ tries to avoid/reduce relationship with you by doing dance:
D7:_____
D8: _____

Step 9C: Reviewing the above dances, which would you rate as:

1. Low quality:(creates more rattles than it avoids): _____
2. Medium quality: (gets rid of some rattles):_____
3. High quality: (not only avoids rattles but also delivers positive or big long term gains): _____

Step 9D: Which particular avoidance dances do you rely on the most?

Dance A: _____

Dance B: _____

Bert, if you completed this step you've just met a couple of your very 'Real Yous.' In order to maintain some independence you must have developed some effective Escape and Avoidance dances.

Step 9E: Now yet again review Steps 1 and 2, if you were to repeat those exercises a year from now what changes would there be? Don't think about it, go with what your gut reporters say.

1. Things will be generally the same or worse: Yes: ____ No: ____
2. Things will generally be better: Yes: ____. No: ____
3. Have trouble making up your mind: Yes: ___; No: _____

Step 9F: Sure a lot of things will likely stay the same, a few get worse, and some get better. Which major parts of your life will likely get better?

1. _____
2. _____

Hint: Review answers to 9D and 9E. Do you get a hunch about whether you're generally optimistic or pessimistic or uncertain? Ask someone who knows you well to give a quick, from their gut, answer to that question. Hey Bert, maybe you've met another of your Very Very Important Real Yous. If in doubt ask Bertha.

CHAPTER 10:

DANCING WITH THE FUTURE

> "Two boxed souls look out through the bars:
> One sees mud, the other sees stars."
> —Eppy

Right down at the bottom of Shippy's notes about 'Dance Cards'—the stuff we told you about in the last chapter—was scribbled a single phrase: 'Dancing With The Future' but nothing more.

Come to think of it most of the dance cards considered so far involved dancing with the present, dancing in the here and now boxes with nary a thought for the long term. But that's the way it is. Most of us don't get into future jigs, except at New Year's Resolution time, or when we get really scared, or deathly sick. Mmmmm. Back we go to Shippy for another intellectual care package.

Cautiously, I edge open the door. Surprise! No yapping, snapping Eppy? Great! But there's poor old Shiplitz back wearing snowshoes. He's in tears. Apparently Eppy swallowed an acorn, got a bowel blockage and almost died. An emergency operation and six hundred dollars later, poor little Eppy lies whimpering in a wee basket on Shippy's lap, while the old man moans: 'He's going to die . . . I know he's going to die.'

Even John, feeling badly, leans over the basket and tenderly strokes Eppy, who feebly raises his little head, bites him, gives a happy little bark and weakly wags his tail.

An euphoric Shippy thanks us for giving Eppy something to live for—a taste of John's blood.

John, with a Kleenex wrapped around his wounded finger, threatens to sue the ass right off Shiplitz unless he gives us some big chunks of wisdom—stuff we can understand.

Shippy puts Eppy's basket on the floor, takes off his snowshoes, wipes his eyes, and promises: 'Anything, I'll tell you anything . . . I owe you . . . I owe you . . .'

DANCING WITH THE FUTURE

So this is what he told us. "It's one thing to dance with the present which takes up most of our dance card, but how do you dance with the future—the unknown and unknowable future? You don't need to be a rocket scientist to appreciate that the future is uncertain. And the further away it is the more unpredictable it becomes." Everyone has at one time or another been savagely goosed by the Fickle-Finger-of-Fate, and will be again. We all know that you can have a Big-Bag-O-Beats, have a great repertoire of Type 1, 2, 3 and 4 dance steps and still fall flat. Who knows when? An acorn for heavens sake, a little no account acorn just about took my Eppy down, just about demolished my life, murdered my future."

We told him it's not that bad. If anything happened to Eppy we'd buy him another dog. Shaking his great head he murmured: "Forgive them Lord, you short-changed these two when you spooned out the little gray cells. But you gave them something even more valuable—you gave them the enduring beat of optimism. Even naïve optimism is better than no optimism at all . . . Did you hear them Lord, 'We'll make everything all better, we'll buy you another dog', or listen to them: 'Give us some good stuff Shippy we're going to write a best-seller.' Lordy, Lordy if they were smarter, if they knew as much as I do, they'd be pessimists too."

Finding the Real You

CONFIDENCE IS IT

Shippy instructs us. If you find an Aladdin's lamp, rub it and when the proverbial Genie pops out and grants you three wishes, here is what to ask for:

Number 1: ask for CONFIDENCE;

Number 2: ask for trusted friends;

Number 3: ask for a normal number of little gray cells in your brain.

But if you are granted only one wish . . . don't even hesitate . . . go for CONFIDENCE.

Notice all three involve trusted forecasts of what comes next—all are forms of confidence: trust in what you're doing; trust in friends; trust in your brain. The old goat is really wound up. He goes on about the biggest space left in your life is the Future. The biggest challenge in life is engaging it with gusto. But we lack reliable information about the future. There are 'experts' who tell you different. Sure, there's tons and tons of unreliable fortune tellers—sincere and insincere—including weather forecasters, stock brokers, doctors, lawyers, scientists, to say nothing of tea cup readers and astrologers.

Of course you can conscientiously try to manage the future by collecting as many B1 news reports and other expert's B2 editorial analyses as you wish. Your brightest B2 editor can add his/her own biases and write you a final report. But by the time you're finished most of the information will be obsolete so you'll have to start all over again . . . as the future glides by relentlessly without you—with you desperately holding onto it's tail.

And still Shippy talks on. "The past is over, the present fleeting, only the future remains. With confidence in that future, and in yourself you've got it made! With a long, strong beat you live 'forever' . . . even if you die tomorrow". Come again?

"Now listen boys, look carefully at any dance card and although it focuses on the present, the future is there. Where? First, it's there in the fact that it's hardly mentioned. It's taken for granted. Like a fish takes water for granted, most of us take the future the same way—that's why we don't have to think about it because we UNCONSCIOUSLY ASSUME it's always going to be there. Til we get shocked or sick. Just as the fish has blind confidence in water, most of us, most of the time, have blind confidence that our future will keep unfolding endlessly ahead of us."

John chirps: "How the hell does that fit into your formula? Bertha will certainly want to know."

"Very simply" says Shippy, and showed us.

THE FORMULA LIVES

In case you've forgotten this unforgettable formula it goes like this:

$$\text{Life} = F3 \ (\text{Your Rhythms} + \text{Their Rhythms})$$

First off Shippy pointed out that the future is represented by F3—Fate's-Fickle-Finger—which periodically shocks us into realizing that the future ain't going to continue unrolling without surprises.

FATE'S FICKLE FINGER

This wake-up call typically arrives in the form of a big rattle or surprising change of direction in your lifeline. The surprise may involve the loss of something or someone you'd assumed would last a long lifetime unfolding smoothly as it should, such as your career, loved one, dog or health.

Conversely, Fate may deliver a pleasant shocker, a winning lottery ticket, a career leap, a late but treasured pregnancy, a medical miracle.

Whether fate's deposit is good or bad, such startling surprises rattle your web, stretch your complacent network of expectations and relationships—some past the breaking point. Recall, that according to Shiplitz our minds are in the business of discovering or constructing consistencies. Inconsistencies, unexpected detours—pleasant or unpleasant-break the beat and force some of Our minds, and Their minds, to work overtime to re-establish a consistent equilibrium. Surprisingly, winning a lottery is like reading a will—it still leaves most of the network unhappy, with some of your Selves and their Selves moaning: 'What about me?'

Pointing at The Formula, Shippy indicated that F3 lies outside the brackets. We, like the fish, can't afford to be constantly worried or wishful about the future, otherwise we can't focus on the daily business of living. So there's a damn good reason for not seeing 'the future' prominently displayed in our dance cards. If it were we'd be like Bert without Bertha—we'd be paralyzed by fearful or wishful analysis or by riding off in all directions at once.

So F3 reserves a place for the unknown future, and our situational brackets protect our small brains, and our fragile network of alliances by keeping that uncertainty outside of consciousness most of the time.

MAPPING THE FUTURE

But in addition, and in a very important way, the future is also represented inside the brackets. How? Well, according to the Herr Doctor Professor the future is embedded in rhythms—Yours and Theirs. That's what a rhythm does, it maps a piece of the future. But people don't call it 'the future'. They call it 'confidence'. Shippy calls it 'blind confidence' because the only way you get it is by: ignoring—bracketing out—most of the real alternative possibilities that always exist in the present and particularly in the future.

He says the real trick of living is not considering all the possibilities—any idiot can raise possibilities. If you actually considered all the real possibilities you'd never leave the house. The greatest challenge facing a human is getting on with their lives in spite of all the negative possibilities. In this sense, ignorance is bliss.

OK. OK. So it's one of those 'too much-too little' puzzles. On the one extreme you have the 'he who hesitates is lost'-the impulsive souls; and on the other the 'stitch in time saves nine' compulsives, with our culture and logic pushing the latter: 'Now Mary, now Johnny, before you make any important decisions consider ALL the possibilities.' Yeah right, just the kind of impossible burden a bear of small brain needs to backpack through life. Just imagine trying to choose a mate, a career, or even buy a pair of socks by considering 'all possibilities'.

Well, if you can't consider ALL the possibilities, then just deal with the important ones. Which are? Which are of course unknowable because they operate in the fuzzy future. Which is why almost all Your and Their dance cards focus on the present and the immediate future—the one we can almost see on tiptoes. We're not completely stupid.

Bertha takes on the roll of cultural town crier, trying to illuminate ALL possibilities by 'yes butting . . .' by interrupting any natural rhythm you get rolling, by questioning your dance, 'Watch out . . . why not do this one . . . don't forget that one . . . you may be wrong.' Of course you may be 'wrong'. That's what bears of small brains have to live with. That's what bears of even bigger brains, like Shippy, eventually learn. But not Bertha, she still assumes that, if only You would consider ALL possibilities, you WILL be right. If only YOU keep your brackets wide open you'll get the whole picture! Nuts, all you'll get is inundated with alternatives. But notice it's YOU not Bertha who must keep an open mind.

John says: "Hey Bert, wherever you are, tell Bertha we bet you haven't got a DOG, instead you've got a witty bitty PET, on a short lease, wearing diapers—gotta close down the possibilities."

Only rarely do we make and stick to long term plans. Mostly, we make our decisions, not by considering all possibilities, or most possibilities, or even obvious possibilities. We make them by unconsciously reducing—bracketing—the situation down to mind size. Typically, we buy our careers, our mates, and our socks because they're close to hand when the emotions are high or the deadline is NOW.

Finding the Real You

Or, if we're a non-decider, we procrastinate, we don't buy, we sit on the edge of life frozen in indecision, or become a critic pointing out possibilities the actual 'players' failed to consider—hello Bertha—or chain ourselves to an active player and ride along on their confidence and wonder: 'How can they be so sure?' Hello Bert.

How can they be so sure? Well confidence rides on rhythm. What kind of Rhythm? You guessed it—a big strong rhythm.' But not all rhythms are strong so the enlarged formula becomes:

Life = F3 [Your Rhythms (Strong & Weak) + Their Rhythms (Strong & Weak)]

To help show you what we mean we mapped the strength of the dance steps of Herman, Shippy, Bertha and Bruney in response to the invitations or demands to dance that they encounter. You can see them in Table 10.1. On the left are the four main types of dances we encountered in the last chapter. The strength of response is rated as high, medium or low.

Starting with Type 1 Standard dances—the ones that fill most of our card—you can see that Bruney has the strongest repertoire of high (confidence) standard steps, followed by Herman and Bertha with Shippy bringing up the rear. The more challenged or clumsy you are in dancing Type 1 Standard Steps, the more you must tune in Types 2 and 3 for damage control. Some of the major challenges might be physical (handicaps, illness, aging); interpersonal (conflicts with family or friends), cultural (status, race, education).

Neil McK. Agnew, Ph.D. and John L. Brown, Ph.D.

Figure 10.1: Strength of Rhythm Repertoire (Confidence)

Dances	Herman	Shippy	Bertha	Bruney	You
Type 1 Standard					
A. Body functions	High	Medium	High	High	?
B. Mates or Special people	High	High	High	High	?
C. Culture/Social	Medium	Low	Medium	High	?
D.					
Type 2: Escape/Avoidance					
H. Mate trouble	High	High	High	High	?
I. Angry authority figures	Low	High	High	High	?
J. General rattles	High	High	Medium	Medium	?
K.					
Type 3: Bully/Lead					
L. Wounded others	High	High	High	Medium	?
M. Uncertain others	High	High	High	Medium	?
N. Strong others	Low	Low	Medium	High	?
Type 4: Explore/Learn					
Q. In small clear spaces	Low	Low	Medium	High	?
R. In large clear spaces	Low	High	Low	High	?
S.					

WHEN STANDARD STEPS ARE WEAK

Because Shippy is relatively weak in performing some Standard steps he has to have strong counter moves for dealing with the resulting rattles. He has to develop extra skills in Type 2 Escape/Avoidance dances. His main jigs involve going into hiding from his mate, the University, from life in general. Similarly, Herman has strong Escape/Avoidance dances except for on-the-spot responses to authority figures—then his mind shuts down with nary a tune to help him, let alone a song to sing. Bruney and Bertha are quite accomplished in keeping up with the Standard dances and on the rare occasions they are challenged, shift readily into Escape/Avoidance alternatives .

The quality of your Type 3 dances (Bullying and Leading others) depends on your partners. If they're wounded, or uncertain, bullying and leading them comes relatively easily as Herman, Shippy and Bertha know only too well. If, however, the other dancer is powerful, then Bruney is the only one of the four who has a large repertoire of strong,

Finding the Real You

and appropriate matching steps. She usually doesn't get defensive or aggressive, because she listens more for the strength of the beat rather than being confused by the lyrics. Consequently she can dance with Dogs or Pets.

Some people unwittingly choose or settle in to careers —a place in the hierarchy—where they can boss or lead other dancers below them who are even more uncertain than they are. A few strong beaters can be leaders almost anywhere. But most of us need the protection of a bureaucratic or social structure —with the dice loaded in our favour by gender, or racial, or professional benefits—helping us sustain our power. One of the appeals of being a therapist or a counselor is that your clients are usually clumsier dancers than you are so they let you 'lead', while they sit there 'yes butting . . . '

FREEDOM DANCES

Now consider the most liberating jigs of all—Type 4 (Exploring and Learning). Bruney once again leads the pack capitalizing on opportunities in both small and large open spaces. Next comes Shippy, who can at times, explore and learn with brilliance in expansive conceptual or abstract spaces—unless he's locked into one of his periods of mental freeze and writer's block—on these occasions he's afraid he's going to fall between the atoms into an endless black hole. Meanwhile, Herman and Bertha are so busy performing Type 1, 2 and 3 dance steps they have little time or skill for significant exploration or learning.

How about you? In the right hand column of figure 10.1 pencil in your first estimates of where your strong rhythms and confidence lie in responding to invitations, commands or opportunities to perform Type 1, 2, 3 and 4 dances. In particular, carefully consider the strength of your Exploring and Learning jigs. Using a bit of graphical license Figure 10.2 displays the four dancers repertoires, highlighting how much Type 1 Standard dances fill most of our cards, and showing that such is the case for all of them, even for Shippy the most 'challenged' of the lot concerning Standard steps.

Figure 10.2 Dance Cards: Rhythm Strength

Percent Highs

Dances	Herman	Shippy	Bertha	Bruney
Type 1 Standard	90	80	90	90
Type 2: Esape/Avoidance	5	10	5	2
Type 3: Bully/Lead	5	5	5	3
Type 4: Explore/Learn	0	5	0	5

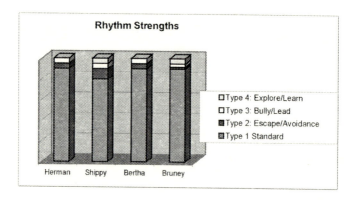

Now examine figure 10.3 which presents a blow-up to highlight the differences in Types 2, 3 and 4 dances, And particularly to display the Exploration and Learning dance repertoire that enable us to explore, both inside and outside, our current boxes and to build better futures.

Finding the Real You

Figure 10.3 Dance Cards: Rhythm Strength Blow-Up

Dances	Number of Highs			
	Herman	Shippy	Bertha	Bruney
Type 1: Standard	2	1	2	3
Type 2: Escape/Avoidance	5	3	2	2
Type 3: Bully/Lead	5	2	6	2
Type 4: Explore/Learn	0	4	0	6

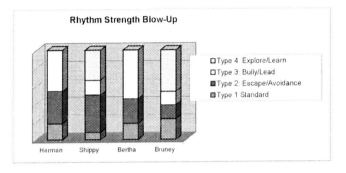

INSIDE YOUR HEAD

Confidence is merely another word for strong rhythms. And notice, a strong beat can carry all kinds of positive feelings and happy lyrics. A good appetite, excitement, and lust all ride on strong, *short* rhythms. Whereas love, commitment, hope, faith and optimism ride on strong, *long* rhythms. We get it . . . finally. Your strong rhythms bully Your weak ones, and Their weak ones. And in return, Their strong ones bully Your weak ones—the lyrics are incidental. And we all stupidly keep thinking that the message is in the logic or in the wording of the lyrics, when all along it's the power of the underlying beat. So your strong rhythms (minds) override your weak ones.

TUNING OUR MINDS

When you have several of your minds battling each other one of your damage control Yous can influence the outcome by manipulating their respective rhythms. Remember? For example, if your conscious mind is bossing one of your 'lower' minds, bullying it with don'ts: 'Don't do it . . . don't even think it!'—notice how one of your Escape minds can sneak a couple of slugs of a cortical depressant — like booze—which helps sedate your high and mighty rational mind. Now, freed from rational restrictions your primitive minds 'have their way', they swing, they sway. Of course if you take too much booze it will not only dampen down your higher brain rhythms but those of your lower brain tempos as well, including speech and motor coordination, sexual potency, and may even shut down your breathing and heart beat leading to coma, even death. Now that's shutting down way-down-deep turtles.

On the other hand, one of your internal bullies or leaders may want to rev up your 'higher' minds and so consumes some cortical stimulant like coffee, chocolate, colas or nicotine—a prized and potent stimulant. Notice what happens to the confidence in your thinking, your logic and your songs and dances? Clear the track!

As we said in an earlier chapter, we don't have to rely on chemical stimulants and depressants to manipulate our rhythms, our confidence. We can rely on other help—imaginary or real. Can you think of examples? As you know a New Year's Resolution is a mild way of trying to strengthen or weaken a rhythm. Joining a supportive group, like AA, is a much better way to increase your beat and confidence. That way a person can have their weak rhythms primed and sustained by those of others. Or you can tie yourself to a strong beater—like Bertha—and ride their rhythms. Or if you're lucky find a compatible significant other where you supplement and expand each other's limited repertoire and confidence—find shelter in each other's boxes, travel into the future riding each other's rhythms.

Don't forget some of the most powerful rhythm masters and confidence builders of all, namely Institutions. An Institution is a big bag of programmed, bullying beats. If you want to be an official and confident member of 'the firm' you have to dance the dance, walk the walk, talk the talk. 'Hey I'm high up in Wall Street'. 'Oh really, well if I can find the time you can visit me at Hawvad'. 'Where's Wall Street? Where's Hawvad? I'm where it's at—Silicon Valley.'

Consider this question: how much of your dance card is determined by strong institutional rhythms: Family ('I'm sorry, I've got to cancel, one of the kid's is sick'): Job ('I know the boss asked for your honest opinion, but let me warn you that's the last thing she wants to hear'); Culture ('Listen, I know he's a nice guy, but you have no idea of the problems you're letting yourself in for with an interracial marriage—think of the kids').

Institutions are the Big Bertha's of the present and the future! Also, don't forget religious and spiritual rhythms that serve to constrain or expand a personal repertoire. Some of us personalize these powerful tempos in various forms, including prayer or meditation, and so sustained are better able to respond with renewed confidence to the rattling demands of the present, and even the scary shadows of the future.

BATTLE OF THE RHYTHMS

So not only does the strength of a given rhythm settle internal mental warfare—enhance or suppress rational constraints—but helps resolve external battles as well—sometimes called the battle of wills. As Bertha, Herman and Shippy know so well, one person's strong rhythms can consistently over-ride another's weak ones.

The only time Bert challenges Bertha is when he's secretly seen an Arnold Schwartzenegger movie, or been into the cooking sherry, thus repressing his rational mind and foresight. Unfortunately, Bertha's tougher than Arnold, so not only do her mental rhythms prevail but her physical ones as well. Poor Bert.

The only time Shippy's wife's rhythms over-ride his occurs when one of her kids is sick—rhythms associated with the physical welfare of her kids turns Ruthy into a clear-the-tracks express train, shunting even Shippy onto a siding. Similarly, Herman's wife over-rides Herman concerning money for ballet lessons and associated travel for their youngest daughter, and bullies him concerning almost everything else when her mother is visiting. But how she pays when Momma goes home.

Finally, what happens when two strong rhythms meet face to face? Conflict is clearly one option, especially, if one dance partner thinks it is their role to prevail and moves into a Type 3 Bully/Lead alternative, and the other partner does not choose to follow, even insists on leading. Or what if one or both parties think the fight is not worth the candle and goes for a Type 2 Escape jig and leaves the floor. The final alternative of course is a Type 4 resolution if the pair can clear some space while they Explore the possibility of a solution that accommodates both of them, rather than opting for 'my way or the highway.'

Wise Bite: The message is in the rhythm. Confidence rides on strong rhythms. The strongest rhythm wins, while the lyric—riding along—takes credit. 'I told em blah, blah, blah, and then I told em blah, blah, blah, and again I told em blah, blah, blah' . . . Forget the lyrics—forget the blah, blah, blahs, listen to the relentless beat underlying the 'I told em . . . I told em . . . I told em'. It's like Bertha's 'Yes but . . . Yes but . . . Yes but . . . ' and the beat goes on and on till you join it or escape physically, mentally or emotionally.

But take note. Strong rhythms can carry positive or negative feelings, can support happy or bleak lyrics. You can have high confidence riding on the trusting tempo of love, compassion, generosity, or optimism, as well as glued to the relentless beat of hate, envy, greed, or pessimism. Anyone who has ever loved or hated—like who hasn't—has taken those rides, knows how fruitless it is to yell 'Whoa!' or 'Stop' til the ride has run it's course.

WEAK RHYTHMS

What about weak rhythms? What rides on them? Obviously tentative feelings of exploration or of uncertainty and the lyrics of doubt like: 'What if . . . '; 'How can you be sure?'; 'I don't know . . . '. Unless, of course, a weak beat catches a ride on a strong one. Then the weak

Finding the Real You

one appears to be strong, like Bert or like the skinny, mouthy kid backed up by his big brother or big sister on the playground. But more on that later.

So if one of Your strong rhythms dances with one of Their weak ones, or visa versa, guess who leads? That's why people who are strongly optimistic or pessimistic about ANYTHING—including a Mountain of Gold in Indonesia or even the End of the World—inevitably attract some followers. There's always a bunch of people with weak beats on the sidelines seeking a strong tempo to ride . . . regardless of the particular lyrics. That's why cults flourish, why many TV hucksters selling 'certainty'-however packaged—giggle all the way to the bank.

So maybe the followers of those glib hucksters aren't stupid or suckers after all. Maybe they just got caught needing a strong beat in a weak-beat slice of their life. Sure, the lyrics don't make sense to an 'outsider' at the time, nor to the groupies after the fleecing, so it must be the beat: 'I just needed a strong beat . . . maybe any strong beat would have done as well . . . crazy!'

EPIPHANIES

Hey, since we've all got some weak rhythms in our bag . . . we're all vulnerable to the big con, or if we're lucky a renaissance . . . a salvation . . . an epiphany! We checked with Shippy on epiphanies. Good News! He claims they're inevitable—little short ones for weak beaters, and big long ones for strong beaters. Weak beaters are almost always looking for a lifeboat and clutching onto whatever is handy. Strong beaters only start really searching for new dance floors when they get repeatedly and strongly stomped on during their regular gigs.

That may help explain Herman's recent renaissance following a run of bad luck. First, he was heavily fined by the IRS for tax fraud; second, he accidentally wounded a friend on a deer hunting expedition; third, because of a dream he became convinced his wife was having an affair—his prerogative, not hers, and finally he developed

Neil McK. Agnew, Ph.D. and John L. Brown, Ph.D.

a bleeding ulcer. When the old ship is breaking apart, when your confidence is low—like Ollie and his sinking ship, you desperately need to 'yump' to find a new place to stood and dance. After some down time Herman rises from the ashes.

One of his hunting buddies—not the one he wounded—operates profitable 'boot camps' for young offenders. He hired Herm, not only as the company accountant, but to run one of the camps where 'he-man' stuff like football, tracking, hunting, and fishing were core curriculum. But also environmental programs—like endangered species and green space—were included. The new fit and lean, glowing with health and confidence Herman became the biggest bully of all in protecting the environment! He developed a hate for poachers and clearcutters, and woebetide any family member who didn't put their Twinkie wrapper in the trash. His wife Gert became the camp 'mother' and even taught the boys dancing. But not ballet—Herman drew a line in the sand about that!

What about his Dreamer? Well, he still sneaks in some of the old lustful fantasies, but mainly his dream themes center around his camp winning ALL the cups and Herman taking over the whole company. In this regard Dreamer tries to tempt Herm into doctoring the books, fortunately his run-in with the IRS, and his new Self as Mr. Lean and Clean, combine forces and keep him honest. For the time being Herman's selves—internal and external—are having a ball. He's finally found a box in which his dance card approaches the ideal . . . if only his camp's academic performance improved then he might just capture all the trophies. For some strange reason he has trouble hiring and keeping good academic staff—Herman and egg-heads don't swing and sway the easy way.

MASTER SET POINT

So Bertha, your most important rhythms, your Queen rhythm, is Big C (Confidence). If Big C equals 100%, indicating all your rhythms are strong, then you have complete confidence in yourself, in your

Finding the Real You

whole dance card, in your future—move over Superwoman. If Big C equals 0%, indicating all your rhythms are weak, then you're not sure about anything, you have no confidence in yourself or your future—hello Casper Milquetoast.

Shippy claims that in order not to get sick and die, in order to avoid brain burn, you've got to have high confidence or trust in the majority of the beats in your bag. How high? Remember Figure 10.1 and how Type 1 Standard or automatic steps fill most of the dance cards.

NINETY-FIVE PERCENT PLUS OR MINUS FOUR

In that regard, The Professor first proposes a Master Set Point of 95%. That means that at any given time you trust 95% of your rhythms, ranging from your heart beat, to your riggy-jigging, to your car starting, to your key opening the front door of your abode, all that you blindly trust will still be where you left it this morning, still occupied by mates and kitty cat . . . no fire, no flood, no terrorism, no earthquake, no Fickle-Finger-of-Fate.

Sure you can dip below that 95% Master Set Point for a bit. Particularly in times of crises, when physical or personal earthquakes strike—maybe even down to 90%. Likewise, it can rise in times of good luck or calm circumstances—maybe to 99.9%, maybe even 100%. Yes, but those times are either followed by a hangover, or very intimate events, so difficult to sustain—even with Viagra. But according to our cranky Guru, in order to live a tolerable life to a reasonable old age you've got to maintain blind trust in about 95% of your rhythms, your dance steps. How ya doin? Yeah, well you've got lotsa company kiddo! John and I have been drinking about it.

John, shaking his head says: "Shiplitz old trout, you're not trying a little experiment are you, seeing how much BS you can get us to sing by repeatedly beating this 95% guff into our little bear brains? You're not really trying to sell us the notion that poor bullied Bert has high confidence in 95% of his jigs steps are you?"

Neil McK. Agnew, Ph.D. and John L. Brown, Ph.D.

Shippy sighed: "Boys, you keep forgetting that pretty well all the Type 1 Steps on your dance card, and most of Type 2 and 3, operate automatically, are hard wired by genes, moms and habit. Therefore, as they go beating along you never even think of them—they typically account for at least 95% of all your beats. Even without Bertha your friend Bert breathes, pees, ties his shoes, says please and thank you, uses a knife and fork, chews-swallows-defecates, speaks and writes English, all with very high confidence. Most of the things you think, do and say are automatic".

The Professor sings on: "The only time you're even aware of most of your jigs is when one of your standard gigs falters or fails—pee won't start or stop, car won't start or stop; you can't get IT up or down; computer crashes; heart bucks and hiccups; a strange lump in the breast appears; loss of a loved one or job. But these rattles are rare, not usually there. Your Yous never notice what runs on automatic till one of them slips or shoves their way into consciousness like almost losing my little Eppy, my poopsy woopsy little love . . ."

Oh boy!

Finally, Shippy, realizing we were still there, resumed his lecture. "As for your friend Bert, as long as he rides Bertha's rhythms . . . let me rephrase that . . . no let it stand you'll remember it better. As long as he rides Bertha's rhythms, and remember she needs him as much as he needs her—bullies are like that—he's probably running at about 99% certainty and 1% doubt. Sure she leads him around from dance to dance. He's got it made . . . no planning. So his trusted decision rule is: 'Follow Bertha's lead.' His big uncertainties only surface when she turns mean or temporarily deserts him. Then maybe he's down to 90%.

We can't buy the crazy idea of Bert being a 99 per-center under any circumstances. John says so: " Shippy old man . . . you're full of it!"

Here we go . . . out the door again with Eppy wobbling crazily after us.

Back at my house we tell Bruney what the old Professor said about Confidence being numero uno.

Finding the Real You

WHAT ABOUT SEX

Bruney asks: "What about sex?"
I replied: "It's a bit early in the day . . . anyway what about John?"
Bruney: " John will have to make his own arrangements."

John explains that Bruney was suggesting that for many people SEX, not confidence, is Number One—certainly Freud thought so.

I stammer: "Of course . . . I knew that . . . I was just. . . .". What do you do when one of your strong rhythms runs into a brick wall and takes a prat fall? Blushing and stammering don't seem to be COOL. Come to think of it, for males sex and confidence go together . . . without confidence . . . 'el droopoh'.

Bruney patted my hand and told John that sex was one our favorite short, strong rhythms . . . sometimes shorter than she'd prefer . . .

Ouch! After two rhythmic smacks in a row I can't find one strong tune in my Bag-O-Beats. Feebly I sing: 'Would anyone else like a Martini?'

John and Bruney ignore me, they're dancing to Shippy's music. John says: "Bruney's right, sex is just one of a bunch of *short*, strong rhythms like hunger, anger, fear, insight, and flatulence."

Bruney chimes in: "John's right" and turning to me adds: " . . . and love is a *long*, strong beat . . . so my blushing mate come back and join the party."

I'm afraid the three of us had a boozy brain stormer during which we analyzed most of our acquaintances, mapping out their formulas, focusing on long, strong rhythms or lack of them, identifying the optimists, pessimists, and flip-floppers. Then the kids arrived home from school and Bruney ordered-in pizza.

But next day neither John nor I could remember how Shippy figured that most of us have a confidence index of 95% or higher. Hung over as we were 5% seemed more like it. Nothing for it but back to Shippy. John would have to apologize, take a peace offering. I suggest a nice chunk of outrageously expensive pate de fois gras for Eppy. His response: 'No way Hozay . . . I can't even afford to eat that ritzy goose grease myself.' We settled for a chunk of liverwurst, with John giggling about feeding one sausage to another.

Once at Shippy's, we warbled seven times how sorry we are for offending him. Have you noticed people demand different levels of apology before letting you back on the dance floor—Shippy's is about seven. Bruney expects about two, but being pessimists Bertha and Herman want you to grovel . . . and they never forget.

Once it was clear Eppy was enjoying his treat, Shippy sort of forgave us. We popped our question— "This 95% about which you spoke so brilliantly. . . ?"

YOU'RE ALWAYS AT SEA

The Professor comes up with yet another damn metaphor . . . vaguely familiar: "Life is like sailing a ship at sea. But in life there are no true dry docks, no safe harbors, you're always sailing in temperamental seas". John says: "What about dancing?" Shippy replies: " For a minute forget dancing. Consistency is the hobgoblin of small minds— you use whatever ideas or metaphors work in the situation. Now back to ships at sea, right?" We both chirp: "RIGHT!" I also realize Shippy's being very patient contending with our clumsy attempts to follow his lead . . . and try to learn his lyrics as we do.

Shippy patiently persists and finally convinces us that he's right, most of us have strong confidence in at least 95% of our dances most of the time.

All right we're back on board our ship at sea. So you're sailing along and you notice something's wrong, say the fridge is broken and the beer's getting warm, or you spring a small leak, or one of the planks is rotting. So you start working on it. Fine. But notice in order to concentrate on that task you've got to assume all the rest of the planks are sound, you've got to believe the rest of the ship is OK, is sea-worthy or life-worthy. You've got to have blind, if temporary, confidence or trust in everything else—or else. Or else you can't focus properly on what you're fixing or learning. That makes sense—right?

Finding the Real You

So it isn't that you have blind confidence in 95% of the same dances all the time. It's that at any given time it's helpful to have blind confidence in the vast majority of your jigs. It may not be the same 95% as this morning, or yesterday. In the morning you may have blind confidence in your digestive system and lack confidence in your appearance. However, after a strange tasting lunch you may lose confidence in your digestive system, and after a visit to your hairdresser gain confidence in your appearance—so a balance of overall confidence is maintained. It's when you lose your lunch, your hair, and your job all together that you fall below 95% and everything seems to start rattling.

As he talks on Shippy raises the bar, convinces himself that we need to trust —have blind confidence in-not 95 but 99% of our world while trying to manage the current 1% that's rattling. Otherwise we're running around like crazy sailors from one plank to another and never getting anything repaired.

You know, just like the 'ship at sea' story, that 99% rule sounds familiar, I think we went back and snuck it into one of the earlier chapters.

Finally, when Shippy runs out of wind, his big ship becalmed John asks him: "Shippy old brain can you work dancing in there somewhere—maybe the Sailor's Hornpipe or something?" The professor is not amused—fires a shot across our bow– we're outa there, a revived Eppy in hot pursuit.

BRUNEY HELPS THEN SHOOTS

We tell Bruney about repairing the ship at sea and the obvious necessity of having confidence or trust in everything you're not repairing or learning. Bruney says: "I get it, you have to have confidence in most of your rhythms, your dance steps, your feelings, your songs, in order to fine-tune a golden oldie, or learn a new one. Otherwise, if you lose confidence or trust in more than a few things at once not only do you sweat blood but you don't get anything fixed. Like the story of the little Dutch boy when there were more holes in the dike than he had fingers to plug them."

John adds: "Yes . . . come to think of it . . . that's pretty well the way we figured it too . . ." No wonder Shippy feels Optimists have it made . . . they're not worrying about the future, about any other planks—optimism is a form of ignorance, is bliss—so you can afford to concentrate on whatever you're doing. But, thinking of Bertha, John does a little Pessimist dance: "What if the optimist is wrong, what if a lot of planks are rotting, what if you trust your feelings and they lead you astray, you fall in love with a phony who breaks your heart?"

Bruney: "Right on John . . . I guess that's why the Professor has the Fickle-Finger-of-Fate in his formula, and why he says, since most of the future is unknown or unknowable why not go with the flow . . . go with your strongest beats . . . which you probably do anyway . . . but sometimes still worry that you're not doing things 'right' . . . or worse not doing the right things, missing something really important . . . so maybe if you could identify and accept your strong rhythms . . . maybe then. . . . Hell I was doing fine before you guys messed up my head. Get offa my ship."

We abandon ship and head back to the office. We must have pushed Bruney below her 95% confidence level, forced her to think about too many weak planks at once. Sure hope Bruney and Bertha don't join forces against us—think of the cannons . . . think of the shrapnel . . . of the demolished planks. . . . of the sharks! Yump Ollie, yump!

BACK ON DRY LAND

We row back to our big island of Optimism—we're not ready to go for this 'Ship at Sea' stuff quite yet—not in our frail little boat. Since you can't control Fate's-Fickle-Finger anyway, Optimist Island is the best dance hall available . . . and it stretches far into the future. We come ashore and I step in something . . . John laughs: "With all this crap around there's gotta be a pony here somewhere!"

Finding the Real You

Bruney calls us at the office: "Have you boys ever thought that your Island of Optimism has no supporting turtles . . . that you're just kidding yourselves . . . that you're really on a big rotting ship on a rough sea, I sure hope you have smooth sailing, but I'd check for storm warnings just in case. If you're wondering why I called it's because you guys ruined my day—you triggered some strong beats with vengeance riding on them. Hope you have life jackets. Enjoy."

Mhhhh. Even basically nice people pull some ugly jigs out of their Bag-O-Beats when someone interrupts their flow, or rains on their parade. I tell John maybe I'll do a little Avoidance Jig and spend the night at his place. He says maybe I won't—his dance card is full. Mhhhh. Back to work.

Quickly changing the lyrics, John says: "We should tell Bert how lucky he is". We phone him: "Bert Old Buddy, we've good news, you're much more confident than you realized, in fact probably higher than the 95% level. That's the normal set point for most people most of the time. Below that level things really start to rattle, and maybe fly apart—like your heart rate, bowels, and credit rating. And of course with Bertha in your corner, you've got the other 5% covered so you're one of the 100 percenters, right???"

What's that Bert? You'll have to ask Bertha? . . . Of course.

HERMAN'S EPIPHANY CONTINUES

John says let's do one more check. Let's ask Herman and see how confident he's feeling now his renaissance has had a few weeks testing. We phone and he reports he's at 100%, he's full of confidence . . . and we think a few other things as well.

Not only is he busy rehabilitating the wayward youth at his boot camp, not only is he head of the local branch of "Keep America Green", but he's become active politically as well. Herm is a Pat Buchanan supporter. He says Pat is misunderstood. John pushes Herm a bit to see if he's done any real exploration of Pat's policies. Surprise! Not only has he explored but also he's put his own twist on some of the stuff.

In fact maybe he should be writing some of Pat's stuff. Herm says: "Neither Pat nor I are racists! We just think that it's high time we looked after our own people before sending our armed forces—our guys and gals—to every trouble spot in the world. You know we have Jews and Blacks and Arabs and Indians and Serbs who are American citizens living right here who need help, who are poor, or being hassled, or persecuted, or ailing. When we've solved these problems at home then we can go gallivanting all over being the world's master fixers." Wow! Herman as a policy advisor to a wannabe President? Holy cow!

If this epiphany of Herm's continues, if his confident optimism, exploration and learning continue we'll have to redraw his dance card—and pray.

How about you treasured reader? Not every minute, but generally speaking are you usually an Optimist, Pessimist, or are you an Uncertain flip-flopper? Bert wonders if there's any simple way to decide without asking Bertha. Shippy suggests asking your mother, or your insurance agent, or your broker. Pessimists buy bonds and lots of insurance. Optimists buy lottery tickets, stocks and ignore insurance. While the Uncertains—the flipper-floppers —delay making up their minds, keep a big cash account, or follow the advice of the last person they talked to, or the decisions of the bully they've currently attached themselves too—Hello Bert.

OPTIMISM BEATS BRAINS

But Bertha, wherever you are, listen to this. Shippy claims optimism is better than brains. If all you've got is brains and no biases you're soon overwhelmed, the news keeps flooding in, the in-basket overflows, you get further and further behind because you're not sure where to file stuff—you lack strong brackets, so you're swamped in a sea of alternatives, an ocean of data. Of course Big Brains, like

Finding the Real You

Shippy, who are on a roll don't call themselves Optimists or Pessimists—just brilliant! But whether the Biggies like it or not, in Science the popular—flavour of the year—theorists are the optimists and their critics are the pessimists. Simple as that. We argue about who should tell Shippy about our brilliant new insight.

So whether you're a citizen or a scientist you're lucky if you've got inside Bullies who are Optimists. That means you harbor senior B2 editors that pick over the news—magnifying the 'good' stuff—news that fits your expectations, while ignoring or trashing the 'bad'—news that doesn't. You're certain there is a pony behind that pile of dung so you go looking for a saddle.

Bertha, you'll be pleased to know that if you can't be an optimist the next best bet is to be a pessimist. How come? Well, because pessimists also have high confidence in the future, they know for sure that the Optimists are wrong. In fact Bertha you've got it made because your B2 editors pick over the news, magnifying the 'bad' stuff while ignoring or trashing the 'good'. You're certain there is no pony, just one pile of do-do after another. But at least you know what to do, namely shovel it on to the Optimist's driveway. Pessimists become amateur or professional critics—hopefully of others. Otherwise, if their senior editor looks inside . . . *bleak time!*.

LIFELINES: DOING THE WHAT COMES NATURALLY

In his recent job shift Herman didn't change himself, he merely changed dance floors. He now performs in halls where his strong beats are more appropriate, where his confidence is high, where he can afford to be more optimistic.

Optimism, pessimism, uncertainty—all three call life's tune. Each of us harbors these three B2 editors. For some, like Shippy and Bertha, their senior editors are their Pessimistic Selves. For others like Bert and Shippy's wife Ruth, their Uncertain Selves write and sing most of their lyrics. But, according to Shippy, Optimistic dance masters call tunes for John and me, and Optimistic editors sing our songs—naive but optimistic.

IF YOU'RE STUCK WITH IT MAKE THE MOST OF IT

If like, Bertha, you're basically a PESSIMIST and if you've got lotsa juice you're a strong beater, you're a high confidence dude. If, like her, you grew up in a home with an uncertain father and strong beat mother, then make the most of it—go out, do your thing, 'Yes Butting. . . . ' everything that moves.

If, like Shippy, you're also basically a PESSIMIST, and if you're a little short of juice—a lower, slower beater, and if you grew up in a patriarchal scholarly home, then crawl with it—hole up, denigrate visitors, and while wearing protective snowshoes create brilliant models of SMALL brains trying to solve BIG problems, and of an eventual collapse of the universe into a tiny speck no bigger than a mouse poop.

If, like John and me, you're basically OPTIMISTIC and you've got sufficient juice —medium beaters—and if you grew up in the pool halls of small prairie towns, long on square dances and short on encyclopedias and ballet, then jig with it. Sashay around busily begging, borrowing, and stealing big ideas and the trappings of culture. Package them up and pretend they're yours.

If, like Ruth and Bert, you're basically UNCERTAIN, and you've got some juice, and if you learned early on that there are many answers to every question and you don't know which ones to believe, then tip-toe with it—team up with a self-appointed 'EXPERT' who knows everything —like Bertha or Shippy. Or better still, hang up your shingle, hire yourself out as a mediator who can point out that there's something to be said for all sides. Or become an announcer or an actor where someone else writes your lines, and you're only uncertain and depressed between scripts.

Finding the Real You

MAGIC LAPEL BUTTONS

We've run out of lyrics so go over to Shippy's. He has some computerniks visiting from MIT. They're designing little badges with tiny computer chips that help people identify kindred spirits and opposites. Still in the early stages of development, they're supposed to play music when people with compatible rhythms come close together and sound like a foghorn when mismatches approach each other.

The nerds tested the badges on John and me—whenever we went near Shippy his badge made the worst noise. The nerds are trying to wire in Shippy's theory about 'rhythms dancing with rhythms'. John asks them can they design a button that plays 'happy days are here again' if he gets close to someone that's on his sexual wave length? We get thrown out.

We're still out of lyrics so we dredge through some of our previously pilfered notes and discover he'd written on the back as well—a whole new treasure trove! We discover that while your most important Yous are those long, strong, confident beats, particularly the ones with Optimism or Pessimism riding on them, you have several assistant Selves giving them a hand.

ASSISTANT DANCE MASTERS

The dance masters—Optimism, Pessimism, and Uncertainty—need help. They get it from a variety of familiar assistant dance masters. As you recall, Herr Docktor Professor Shiplitz has pronounced:

1. Everyone needs a strong lifeline, one grand passion carrying optimism or pessimism;
2. In order to protect our small brains, we have to say 'NO' most of the time, we have to avoid, avoid, avoid most stuff;
3. The Dance Master of the grand passion needs a few Assistant Dance masters to keep the band in tune and the show on the road.

Neil McK. Agnew, Ph.D. and John L. Brown, Ph.D.

These assistants operate in the middle, between the compelling 'YES' and all those 'NOs'. These assistants are middlers, the 'roadies' who make deals with the devil —strategically rationing out the precious yes's and liberally dispensing the endless supply of no's... the no's that help keep your ship on course. These assistants come in pairs.

We'll discuss a couple of our favorite pairs of these wheeler-dealers and you can add others. Our favorites are the Ends and the Means twins; and the Aggressive and the Passive duo.

ENDS VS MEANS

Of course people can be optimistic, or pessimistic, or uncertain about different things. None of these Dance Masters can manage everything so they work with specialists. Some specialize on Ends, like choosing a holiday destination or deciding when to retire. While others specialize on Means, on how to get there, how to get anywhere. Because we're bears of small brain we can't think of everything so we have to specialize, one of these selves typically bullies the other.

Who is boss inside your head? Are you an Optimistic Ends person—a positive goal setter? You have no trouble selecting your destination but you invariably get lost en route? Or are you an Optimistic Ways and Means cat? Once someone sets a goal you're positive about how to get there, and by the shortest means. You're a navigator instead of a goal setter.

Consider pairs of people instead of pairs of Selves. For example, consider having children. Have you ever noticed that males are enthusiastic participants at the very first dance step along the way, but after that jig they delegate the rest of the ways and means to the female? With pairs of people, have you ever encountered the couple where one chooses the destination and the other maps the route serving as navigator? Sometimes they even try to 'help' each other out: "It would be nice if you told me about the turnoff a bit before we came to it, not after we've passed it." The other replies: "It would be

Finding the Real You

nice if you stopped driving like we're in the Indy 500 . . . Ohhhh. . . . we just flashed by another historic sight . . ."

Herman's son just got his driver's license. He doesn't care about where anyone is going as long as he can drive them there—he's a pure ways and means guy. Conversely, his sister doesn't care about driving —about means—she just wants to get there. Similarly, she just wants to buy the new CD then get home and listen to it. Well, listen to it after her brother puts the CD player back together.

According to Shiplitz, John and I are strong on Ends and weak on Means. We're Optimists who focus on a goal (writing a bestseller) without a clear plan of how to get there. He says we rely on a kind of random walk strategy. John tells him a random walk is better than being frozen stiff . . . better than writer's block. Oh Boy! Yump Ollie, Yump!

Before we were banished Shippy waxes poetic about Bruney—he says she aims for less grandiose goals than he does and has a good travel-agent-self helping her get there. He says she's a more anchored optimist (she's writing and publishing a science column every month) and she tenaciously follows a rough map—(does research and writes an hour a day) even if it has to be after midnight or at five in the morning, while periodically creating family panic as her deadline approaches. You could learn to hate a person like that—except she breaks up at our jokes.

Now you take Shippy.—and welcome to him. He's a pessimist with grandiose if often bleak goals—modeling how everything in the world is running down, how not only our sun but all suns are burning out, how the universe is gradually becoming dark and cold. Fortunately for us, and unfortunately for him, he has writer's block, his ways and means dance is weak—unlike Bruney's. She defends him pointing out that his goal—explaining everything—is a lot bigger than her's. She asks, 'how do you map and follow a path to everything, everywhere'? What is your answer to that? God's will? Physics? Winning a sweepstake?

We suggest the answer to Shippy's failing universe is a defective Geiger counter—he always forgets to replace the batteries.

Neil McK. Agnew, Ph.D. and John L. Brown, Ph.D.

The world is fine . . . always will be. It's not the world that's running down it's just that Shippy's too cheap to buy new batteries. Being a confirmed pessimist Bertha believes Shippy's dismal predictions. She's got two years supply of wheat germ, honey and mineral water in her basement. Bert's invited us over in case the world goes dark. Yeah right!

THE AGGRESSIVE VS THE PASSIVE

As well as the Ends vs. Means Selves, we also harbor Aggressive Vs Passive Selves. Now Bertha will probably say these are the same as Strong Vs Weak beats, and in a way she is right. John says she's absolutely right. Nevertheless, I sneak it in. You will see that although it looks obvious there is a surprising twist.

Quickly, let's cover the obvious. Aggressive Optimists or Pessimists are typically strong beaters. But not all strong beaters are aggressive. They can just be quietly but persistently pursuing a goal or a means. All right? Like a turtle with a long, strong beat. Turtles aren't aggressive but they get there. O.K.? What's that? Someone in the cheap seats just said: 'Yeah they end up in the soup.' Well fella, remember, nobody likes a smart ass!

But now to the twist. The most interesting of these selves are the **Passive Aggressives (PAs)**. After much casual study of these smoothies we can assure you they're powerful stuff—keep em off your dance card if you can. We've seen them bring strong, aggressive Optimistic and Pessimistic dancers to their knees, right out on center stage. It may take several years, but they can do it.

BERTHA IS NOT A PA

Now **PAs** are not like Bertha. She's straight out and out an aggressive Pessimist who will 'YES BUT . . .' into submission any End or Ways and Means you generate. Conversely, but even more effectively, the skilled Passive Aggressive operates like the Chinese Water Torture—

Finding the Real You

one drop at a time . . . in the same place. They have an uncanny knack for finding the tender spots.

When you're dancing with a skillful **PA** you rarely notice when they oh so gently lead you off your rhythm. You never notice you've been led astray or 'yes butted..' til it's too late. They're so subtle you miss it . . . then gradually you realize you've been had . . . you lose your rhythm . . . you feel cranky . . . but there's no enemy in sight . . . no weapon in evidence . . . so you can't strike back. Only an outsider can see what's happening. Check the following scenario:

You: 'Let's go to the Caribbean for our holiday.'
PA: 'Good idea . . . I was just wondering. . . .'
You: 'What?'
PA: 'Oh it's probably nothing . . . I'm sure it's nothing . . .'
You: 'What is it.'
PA: ' It's really nothing . . . forget about it.'
You: 'FORGET ABOUT WHAT?'
PA: 'Now you're getting worked up about nothing . . . I really want to go . I . . . . .really do.'

Guess where they're not going for a holiday? And if they do, guess what kind of time they'll have: "The fruit is really inexpensive, isn't that great. They grow it right on the island. Someone said they use human manure.. . . ?"

Dealing with a **PA** is like fighting a mean ghost. If you've got one at home give up or get out. If you are one, you've got it made! You own the box.

THE UNCERTAIN DANCER

When dealing with Optimists or Pessimists you may not know 'the score' or the lyrics but you know the theme—good news or bad news. With these cats you can at least predict their favorite rhythms

But what do you do when an Uncertain comes on the dance floor?

Neil McK. Agnew, Ph.D. and John L. Brown, Ph.D.

What can you predict? Uncertains don't have any strong B2 editors. They have to rely on someone else's. The only thing you can conclude is: 'Don't bet on them. Well you can bet that the outcome, if there is one, will be based on the last thing they heard, likely the song and dance routines of the Optimist or Pessimist they've attached themselves to for the moment. In order to survive—psychologically—Uncertains typically march to a different drummer. It's just that it is someone else's drummer. They become camp followers—like Bert. The camp he follows is Bertha.

MIND DEPOSIT #10

If all this seems too complicated, triggers you to say 'to hell with it' then take the simple route. Simply ask yourself: 'Do I generally go for Dogs or Pets?' For the 'rough and tumble' or 'the neat and tidy'. Do you want to see what's over the horizon, or does the route look scary, and most likely there isn't much over there anyway. If you go for the rough and tumble, if you frequently take risks, you're probably a strong beating optimist, or tied to one. If you go for 'the neat and tidy', you're probably a pessimist. If you can't decide, you're probably an Uncertain without a 'Bertha' bullying or leading you at the moment.

If you want to go beyond the quick and dirty classification above, then read on.

When we bears of small brain go looking for our real Selves we'd best limit the search to a precious few. First, try to identify your way down deep turtles, your Dance Masters, your long, strong beaters: 1. Optimist; 2. Pessimist; 3.Uncertain.

Then, identify their major Assistants: 1. Ends or Means; 2. Aggressive or Passive; 3. Passive Aggressive. If you have some personal favorites write them down. And if you like, let us know. We're making a list of Assistants.

Now you're in a position to write your personal code using just three or four letters. Shippy says John's and mine are: O.E.A. (Optimistic, Ends oriented, Aggressors). Bertha's is: P.M.A. (Pessimistic,

Finding the Real You

Means oriented, Aggressor). Bert's, when he's alone, is U.E.P. (Uncertain, Ends oriented, Passive). When he's with Bertha it's the same as her's. Herman? If he has a good day and not too many single malts he will seem like an O.G.A (Optimistic, Goal oriented Aggressor) but push him or let him tip the glass once too often and you see he is really a closet P.M.A. (Pessimistic, Means oriented Aggressor). If you want to get fancy you can use small letters to indicate less strength like a small 'a' for Bruney's aggressiveness. Bruney's code becomes O.E & M.a (Optimistic Ends and Means oriented aggressor.)—she can afford a larger repertoire because she doesn't waste quite as much time as the rest of us doing Escape, Avoidance, and Bullying jigs.

In the next chapter we give you Shippy's latest discovery. Namely, how to get your Master Set Point back up when it's knocked below the 95% level, and also, how to raise it above that level—EPIPHANY!

"YES BUT ... you *@#&%@$&* twits ... when I finish with you there'll be no epiphany the closest you'll get to a spiritual experience will be singing in a boys choir. I don't know what you've been telling my Bert but he had the nerve to tell me I needed him more that he needed me...! Well let me tell you we soon straightened out that little misunderstanding. You can pick him up your way to choir practice.
      Furthermore, you'll need some new letters to write my code properly, something like B.B.A.TTT.&L (Brainy, Beautiful, Amazonian, Truth-Telling Teacher and Leader).
      I'll be watching and if you use my code in your next chapter I'll sue your pretty little buns off... well, John's anyway."

WELL YES . . . but Bertha don't get mad at us. All those ideas come from Professor Shiplitz . . . he's the one you should . . . you know . . . whatever it is you have in mind.

Neil McK. Agnew, Ph.D. and John L. Brown, Ph.D.

MIND MAP # 10

O.K. time to write your secret code that displays your Real Yous, and that of a 'significant other'. Try not to use more than 3 or 4 letters—remember we're Bears of Small Brain. Also after the code write down what it stands for. For example, for John and me, the code is O.G.A (Optimistic, Goal oriented, Aggressives)—we're weak on Ways & Means.

Mind Map #10a:
My Code 1st try: _____. (_____)
My Code, second try: _____. (_____)

Mind Map # 10b: Now code your mate or special other:
Significant. Other 1st try: _____. (_____)
Sig. Other 2nd try: _____. (_____)

Mind Map # 10c: Now estimate some of your Set Points.

According to Shippy the Ideal is 99% with 1% going to damage control, exploration and learning . . . he should talk. We think that's unrealistically high. We propose the normal should be 95% high confidence dances with 4% going for damage control and 1% for exploration and learning. If you're between 93 and 95% then you're probably dealing with some unusual crises but you can climb back up to normal as long as it doesn't last too long. Below 93% some of your trusted turtles are thrashing about, even swimming away . . . you need to beg, borrow, or buy extra escape, avoidance, and leadership dance routines or face chronic physical or emotional disability.

Finding the Real You

Estimate your average or Master Set Point: _____%
Comment:(_____)
Estimate average Set Point during the Week: _____%
Estimated average Set Point on weekends: _____%
Estimated average Set Point on holidays: _____% (If it's not higher than the weekday Average then you're going to the wrong place with the wrong people.)

Mind Map # 10d. When your set point gets knocked down what are the three most likely Selves or Others responsible—your depressors?

Most common downer: _____
Next: _____
Next: _____

Mind Map # 10e. When your Set point gets knocked down indicate the three most frequent Selves or Others helping to get it back up—your elevators?

Most Common lifter: _____
Next most frequent: _____
Next most frequent: _____

Mind Map # 10f. Go back to figure 10.1 and make any changes in your column that you feel are appropriate.

CHAPTER 11:

RIGGY JIGGING WITH THE UNIVERSE

> "Heard melodies are sweet, but those unheard are sweeter."
> —Keats

John is working away at something. I ask him if it's Chapter 11. He says never mind. I sneek a peek—it turns out to be a poem for his love, titled: 'The soft melody of her smile.'

Hey, that's kinda sweet, and fits right in with everything being based on rhythms, even smiles. John's kinda embarrassed, stuffs it away in his pocket and we start horsing around, throwing musical phrases back and forth:

'The crashing beat of his anger'
'The mechanical pounding of his lust'
'The slow surfing of her sadness'

Enough already. Back to work. We need a title for this final chapter that reflects the grandest rhythm of all: 'The Music of Life' . . . 'The

Dance of Life'.... Finally it came to us: **'Riggy Jigging With the Universe'**. Now there's a title that does justice to Shippy's formula that explains EVERTHING in terms of rhythms—ranging from our cells dancing to the music of life, all the way up to our planet dancing to the music of the universe. If either our cells or our minds or our planet get out of step ... Rattle ... Rattle ... Rattle!

OK we've got a title, now what?

Well, last chapters are supposed to do two things: tie everything together; and then close on a resounding note that propels us all into a fabulous future. First we take a crack at tying things together. Then we'll visit Shippy and beg, borrow or steal that brilliant chunk of resounding wisdom that makes IT worthwhile.

PUTTING HUMPTY TOGETHER AGAIN

The western way of finding out how something works is what? Take it apart!

As anyone who has ever dismantled any piece of machinery knows, it's easier to take something apart than to put it back together. Dr. Frankenstein found that out when he tried to reassemble his monster—not only did it walk and talk funny but the stitches showed. In order to succeed you not only need to number the parts, you need a master blueprint—which in our case is The Shiplitz Formula.

Life = F3 (Your Rhythms (Strong & Weak))
+ Their Rhythms (Strong & Weak))

The promise of this book is to help find the Real You. In the early chapters we scattered some of life's parts before you. They were done in a linear fashion the way book chapters are written. One chapter followed by the next until the last chapter. This one. Think of these chapters as the numbered parts of the Real You. Well-numbered parts like the following:

Neil McK. Agnew, Ph.D. and John L. Brown, Ph.D.

1. The Zero, The One, **The Many**, with us beating for many minds (many rhythms, many selves) Yours and Theirs. And, with Bertha beating for The One. Which answer are you beating for?
2. You can think of these many minds as a **Family of Minds** formed into concentric circles, into **Islands of Consistency**, constructed out of the flood of sensations (rhythms) as they flow by. We gradually bracket these rhythms, gradually build up our personal islands: a) our mental categories (male, female, cats, dogs, Republican, Democrat); b) our stereotypes (chauvinist pigs, feminist witches, red necks, bleeding heart liberals); and c) our cause-effect chains of, if A then B, (If male then sex hound; If female then illogical). The important ones, we place at the center, the less important are assigned to our outer islands. And we hire immigration agents and squads of defenders to keep our islands safe and undisturbed. Have you been able to figure out which islands you placed at the center of your circle? And where do you reside on the islands of significant others, central or out on the outer atoll?
3. Because we're **bears of small brain** we can't handle too much complexity, that's why most of our minds or islands are constructed of simple consistencies (men are . . . women are . . .). That's why we rely so heavily on stereotypes and habits—our automatic dance routines. They require relatively little brainpower. We ration it like any limited resource, trying to reserve a precious bit for a more detailed mapping of a few special people and projects. But that is also why the impact is so great when our automatic responses fail. When one of life's hurricanes shakes up our center islands—then almost all our resources gravitate around damage repair. How about you . . . any hurricanes ravaged your core islands lately?
4. Your various selves or islands consist of a **network of alliances**—short and long term—which provide sustaining stability. However, they also constrain what your various Yous and Thems can and cannot think and do. One of the most important alliances is the

Finding the Real You

one you've built between the mental islands inside your own head. But as in all families, our many selves do not always live in gentle harmony. Living involves maintaining a precarious balance between our many selves, including those attached to the selves of others. Earlier we asked you to take a crack at mapping your society of minds and adjust it as you went along. How have you done? Any major changes taken place lately?

5. Our **internal,** inter-island alliances gives us a personal sense of stability and integrity, our character. Our **external,** inter-island alliances, linking our central selves with the multiple selves of others, gives us a stable sense of interpersonal and social belonging. Living involves maintaining a precarious balance between independence and belonging, between **defending and linking** our islands. Throwing 'whys' at a consistency or belief is one way to check out the strength of our own and other's defenses. If you haven't tossed three whys in a row recently, target a schmuck and test their mettle.

6. Because life can be uncertain and rough we need a few strong, trusted **places to stood**—both internal and external, both personal and social. When we look at our island network what do we find? We find some private core islands, surrounded by floaters, plus supporting and hostile social networks. Hopefully some of our islands and our alliances are 'safe' and built on solid foundations, on a **Tower of Trusted Turtles**. The Real You is the core group of **Safe Islands**, private ones, plus solid alliances. How much confidence do you have in your current mind map? Which core islands are written in ink? Which in pencil?

7. We now have a picture of the Real You. Or at least a way to make the picture. But that is what it is, a picture that needs animation to give the Real You life. We said that it is not possible to solve significant problems at the same level of thinking that created them—that's why we often need to shift out of our familiar boxes. Life is just a series of one damn nine-dot puzzle after another.

   To make the Real Yous swing and sway people have to understand how the minds of the Real You work. The essence of **Our**

Minds and **Their Minds** is the beat, the flow—yet so often we get seduced by misleading lyrics ('I love you . . . ', 'Believe me when I say . . . ' But remember what dear old Gran said: 'I can't hear what you're saying for what you're doing'). Once you see You and Them as a **repertoire of rhythms** you're outa the box, you swing, you sway, you're on your way.

8. The brilliant blueprint that ties the rhythms together, that takes these bits-o-beats and makes music is: Da-Dah—**The Shiplitz Formula.** The formula simply says that life consists of Your rhythms dancing with Theirs. Which particular You dances at any given time depends a lot on the situation—on which bracketed dance floor you happen to be jigging—and with which partner, internal or external. It also depends on your own **Tower of Rhythms** and the strength of the life force beating at its base. Is it strong, tied to big long-term goals, or are you into the old waver and flicker routine of pressing short-term gigs?

    In order to get on with the dance of life, we necessarily and unconsciously ignore the **F3** in the formula, **Fates-Fickle-Finger** until he/she/it breaks through our protective brackets and gives us the goose We've included Figure 11.1 to summarize Shippy's formula and included some examples.

Finding the Real You

Fig 11.1 - The Shiplitz Formula

Life =	F^3	(brackets)	Your R's	Their R's
	Fate (Destiny?)	**Boxes:** Sensing, Thinking Acting	*Your Repertoire of rhythms and lyrics	*Their Repertoire of rhythms and lyrics

	* Suprises - Good or Bad
	- Lover cheats
	- Get fired
	- Win sweepstake
	- Brakes fail
	* Bracket penetrators
	  or breakers
	- Unpredictable or
	  unconscios Selves
	- 'Lose it…'
	- 'Fall' in love
	- Have heart attack
		* Categories
		* Stereotypes
		* Bounded Islands of
		  Consistency
		* Internal & External
		  dance floors
		- situations
		- moods
		- bears of small brain
		* Constraints on what
		  you sense, think feel
		  and do
		- Herman's machoism
		- Bertha's pessimisim
		- John's optimisim
		- Bert's uncertainty
		- Yesterday's myths
		  and logic
		- Today's Religious &
		  Scientific assumptions
		  'presumptions'
			* Types
			- Standard
			- Escape/Avoid
			- Bully/Lead
			- Explore/Learn
			* Weak & Strong
			* The dances your
			  various selves do
			  internally with each
			  other, and externally
			  with other Selves, in
			  different situations -
			  on different dance
			  floors
				* Types
				- Standard
				- Escape/Avoid
				- Bully/Lead
				- Explore/Learn
				* Weak & Strong
				* Their dances
				* Other Selves
				- Internal & external
				- Bertha on Bert
				- Herman on cadets
				- Bruce on Shippy
				  her own family, etc.
				- Eppy on Shippy
				- Shippy on John and me
				- Shippy's doubting Selves
				  on his writing Selves
				  and snow shoes.

9. As bears of small brain, and limited to five frail senses that restrict and filter the flow, we have no unedited access to the rhythms in the **REAL WORLD**. We can't reach the world stripped clean of our sensory limitations, their distortions, and of our stereotypes. The only worlds we can know come to us strained through our bread-in-the-bone senses, bracketed by our culturally programmed psychological niches (one color of skin good, a different color only once in awhile).

The unfiltered world does not exist, we can subtract it from our vocabulary, so we call it **(-1) World**. Since we're bears of small brains we never get unedited access to the whole bag-o-beats, to the whole story. Nevertheless, we do get access to two smaller bags. **World (1)** consists of a chaotic array of news fragments (short beats) collected by our **B1 Reporters**. Our **B2 Editors** use these news fragments to construct patterns and plausible stories (longer beats), mental symphonies to keep our dancers busy. Which of your **B2 Editors** rule the roost, which news fragments get selected, tied together, and delivered into consciousness: sex, fashion, sports, children, politics, money, illness?

10. To make sense of our worlds we must take tiny samples from the buzz of sensations continuously assaulting us and freeze them in time and place, at least for an instant. We transform the excitement of verbs into the safety of nouns. The nouns are like stones, tightly corseted and bracketed. The verbs are like water, they flow. Some beats are weak, some strong; some are short, some are long, some are fast, some slow. The slow, strong ones are like nouns. Fast ones are more like verbs. Dancing with stones and nouns is safe but boring. Dancing with water and verbs is exciting but exhausting. To maintain our brackets or establish order in our worlds—on our dance floors—we rely mainly on **the logic of stones**. To court excitement, or to manage bracket-breaking crises, we must rely on **the logic of water.** The logic of water requires a lot of brainpower—it's like herding cats—so we can't use it too often or for too long. When you mapped your own basic beat what was it on average: fast, medium or slow?

11. When Your repertoire of rhythms dances with Theirs you create an unfolding **dance card** called living. When one of your Selves or Theirs invites or commands one of your Yous to dance then, away you go—gracefully, clumsily, aggressively, or maybe gliding or sneaking right off the floor. Every dance card includes **four types of steps**: Type 1 **Standard Steps** that are automatic and occupy most of our dance card _ ninety-five percent. When any of those basic steps fail you go into damage control relying on Type 2 **Escape and Avoidance** jigs or Type 3 **Bullying and Leading** tangos. And when we're lucky or clever we create a bit of open space and expand our repertoire through Type 4 **Exploring and Learning** mambos.

    The ideal dance card is mainly filled with Standard steps. In the typical card, Standard steps bounce around between 90 and

Finding the Real You

95%, with Escape/Avoidance and Bully/Leading jigs mending planks and bailing water to re-establish stability. Hopefully, you have also discovered enough time and space to try out a new Exploring and Learning dance. Pray what kind of dance card did you display today?

12. Since life involves Your rhythms dancing with Their rhythms, and since all rhythms provide short or long forecasts of what comes next, then all rhythms involve **dancing with the future**. And if you only have one wish about what treasure to take on your journey into the future take **CONFIDENCE.** Confidence and trust ride on strong rhythms, uncertainty rides on weak ones. Weak rhythms provide weak or uncertain forecasts, strong rhythms provide strong forecasts, strong steps.

To successfully navigate the sea of life we must have strong or blind confidence in most of our ventures. To be able to concentrate our limited resources on repairing one rotting plank we must trust that the rest of the ship is sound. Furthermore, to reduce a ship's rattles you must tune its Rpms to find it's **Master Set Point**, it's sweet point.

So too in life, we gradually learn to adjust our Rpms to locate our set points, our sweet points in various situations. If we're lucky, we do so by capitalizing on what comes naturally, by finding a dance hall where our personal—if unique—repertoire of rhythms works, where most of our main and supplementary dance steps are rewarded, or at least tolerated. Hello Herman.

How high should our confidence be? Shippy recommends a **Master Set Point** of at least 95%. He says that in order to keep the rattles to a brain-tolerable level you need to trust 95% of the rhythms in your bag-o-beats _ most of the time. You may be naively optimistic like us, or brutally pessimistic, like Bertha, but if your confidence is high then your life's traffic will flow rather than hiccup and jam. Watcha think? Are you more like John, or Bertha, or Bert, or even like Bruney?

Now it's time to extract our final intellectual care packages from

Neil McK. Agnew, Ph.D. and John L. Brown, Ph.D.

Shippy, and find out how you locate set points, not only for little local dance floors, but Big Ones that help you establish a master dance card that lasts you a long, sweet lifetime.

DANCING THROUGH TIME

Shippy's in a good mood these days. No wonder, with Bruney's help he's actually completed a major manuscript on The Elasticity of Time. In Bruney, he's finally found a co-author he can swing with. Not only is she smart enough to extract meaning out of his mental river of brilliance laced with nonsense, but she's also secure and tough enough to keep him civil. Whenever he throws a tantrum she simply tears up the pages they've just completed and comes home. Within minutes he's at our back door and pleading with her to come back, promising he'll be good, and also promising that he'll stop feeding Eppy garlic sausage—for such a small dog Eppy can deliver brain-numbing flatulence.

When Bruney told us about Shippy's theory concerning The Elasticity of Time, John and I looked at each other, let out a whoop, and took turns sashaying Bruney around the kitchen. That's it! We can use the elasticity stuff to wind up the book in a blaze of glory.

Never mind that the stuff Shippy and Bruney were talking about was airy-fairy theoretical physics, our B1 Reporters now know how to borrow bits and pieces, and our B2 Editors are spin masters who can weave them into a symphony of rhythms providing a beat on which you and we can ride with low rattles and high confidence into a fun and sun filled future.

You already know something about The Elasticity of Time—from personal experience. It can slow down—like when you're waiting for the dentist, or speed up—like when you're making love ('Was that good for you?'; 'I'm not sure . . . it happened so fast') Of course it depends on the partner—most guys seem to think if anything's worth doing it's worth doing fast.

We obviously don't really dig Shippy's new stuff, otherwise we

Finding the Real You

wouldn't have run out of lyrics so soon. So off we go, hats in hand. We find the Professor and Eppy, sans snowshoes,—enjoying their lunch—beer and garlic sausage. When Eppy drinks beer he sneezes because of the fizz. Shippy thinks it's hilarious. We think it's messy. We tell Shippy our problem and he condescends to give us The Answer.

First he reminds us of the paradoxical fact that the faster your personal Rpms the slower time flows—hence for two people making love there are three times: 1) clock time of ten minutes; 2) The fast Rpm male estimates elapsed time as twenty minutes; 3) The slower Rpm gal estimates elapsed times as two minutes. Which Time is 'correct'? If you're a MANY-minded person you answer 'all of them'. If you're a One-minded person you must choose. Which ONE did you select?

Shippy also reminds us that for people on sedatives—slowed Rpms—time speeds up. For those on stimulants—faster Rpms—time slows down.

We tell him yeah, yeah we remember all that but we need more stuff—more islands, more bridges, more turtles providing trusted stepping stones into a healthy, wealthy future. Because that's what we promised you—all your Yous. Shippy sighs, empties his stein, feeds Eppy the last bit of garlic sausage and tells us that an anthropologist—guy named Ed Hall—has done the best work on how, not only individuals, but different cultures construct their rhythms, their space/time frames . . . their dance halls. Hey Bertha hear that? Not just ONE time, but MANY!

John asks The Professor if he stole the so-called Shiplitz Formula from this chap named Hall? Oh! Oh!

Shippy screams: "It's MINE .. it's MINE . . . it's ALL MINE! Get out . . . get out . . .'

Seems like a good idea. We leave.

Neil McK. Agnew, Ph.D. and John L. Brown, Ph.D.

ELASTIC TIME

Bruney's just back from a conference in Paris—jet lag! French Clock Time was out of sync with her Biological Time—eating, sleeping, meetings all took place at 'the wrong time.' She finally stretched her biological beater to fit Paris clock time. Then, of course, when she got back home she had to reset her biological clocks all over again. So you have two kinds of time right there: clock time and biological time which may or may not be in sync, which may or may not find a sweet set point.

We get rattles when those two times step on each other's toes. But you don't have to do air travel to experience that kind of dislocation. Some of us operate permanently on a biological time that runs either several hours ahead or behind clock time (the early birds and the nighthawks.) Shippy does his best work between midnight and four in the morning. Bruney's rises with the sun, is zinging around by six while I'm barely intelligible by nine. Learning to dance with clock time is the first jig babies have to learn . . . 'glory be little Audrey slept right through . . . no four o-clock feeding' . . . 'Hallelujah . . . we've finally got little Berty to go potty before he goes to Playskool.' . . . 'Hey, hey it must be Sunday . . . we had sex last night.'

So how are you doing in dancing to Clock time? Do your Standard dances fit The Clock or are you forever stretching one or more of your Selves out of shape to cut down the rattles? John has elaborate dances to escape or avoid the cacophony of the alarm clock in the morning, and also to avoid 'Bed Time' at night. Herman uses clock time as a weapon to bully his family and now his poor cadets. Never be late with Herman.

We tell Bruney that Shippy threw us out yet again, and about this anthropologist who studied the different kinds of clocks humans run on. She'd heard about it, and told us that the idea that the Universe is nothing more than a bag of rhythms is now 'in the air' and to expect to see it start popping out all over the place . . . Shippy's just a bit ahead of the time.

Finding the Real You

We find a new bottle of Beefeater gin, make a batch of Toonies and scribble out a list of some of the obvious times we dance to:
>Clock Time
>Einstein Time
>Biological Time
>Psychological Time
>Institutional and Cultural Time
>Economic Time

If you're going to use Shippy's formula to understand the meaning of life it helps if we know the kind of TIME your Selves and their Selves are dancing to in a given situation, within a given set of brackets. Maybe that's the single most important thing to know? Maybe that's the answer to EVERYTHING?

For example, notice how Institutional Time bullies most of the others. Institutions love clock time when it suits their purpose. And when it doesn't the big bosses invent new tricks to stretch it both ways—breakfast meetings, dinner meetings, emergency meetings, deadlines— 'deadlines' . . . isn't that a cheery word? How are you doing in your dances with Institutional Time? Are you one of the lucky ones who has located institutional dance floors that fit your repertoire of personal Rpms? Some institutions are 'looser' than others—like most government departments, and also universities, that provide enough slack time to accommodate almost everyone's rhythms except those of their clients—the paying public.

Institutions adopt the computerized telephone answering system—with that phony: "Your call is important to us, please stay on the line." Ha . . . the thing that's important is not us, but rather finding yet another means of forcing us to humbly jig to Their Institutional Time.

Notice how Clock Time and Institutional Time constrain and program our biological rhythms early in life. We place our kids in 'educational boxes' as young as possible. If not nursery schools then marching to the TV SCHEDULE. At school, how many of you had a teacher that lead you in the mindless recitation of some lyrics in which the hero—big bad Time—is already tailgating your young life?

In our small town upbringing John and I and the rest of our class opened every school day with an indoctrination-: " So here doth come dawning another blue day, think . . . wilt thou let it slip useless away?" Bruney, growing up in a metropolis, was led in reciting—in unison—Kipling's IF, with those immortal lines: "If you can fill each unforgiving minute with sixty seconds worth of distance run . . ." And remember the terror of being: 'LATE FOR SCHOOL?'

There we have the foundations for scary islands of consistency—programming our Turtles to Tick, making Time an unforgiving task master, a persistent tailgater, certainly not a gentle enveloping friend or lover. Here we see 'Clock Time' and it's Nazi henchman 'Institutional Time' bullying all other times—particularly 'Biological Time'. No wonder we rely on so many quick fixes to manipulate our biological Rpms to try to accommodate, escape or avoid those bullies, to keep jigging just ahead of the pushy monster or blot it out of our awareness.

CULTURE TIME

Individuals and institutions within a given culture dance to different drummers—**wildly** at home with small children and also in small entrepreneurial shops, **busily** in large Corporations, **sedately** in Government departments, and **casually** in Universities.

Not only do we see differences within a given culture but also between cultures, like the U.S. and Japan. Until recently the Japanese worker had a guaranteed dance floor for life. After a day's work Japanese executives are supposed to socialize (network) over food, drink, and 'entertainment' arriving home gently or profoundly soused long after the children are to bed—family time, biological time be damned. Mediterranean and South American cultural rhythms are more in tune with biological time, and with solar time as reflected in the seasons, the sun, moon and tides—which of course spawned our primitive biological or circadian rhythms.

Finding the Real You

So... in terms of core solar and Biological Time—the times our deepest turtles dance to—how are ya doin? Do you have any safe-place islands where some of Your Selves and maybe some of Theirs can swing and sway the natural way? Any friendly islands where you can get off the institutional express and smell Your flowers, Their flowers, and then rub pollen laced noses?

In checking your dance card how many, if any, of your dance floors and dances reflect natural biological rather than compressed clock and institutional time: sleeping, eating, loving, thinking, sailing?

One of the biggest bullies employed by THE Clock and Institutions is Economic Time—now there's a tailgater! Check your dance card again—how much of it is devoted to jigging for the Yankee Dolla? What kind of payoffs are you getting? Is it a fair exchange? Not only in providing user friendly islands operating on compatible Biological Time, but if you're really lucky you have an accessible island operating on the most flexible and liberating time of all—Transcendental Time—a time that transcends all other times, Clock, Institutional, Economic, and even Biological. But more on that freedom fighter later.

But how do these different times fit together? Trust John to have an answer as he pulled out yet another handful of pilfered notes from Shippy's office.

HIERARCHY OF RHYTHMS AND OUR PERSONAL TIME MACHINE

Shippy claims that all Our rhythms and Theirs are running all the time, but at different levels of awareness. Furthermore, we each have our own personal time machine for travelling between them. Like? Well like when we daydream during a meeting. To others it looks like we're operating on Institutional Time listening to the speaker's song punctuated by the regular drumbeats of colored slides. At one level we are paying attention. A bit of our brain is tapping its cane to every tenth beat. However, most of our awareness has shifted to daydream music—shifted either up a level to swing with dreams of glory, or down several levels to riggy jig with a shameful sexual fantasy.

And here we thought a Time Machine was Science Fiction nonsense, and yet we've all got one tucked safely between our ears. One that can beam us up to dreamy fame and fortune or down to richly fantasized lust and thrust, launch us forward into fabulous futures or slide us back into private pasts.

And of course, our time machines control rhythms at all levels of consciousness—high and low. Those magic machines must operate and coordinate vital rhythms that lie beyond our awareness, including a myriad of biological dances like high frequency nerve transmissions, brain waves, digestion, wake-sleep cycles, growth, menstruation, sperm and dandruff production, aging, dying—we have an extensive tribe of networked timekeepers.

TRANSCENDENTAL TIME

Earlier we mentioned a time that transcends all others.

Bertha says: "What's this Transcendental Time? Keep Religion out of it—that's a private matter, none of your snoopy business".

Well Bertha, yes and no. We know a couple who are regular churchgoers—they religiously follow the Institutional Time—including the Clock Time—of their church. In the case of the guy he's doing a ritual institutional dance that also jives nicely with Economic Time—he sells insurance, so each parishoner is a potential customer. What about for her? Well, she also follows the Institutional and Clock Time of their church—they arrive and leave 'on time' during which she gains access to Transcendental Time . . . not Angels, not Heaven . . . but something very personal . . . better than hot fudge sundaes . . . better than sex. When asked about it she can't give a very articulate answer—she kind of mumbles: 'I don't know . . . but for a few precious minutes I kind of understand what it ALL means.'

From the outside these two look like a civilized couple sharing a mutual and dedicated religious experience. But notice they're only

Finding the Real You

sharing—keeping mutual time to—a small number of the church's institutional beats. Between those beats each of them is playing hooky—he jigging to Economic Time, she swinging to a Transcendental beat, one beyond clock, institutional, even biological time.

So, no Bertha, we're certainly not talking about big R RELIGION and all it's odious organizational trappings and priestly frailty. I know it's none of our business, but ask yourself: does your religion include any islands operating on transcendental time? Islands or dance floors where time is so elastic that one of your Yous can escape all other clocks, all other jig masters, and swing and sway to the music of the universe, to the chords of the cosmos—and without snowshoes?

WHAT DOES IT ALL MEAN

Most of us have been taught that happiness is the name of the game. If we can only get our dance card filled with the right partners, stop the rattles, and find our Master Set Point we'll have it made. Nothing wrong with happiness when it comes. But the damn stuff also goes—comes and goes, comes and goes. Unfortunately, try as you may, you can't lock in it's set point, can't capture it between trusted brackets, can't noun it. Happiness doesn't follow the logic of stones . . . it follows the logic of water. It is forever on the move, here today, gone tomorrow, or hey I think I see it over there.

Great feeling when you dance in sync with Biological or Institutional Time, and it's ecstasy when you can swing to both at once—as Presidents of countries and corporations know, power is the greatest aphrodisiac of all. Talk about a 99.9% confidence level, talk about rhythm strength—Wow-zippers away! Panties astray! But soon the logic of water—of change— prevails, happiness takes a holiday, happy rhythms weaken, life flows on, up and down, up and down.

Neil McK. Agnew, Ph.D. and John L. Brown, Ph.D.

BUT IF HAPPINESS ISN'T IT, WHAT IS

But if not Happiness, what? How can anyone dance in psychological sync with the inevitable rise and fall of both biological and institutional rhythms?

Notice, we just created a nine-dot puzzle for ourselves. As Uncle Albert told us: 'You can't solve a puzzle at the same level at which it was created'. To solve it we must somehow shift levels, get outside the box, must catch and ride a rhythm strong enough to break through. Like? Well if you can't have Happiness NOW then go for Certainty in the future. Shippy claims that John and I solve here and now problems by shifting time frames, by riding a strong rhythm, or beat, out of the here and now box, and cycling forth on naïve optimism. Bertha rides out of the now on a strong rhythm of cynicism—convinced that everyone she meets is wrong, and she can tell them, how, when and where.

We corner Shippy and ask him if that's the kind of thing he has in mind when he talks about Transcendental Time. He shakes his head and takes Eppy for a walk.

We go and ask Bruney and she says well sort of but not really. Well then, for heaven's sake tell us about 'Really'!

Bruney explains that we're right about shifting from one time scale to another, but she suspects that when most optimists face a terminal illness—their own or a loved one's—they 'lose it' and become Uncertains. Typically in the face of such disasters their confidence level plumets and everything rattles. Similarly with most pessimists, when they're confronted with their own mortality they lose their blasé cool, reach desperately for straws, even becoming last minute born again true believers. We may talk a good game but when ye old fickle finger delivers the goose few of us have a sustaining confidence, a confidence that transcends the total collapse of say, our investment portfolio, or the ominous wing beats of the angel of death.

Bruney continues: "Yes, threats to our core selves invariably rattle our networks, frightens our turtles. But some of us transcend those storms better than others. How come? Certainly everyone hurts, sure everyone suffers, but some seem able to 'play through the pain', to accept such poop storms as just one more of the Fickle Finger' periodic jabs. Their brackets seem to include a tougher set of damage control steps. It's as if some of their Yous unconsciously understand it's not a question of IF the Fickle Finger's will strike, but only a question of when. That's the kind of transcendental time scale Shippy is talking about. A time scale that you can jive to, no matter how out of sync you become with biological and/or institutional time".

REINCARNATION

John: "You mean like believing in reincarnation?"

Bruney: "Well . . . that would be only an example but one foreign to most of us. I think Shippy has in mind even more mundane kinds of a time scale that transcend and bully all other Times—biological or institutional—and that somewhere each of us harbors such magical dances in our repertoire of rhythms. Like? Well, for example Shippy's constant search for The Big Picture. It certainly doesn't make him happy, but it's his strongest rhythm by far, the most common dance on his card. I'll bet that on his deathbed his trembling hand will be making spidery scribbles about The TRUTH."

"Oh great . . ." cries John "You've got to be a ruddy genius to dance to transcendental time, otherwise you're down here desperately jigging to chronic indigestion, periodic impotence, interminable committee meetings and IRS deadlines."

MUMS HAVE IT

But Bruney reassures us by giving examples of how common folk like us go transcendental. Most mothers have access to transcendental time in spades. They're not always happy but there's no doubt about what dances and what Time hold the priority places on her dance card—those of her kids. Maternal Time trumps Biological

Neil McK. Agnew, Ph.D. and John L. Brown, Ph.D.

Time, Institutional Time, Economic Time, Mate Time. Most Mums will die for their kids, live for them, and continue living through them—a kind of reincarnation.

Anyone emotionally committed to the young—some fathers, dedicated teachers, loving grandparents, sincere mentors—all compulsively dance to a child's rhythms, in the present and into the future In doing so they're not necessarily happy, in fact some of those dances hurt awfully. But for those so engaged it's CERTAIN, the compulsion automatically sets priorities and illuminates what IT all means. You have no choice but to go with that flow—you may not articulate it but you experience it. You are at the not so tender mercy of the irresistible logic of the tides of childhood.

John asks: 'What if you don't like children?'

Bruney: "John, that's awful. You're not alone. You can do like Shippy, get a dog. He has two Transcendental Times to dance to—The Truth and Eppy. Don't laugh, in America pets rank almost as high as kids in generating transcendental time for their owners. For their pets people will stretch Economic time, will challenge Insititutional time, will ignore Biological time—will brave smoke and fire to rescue a pet."

Bruney bids us bye-bye, thanking us for giving her an idea for her next column. John and I keep wrestling with Transcendental Time. It seems to be any time or rhythm that consistently trumps all other times. Like? Like being in love. But that usually only lasts a relatively short time, and then biological, institutional and economic time regain control. Some scientists and environmentalists catch it and become convinced that all things are related and that they themselves will continue to exist forever with their molecules recycling through everything—even broccoli.

Real True Believers have it. John and I decide we'll attain imortality because the ideas of this book will be incorporated into world thinking and continue forever cycling down the corridors of time—like Bing Crosby's White Christmas.

How about you? Do you have any access to Transcendental Time?

Finding the Real You

If not, better get cracking. As you know Biological Time doesn't beat on forever.

Hint: To get started do like Herman—identify your strongest rhythms—repulsive or otherwise—and go with the flow. In a sense your current Transcendental Time is nothing more nor less than your strongest beat, your biggest internal bully. The trick is to locate a place to practice it, get paid, and stay out of jail—like Herman. Shippy claims that as long as you're practicing a strong rhythm it will gradually bring other times into sync, and get this: 'Will automatically generate higher order rhythms, higher order transcendental times — peak experiences that beat hot fudge sundaes and riggy jigging—well sometimes.'

So you may, like the Herman of old, be operating with a kindergarten or grade 1 level of Transcendental Time. But like the new Herman, merely by locating a compelling dance floor on which to practice your currently strongest rhythm, you will automatically evolve higher and higher orders of time—Grade 2 . . . 3 . . . 4. . . . and away you go. With increasing frequency you'll experience a cognitive orgasm—an ecstatic sense of 'What It All Means.' But don't try to write it down. Not at first anyway. Early in your ascension the lyrics are usually awful. As you may have noticed earlier in this book.

What about Bertha? How can she find a meangful beat to ride over the rainbow? She should become a professional critic—get paid for doing what comes naturally rather than doing it for free. Bert? He'd be an ideal counsellor—someone who listens, tells you what you just said, and then charges you two hundred bucks an hour. Shippy's wife Ruth? She mothers anything that moves—she's doing OK right where she is—and probably has access to levels of Transcendental Time that Shippy's never dreamed of. And Bruney, she's got it made: great biological rhythms; big strong Maternal Time (driven by the kids, the dog and me); and in sync with Institutional Time with her column. You could learn to dislike a person like that—well not me, I get to go along for most of the ride. She's my strong attractor who helps create order and compelling futures out of chaos.

Neil McK. Agnew, Ph.D. and John L. Brown, Ph.D.

STRINGS ARE IT

Bruney advises us to pry one more gem out of Shippy. He may be leaving. He's been offered a prestigeous job at a California Think Tank. Before he goes, ask him about his new pet theory that explains everything—String Theory.

We try. He's still riding high, welcomes us, more beer and wurst, and Eppy gas! Shippy calls it 'Demon Wind'.

John says: "Shippy, What's about String Theory?"

Shippy: "No, no . . . that's way out of your league, even Einstein's . . . But you've reminded me of something that would be helpful for your little book".

THE STRING'S THE THING

"When you were young I'll bet someone showed you how to hang a piece of string in a glass of water saturated with salt. And you saw how the dissolved and invisible salt molecules crystalized so beautifully around the string. Magically, that string created a lovely order out of 'nothing'—out of a chaos of unseen salt molecules."

We say: "So?"

Shipplitz: "So . . . think of that lifeline you're looking for—the Real You—as a string you throw into the future. Think of it as a 'line of life' around which the chaos of experience crystalizes into images, ideas, hopes. Strong strings with complex niches create strong realities. Weak strings with fuzzy niches create weak realities."

John asks: "What are these Lines of Life?"

The professor: "Think for a minute, what kinds of strings or lines attract order, construct order out of the buzzing confusion of living, out of chaos?"

We say: "What kinds?"

Shipplitz: "Eppy, for God's sake tell them!"

Eppy barks, laps up some beer and finishes off his wurst.

We say:"Beer and liverwurst?"

Finding the Real You

"Well not good, but not bad. Thirst, hunger, and seeking a bit of a buzz certainly are lines, or minds, that we throw into the future, lines of attention around which particles of experience crystalize: H20 becomes a drink, protein molecules become food, and lysergic diethelamide becomes 'Lucy in the Sky with Diamonds'.

John says:"Come on Shippy, stop with the chemistry and give us the goods."

"You're right. You boys don't have the strings and I don't have the patience to crystalize this wisdom. Get out!"

We bow, whine, plead: "Please . . . please . . . just a quick summary on strings and Real Yous and we promise not to bother you for a whole month."

Shippy says: "Make it two months."

We say: "Right. OK. Cross our hearts."

STRANGE ATTRACTORS

Shiplitz: "The string is an attractor, it provides niches into which salt molecules fit. Other kinds of molecules won't fit those particular niches so remain free, remain chaotic. Now think of your various minds as strings of attention, as attractors for particular kinds of multi-faceted experience—for particularly shaped psychological 'molecules'. In some cases only one facet of the experience fragment will fit the multi-faceted niche—a superficial match, one easily dislodged in the heat of experience."

John: "Like new telephone numbers and one-night stands?"

Shippy ignores him: " In other cases many facets of the experience fit the structure of the niche and become permanently attached—maybe becoming tenacious body fat (ugly love handles), or becoming part of long term memory (the rich images of a lover or pet). In still others instances no facets fit, or, like most of the universe, remain out of reach. The Transcendental Time you mentioned is a magic string creating higher order wonder and hope out of disorder."

Neil McK. Agnew, Ph.D. and John L. Brown, Ph.D.

John shouts: "I get it. I get. It's . . . like a grand slam homer in the ninth inning, or a hole in one, or a real friend."

Shippy nods: "Yes, well . . . stop interrupting! Being bears of small brain most of REALITY eludes us (remember World (-1))? It's 'molecules' are too big, too small, too low frequency, or too high frequency (maybe O.K. for bats), or too complex to find a compatible niche on crude human strings. So we can only capture and retain relatively simple mental and environmental frequencies: proteins, sounds, images, ideas, biases that we crystalize into our World 1 and World 2."

I ask: "I don't . . ."

The Professor: "Shush! The stability of the structure of your string, the number, the complexity of it's facets determine which fragments of experience will crystalize and which won't. Both Bertha and Herman have strong but relatively simple and predictable facets on their main string or lifeline."

John says: "And Bert has mushy facets into which almost anything will fit till another molecule comes along and displaces it. And Bruney has complex, mutifaceted niches so she can crystalize a bunch of different experiences. Hey hey . . . I've got it. I've got it."

Shippy: "Well let's not get carried away. You're getting within shouting distance, but you're not there yet. The string analogy cuts the problem down to bear-brain size but is too rigid, and too simple. We have to shift up a level, as Einstein advised, to better do justice to the problem."

John: "Take it easy Shippy, we're barely holding on . . ."

Shiplitz: "Can't be helped, to understand the puzzle we have to shift up from the logic of stones to the logic of water. Keeping the analogy of the string and crystalization in mind, now add in my Formula, add in rhythm. Not only are niches attractors, and rejectors but they're not static, they're RHYTHMIC. So think of the facets in the niches as having rhythms. Intuitively you know that—some of your niches attract stuff before you eat but not after, before sex but not after, before education but not after. In brief the logic of stones doesn't work for most of our niches because they dance to temporal patterns.

Finding the Real You

Some simple niches will be predictable in the short run but not the long (honeymoon). More complex, dynamic niches will only be predictable in the long run (marriage, divorce, Truth, transcendental time), and some not at all. (what do women really want? The beginning or the end of the Universe?) That's why getting to 'know' any living organism takes time—they're not a thing, they're an evolving symphony."

John: "Ah ha! So the logic of stones formula would be:' Your facets fitting or not fitting my facets', but the logic of water says: 'Your rhythms dancing with my rhythms'. So the stoney logic works OK with simple or dead stuff—stuff that stays where you leave it—but you need liquid logic to work with living stuff. But Einstein says that all stuff is living stuff—stones just dance real slow."

Shippy: "Those computer scientists from MIT with their magic badges are still relying on the logic of stones. To keep it technically manageable they assume the facets in the niches are stable. So when you approach someone and your badge signals a match or a mismatch it will be a very crude fit—based on one or two simple facets. They're interested in my Formula to enable them to make more sophisticated, dynamic matches. It's like meeting someone and you think they're great because they hate Clinton, or like martinis, or math, but after a few meetings you can't stand them—not only are there too few facets matching, but the rhythms are wrong."

John: "What about Real Yous and Thems."

Shippy: "What you need is a master rhythm strong enough to last you a long lifetime. Think of it as your Real You if you like. Think of it as a master string stretching beyond the horizon, one from which smaller strings branch, but all are covered with niches containing simple and complex rhythmic facets. Now turn it on and experience Your strings dancing with Their strings, a continual trial and error process of accepting and rejecting: viruses, proteins, caffeine, things, moods, ideas, people, TRUTH."

John: "I'm losing hold, I'm falling off . . ."

Shippy: "Sorry, I keep forgetting who I'm talking to. Those master strings are lifelines—like optimism and pessimism. They're strange dynamic attractors which create patterns in the rough and tumble of living, that create order in the surrounding chaos—that crystalize your experience. The Real Yous are those strings, those lifelines, those strange attractors, that discover or create order in what would otherwise be confusion and noise."

John: "So Bert's string is Bertha. So Herman's string is Macho Man. So your string is FINDING THE BIGGEST STRING OF ALL but you keep getting it all tangled, right?"

Oh boy . . . away we go . . . another pant cuff for Eppy's collection.

Back at my place we try to tell Bruney about all the stuff Shippy said.

John adds: "We promised the readers we'd help them find their Real You . . . what can we tell them now?"

Mind Deposit #11

Bruney: "Tell them their Real You is water, not stone. Tell them their Real You is time lapse, not snap shot. Tell them their Real You is evolving, here today, different tomorrow, and who knows what epiphany next week, next month, next year. Tell them 'they ain't seen nothing yet'".

John:: "But Bruney, if we're all bears of small brain, how do we ensure those epiphanies, what can one bear do?"

Bruney: "One bear, any bear, can only start by riding the rhythms they've got. But their freedom lies in—by foul means or fair—increasing the strength of their core beats so that their attractors don't languish in the past or present, but robustly flow into the future."

I say:" And pray how do they do that? "

Bruney: "You've been nattering about how to do it all through your book."

John: "We have?"

Bruney: "Oh Gawd! Don't you remember?"

Finding the Real You

1. By tuning your Rpms any way you can to locate set points . . . sweet points.
2. Use whatever Escape/Avoidance and Bully/Leader steps you have to change dance floors.
3. Use whatever Exploring/Learning steps in your repertoire to find some transcendental time—to send Your STRING dancing into the future.

John: "How do you know when you're on the right track?"

Bruney: "The same way you know anything, the ground trembles, the angels dance, poets speak, you laugh deep in your guts, you cry out loud in the movie from joy or universal sadness. You'll know. You'll know because you'll hear the voice of your turtles, your deep, down turtles, and they'll be singing, they'll be whooping . . . they'll be TRANSCENDING".

Well yes . . . there is a trial and error component in making any changes in your dance card. Shippy says that's why non-rational stuff like Optimism, Pessimism, and Rpms are it. They constitute your emotional intelligence. They determine how much space and time Exploration and Learning dances capture on the card. Therefore, they determine what level of Transcendental Time you can reach. The stronger and longer the STRING, the stronger and longer the Rpms, the stronger and longer the epiphanies.

(**P.S.** Herman is now Vice-President of Wayward Rangers, a profitable retraining program for teens in trouble. Bertha is now Director of the Municipal Welfare office and is in danger of working herself out of a job as she merrily cuts back the rolls. Bert runs a grant-supported counseling center and 24 hour hotline for abused husbands. Meanwhile John and I are optimistically looking for a publisher.)

MIND MAP #11

You now have a pretty good idea who the current Real You is—the one who most consistently bullies all your other Yous, the dance master of the important dance floors, the one who fills in most of your dance card. Or there may be several Real Yous. Right Bertha?

Yes but ... Bertha can't talk to you at the moment. She just lost her job as book critic for the Yellow Grass Gazette - the editor is a stupid man. But she thinks she's got a new job at City Hall evaluating applicants for welfare. I'm going to take a night course on counseling, but can't decide which one to take - I'll ask Bertha when she gets home...

Now we're ready for the next big question, namely, who is the future Real You going to be? Maybe the answer lies in the following: *"Work like you don't need the money, love like you've never been hurt, dance like there's nobody watching."*

This gem of a quotation came over the e-mail from a wise friend. It contains an impossible set of proposals. They all presume a certain level of Transcendental Time, they presume you've been able to escape from: Clock Time; Biological Time; Institutional Time; Eco-

Finding the Real You

nomic Time. Impossible! Well maybe not, since according to the Shiplitz Formula they all involve dancing. So all you have to do, some of the time, is work, love, and play as if you're not being watched, not being timed, not being tailgated by someone or something. If you do it already, it sounds like you've found and protected some safe places for Exploring and Learning.

MAP 11a: A chappy named Abe Maslow arranged dance floors on an ascending scale. While taking gross liberties with Abbie Babby's hierarchy we present the following to identify the dance floors where you do your best jigs:

Level 1: Physical survival: a good working relationship with Biological Time _____.
Level 2: Psychological identity: Most of your Yous accept each other _____.
Level 3: Group Membership: Most of Your Yous are accepted by Their Yous _____.
Level 4: Group Leadership: Your bullies control/lead Their bullies _____.
Level 5: Self-Actualization: Traditional times are working in sync _____.
We add:
Level 6: Soul Actualization: Dancing to Transcendental Time _____.

In the space provided pencil in H (high); M (medium); or L (low) to indicate how well you're currently doing at the six levels in the hierarchy. Now put a tick mark at the level where you'd like to increase the quality of your dancing. Finally, employing some of your Escape strategies, skip to Level 6 and try a few jigs—even if you merely lie in a warm bath improving the quality of your day dreaming.

Maslow assumed you had to have it made at one level before you could move up to the next. Without thinking, most people would

Neil McK. Agnew, Ph.D. and John L. Brown, Ph.D.

agree that you have at least to be dancing well at Level 1 before you can go to any other level. We don't agree. Look at Stephen Hawking—the black hole guy in a wheel chair who talks eerily through a computer synthesizer—who works on all levels, most of his time at grade gazillion! Also, consider some terminally ill people who are so deeply into Transcendental Time that they escape the bleak drumbeat of their biological decline and thumb their nose at the undertaker as their soul riggy-jigs with the cosmos, or their pet, or images of the grandchildren projected in time.

To get in the mood for the next Map start humming that great song 'Born Free' or any music that gives you a lift.

MAP 11b: List three situations—dance floors—where you feel free, feel like you're dancing without being watched or tailgated . . . even if you're not alone.

Dance floor #1: _____
Dance Floor #2: _____
Dance Floor #3: _____

MAP 11c: By definition 'freedom' means you're not being bullied or tailgated, so at some level you're dancing to Transcendental Time. The level you reach depends on how many of the other times you've 'escaped' and on the kinds of dances you do. Through day dreaming Herman escapes from all other times, but then does pretty primitive fantasy jigs. On the other hand, Shippy when he escapes into high level thinking does some impressive Exploration and Learning waltzes. The rest of us probably perform on transcendental dance floors not quite as low down as Herman's nor as ethereal as Shippy's.

What kinds of dances do you typically do when you've escaped from the constraints of some traditional time and 'feel free'? Rank the following from 1 to 5, with 1 being most and 5 least frequent:

Finding the Real You

Day dreaming: _____
Standard comfortable dances
(e.g., cleaning the house, watching TV): _____
Working on a hobby: _____
Hanging out with friends: _____
Exploring and Learning new stuff: _____
Other: _____

MAP IId: Daydreaming is the fastest route into Transcendental Time even if it's low-grade stuff. To reach the higher levels you may be able to fall in love—with a dog, children, a mate, or 'god'. But you can't just buy LOVE off the rack, so you need a fall back position. Exploring and learning new stuff is one of most effective ways to build strong, long rhythms that last a lifetime and that transcend other times.

List three of your dance floors where Exploring and Learning is most likely to occur:

Dance floor #1_____.
Dance floor #2 _____.
Dance floor #3 _____.

MAP 11c: Take out your dance card, cancel out at least one negative payoff dance a [+] or a [—] from Mind Map #1 way back in the first chapter, and replace it with one of the above, and get ready for a little Level 6 Soul Actualization.

MAP 11d: This idea comes from Gert, Herman's wife. She says there are three simple ways to increase your repertoire of rhythms, and in doing so expand and extend your horizons. The three ways are: 1) Dance; 2) Dance; and 3) Dance. The more you dance to different tunes—literally bounce around to the music—the more rhythms you add to your psychological repertoire, the more of life's dance floors welcome you, the more partners you can swing with—follow, lead, understand, enjoy, the more epiphanies you generate, the more time and space you TRANSCEND. Hey, she's right.

I say: 'How come we didn't think of that?'

John says: "Don't forget to tell them how they can get a gold embossed certificate by taking a crack at all the mind maps—a certificate signed by Shippy, and US." Wow! Also, we're trying to talk Shippy into setting up a web site so you can have access to his latest intellectual care packages, maybe even signed autographs by him, and Eppy. Check out www.RealYou.ca

End

BVG